GIFTED
AND
TALENTED EDUCATION

GIFTED
AND
TALENTED EDUCATION

By

Kondru Subba Rao

M.Sc., M.Ed., M.Phil., (Ph.D)
Principal
A.S.R College of Education
Kovvuru–534 250 (A.P)

General Editor

Dr. Digumarti Bhaskara Rao

M.Sc., M.A., M.A., M.Ed., Ph.D.
Reader
R.V.R. College of Education
Srinivasa Nagar Colony
Guntur–522 006
Andhra Pradesh
India

SONALI PUBLICATIONS
NEW DELHI-110002

Edition - 2023

ISBN 81-88836-59-1

Published by

SONALI PUBLICATIONS
4228/1, Ansari Road,
New Delhi-110 002 (India)
Phone: 23266109, 23279245 • Fax: 91-11-23253475

Printed by -
Navya Digital
Delhi - 110092

PREFACE

Two major social concerns of recent years have placed in sharp focus the quality of school efforts to identify and develop the high potential of gifted students. One of these is the sharpened sense of challenge from the Soviet Union, arising primarily from its scientific success in atomic and space technology. The other is an awakened national conscience disturbed by the failure of an affluent society to root out poverty and ignorance. With respect to scientific competition with Russia, schools are asked whether they are discovering all students of intellectual promise and whether they are stimulating them to adequate performance. As regards underprivileged segments of the population, schools must answer whether they are identifying talent that is hidden by the effects of poverty, and whether schools are compensating through their programs for these effects.

The tasks of developing talent and providing opportunity for the disadvantaged are not new assignments for the schools. The urgency of present needs places new emphasis on these long-established functions. As never before, schools must look about them to define new requirements, to formulate new plans, and to set in motion new programs.

Since 1950, a wealth of reports has accumulated in areas such as creativity, motivation and achievement, guidance of the gifted, the potential of underprivileged groups, characteristics of the gifted, application of new teaching methods, and employment of new curricula in the schools. Much of this research is still fragmentary and suggestive rather than conclusive, or on too small a scale to warrant definitive conclusions. However, so much has been reported that it is time to try to relate theoretical research and demonstration of practices in actual situations to problems in education of the gifted. New problems are not solved by applying old formulae which were discarded because they did not work in the past. An enhanced education of the gifted depends upon fresh perspectives tested in a crucible of objective research.

A large number of studies have been called upon in preparation of this volume. Space does not permit full discussion of many of these projects, but the editor hopes that brief descriptions will, in many cases, whether the reader's appetite for fascinating encounters with much of the primary source material. Acknowledgment is due here to the many authors whose work is cited throughout this book.

Editor

CONTENTS

1

VARIETIES OF GIFTEDNESS IN CHILDREN

Any systematic consideration of giftedness in children must begin with reference, however brief, to the monumental studies by the late Lewis M. Terman. Prior to his work— and to some extent even since, for stereotypes die hard— the gifted student was portrayed as an unattractive, bespectacled, badly coordinated, if not altogether anemic child, who was an outcast among both other children and adults. Terman's studies contradicted all this. The gifted student was found to be healthier than the average, more attractive personally, better coordinated, and in general to be enjoying a richer and fuller life.

To those interested in studying giftedness in children, Terman left a research model that was both simple and powerful. Briefly stated, here is the basis of Terman's procedure. He entered the schools of a particular area— in his case, California— and, applying group or individual intelligence tests, selected children in the top 1 or 2 or 3 per cent in IQ. Calling these children "gifted," he proceeded to pose the question: What other qualities are associated with this exceptional intellectual ability ("exceptional intellectual ability" being of course defined by the high IQ)? It was not long before other investigators were applying this model to other populations– invariably using the IQ metric, relating it to other qualities, and finding essentially what Terman had found. Information about the child with a high IQ accumulated rapidly.

Some efforts have been made to collect and summarize the overall findings, to take inventory, as it were, of what we have been up to in these studies of gifted children. Typical is a 1954, symposium whose participants included Terman himself, his associate Melita Oden, Margaret Mead, Ruth Strang, Paul Witty, and others who have done significant work in this area. The task of the symposium was to bring us up to date– some 30 years after Terman's first publications– on what was known about the gifted student. The most striking conclusion from the collection of papers is that the things that could be said with certainty in 1954 about the gifted child did not differ substantially from Terman's earliest findings. Although each paper is excellent in its own right, together they reflect a slackening of progress in our understanding of giftedness in children. Many of the statements made tentatively by Terman in 1925 could be made with greater conviction, and the importance of this should not be minimized. Yet by and large, further conceptual development and fundamental knowledge seems not to have been forthcoming. The crucial problem, for us, became "why."

It seemed that the primary block to further work lay in epitomizing giftedness in children within the one concept of intelligence as represented by the IQ metric. In most studies, the word "gifted" was synonymous with "high IQ," and the term "gifted child" was for all intents and purposes only a shorthand way of saying "child with a high IQ." A child who did not have a high IQ, no matter how accomplished in other respects, was not considered "gifted." Although this psychometric definition has great heuristic value, it is not without at least three severe limitations.

First, it suggests that the common intelligence test samples all, or at least a sufficiently broad range, of known cognitive abilities. It thus discourages the observation of other types of cognitive functioning. On the contrary, the items on the typical intelligence test seemed to us to represent a rather narrow band of intellectual tasks, relying chiefly on those requiring in Guilford's terms "convergent thinking" and neglecting those requiring "divergent thinking." To do well on the typical intelligence test, the subject must be able to recall and to recognize, perhaps even to solve; he need not necessarily be able to invent or innovate.

Second, although the correlation between the IQ and learning is positive— and we ought to say at once that we recognize the IQ as probably the best single measure we have— it nevertheless rarely accounts for more than one-quarter of the variance in such crucial factors as school achievement and academic performance. The student with a higher IQ who is doing poorly in school and the student with a lower IQ who is doing well appear too often for the IQ to stand as the only predictive measure of intellectual ability or as the sole criterion of giftedness. Moreover, it is commonly observed that many children who are very high in intelligence as measured by IQ are not concomitantly high in such other intellectual functions as creativity, and many children who are very high in creativity are not concomitantly high in intelligence as measured by IQ.

And third, the IQ metric has been peculiarly immune to advances in our understanding of thinking and behavior. Despite significant transformations in our theories of cognition, learning, and problem solving, the conceptual base of the intelligence test has remained unaltered. The soundness of a new intelligence test is often measured by the degree of its correlation with an old intelligence test, that is, the new test must measure the same mental processes as the old test. This procedure effectively perpetuates the original conception of intelligence and guards it from serious theoretical and empirical scrutiny.

These considerations, among others, led us to wonder whether the slackening of progress in the understanding of gifted children might not be due to the too-heavy reliance on the concept of intelligence as reflected in the intelligence test. Are there not other intellectual qualities— qualities not presently sampled by the intelligence test— that are also representative of giftedness? Is not creativity just such a quality? The assumption of most studies of giftedness is that intelligence and creativity are so highly correlated that the highly intelligent student is also the highly creative student. Is the assumption tenable?

That creativity and intelligence might not be closely related was suggested in psychological literature even before the intelligence test as we now know it had been developed. As early as 1898, Dearborn studied the imaginative responses of Harvard students and faculty to a series of inkblots. In discussing his results, he commented that two of the poorest records were made by "students of decidedly 'intellectual type.' " Several years later Colvin studied "inventiveness" in the English compositions of grade-school children. Two of his scoring categories were "logical power" and "spontaneity," the one referring to organizational ability and the other to imaginative ability. Colvin concluded, "If we further study the results we will see that for both boys and girls logical power varies largely with the extent of the composition, but does not seem to accompany any particular element of spontaneity." In 1906 Colvin and Meyer repeated the original study with the same results. "Logical power shows no pronounced relation to any type of imagination except the visual," they reiterated. In 1916, to give one other instance of these early investigations, Laura Chassel studied a number of different tests, ranging from tests of word building and coding to those requiring unusual and original responses to novel situations. The former tasks were quite similar to those included in many present tests of intelligence, the latter quite similar to many present tests of "divergent thinking" or creativity. Chassel found that performance on the IQ tasks bore relatively little relation to performance on the creativity tasks.

By 1920 the intelligence test in its standard form was very much with us. It had been used in military selection, and was being widely applied to all sorts of decisions involving children. Terman's own studies were under way. From the beginning, effectiveness of the IQ as a comprehensive measure of cognitive functioning was challenged by a number of people. R. M. Simpson, writing for the *American Journal of Psychology* in 1922, had this to say.

> *Tests devised to ascertain either native intelligence or acquired knowledge are certainly valuable to an employer .However there are no elements in them to extract from the mind of the individual his powers of creative productivity and his tendencies toward originality. If his creative ability is expressed in many of these tests, the methods of scoring have failed to take it into consideration. It is evident that we need tests designed to give us more direct and dependable information upon this essential element of progress – creative imagination.*

He went on to develop a number of tests of creativity and to try them out on several samples of school children. He concluded that such "creative tests" should be given as a supplement to tests of general intelligence if we wished to obtain "a more accurate statement of the worth of the individual."

These early statements of belief and tentative empirical observations were followed in due course by more direct studies comparing performance on tests of imagination or originality and tests of intelligence. In 1930 Elizabeth Andrews developed three tests of imagination (e.g. originality of reactions to visual stimuli), and administered them to a sample of pre-school children. The correlation coefficients between the children's intelligence test scores and their scores on the three tests of imagination were .15, .02, and .03. In 1931 McCloy and Meier administered to seventy-nine school children a test of "re-creative imagination," requiring the subjects to respond to the symbolism in abstract paintings, and correlated the quality of their responses with their IQ scores. The correlation was .22. Sporadically through the years other correlational studies produced the same results. For example, in 1946 Welch administered to forty-eight college students a test requiring the reconstruction of ideas into new and original patterns, and correlated the originality of their responses with their performance on the Wonderlic Intelligence Test. The correlation was .27. The casual observation by Dearborn in 1898 had become a commonplace research finding— giftedness in intelligence and giftedness in creativity were by no means synonymous.

Despite this the intelligence test remained essentially the same, emphasizing learning ability and school achievement, and neglecting creative ability. And for all intents and purposes— surely in the school situation— the intelligence test score was most often presumed to be a comprehensive representation of the child's intellectual capacity, both of his mind *and* imagination, as it were. The crucial question as to whether creative ability might not of itself be related to school achievement was simply never raised. This question aside, Stephenson's statement of the significant issue between intelligence tests and creativity in his *Testing School Children* is well worth noting.

> *All well-made Intelligence Tests are exercises in 'objective' thinking, and it is far from true that the most intelligent person*

> *writes the best poetry. How to distinguish between creative and merely intelligent work is the crucial matter, and I am not likely to succeed in a description of the difference, except perhaps to say that the one is characterized by cognitive complexity, and the other by its 'pregnancy with newly expressed emotions.'*

We may conclude this very abbreviated and illustrative summary of relevant research and comment by citing several excerpts from J. P. Guilford's 1950 presidential address to the American Psychological Association. The observations are not only "official" but seem to us very well-taken.

> *Examination of the content of intelligence tests reveals very little that is of an obviously creative nature. Many believe that creative talent is to be accounted for in terms of high intelligence or IQ. This conception is not only inadequate but has been largely responsible for the lack of progress in the understanding of creative people.*
>
> *If the correlation between intelligence test scores and many types of creative performance are only moderate or low, and I predict that such correlation will be found, it is because the primary abilities represented in those tests are not all important for creative behavior. It is also because some of the primary abilities important for creative behavior are not represented in the test at all. In other words, we must look well beyond the boundaries of the IQ if we are to fathom the domain of creativity.*

Our argument then is this. Giftedness in children has most frequently been defined as a score on an intelligence test, and typically the study of the so-called gifted child has been equated with the study of the single IQ variable. Involved in this definition of giftedness are several types of confusion, if not of outright error. First, there is the limitation of the single metric itself, which not only restricts our perspective of the more general phenomenon, but places on the one concept a greater theoretical and predictive burden than it was intended to carry. For all practical purposes, the term "gifted child" has become synonymous with the expression "child with a high IQ," thus blinding us to other forms of excellence. And second, within the universe of intellectual functions themselves, we have most often behaved as if the intelligence test represented an adequate sampling of all mental abilities and cognitive processes. Despite the already substantial and increasing literature regarding the intellectual functions closely allied to creativity, we still treat the latter concept as applicable only to performance in one or more of the arts to the exclusion of other types of achievement requiring inventiveness, originality, and perfection. The term "creative child," in becoming synonymous with the expression "child with artistic talents," has limited our attempts to identify and foster cognitive abilities related to creative functioning in areas other than the arts.

Despite its longevity there is after all nothing inevitable about the use of IQ in defining giftedness. Indeed we might argue that in many ways this definition is only a historical accident— a consequence of the fact that early inquiries in the field had as their context the classroom and its attendant concern with academic abilities and achievement. If we were to move the focus of inquiry from the classroom setting, we might identify cognitive qualities defining giftedness for other situations just as the IQ did in the classroom. Should we change only the original criteria of learning, we might change the cognitive qualities defining giftedness even in the classroom. For example, if we recognize that learning involves the production of novelty as well as the remembrance of course content— *discovering* as well as *recalling*— measures of creativity as well as IQ become appropriate defining characteristics of giftedness. Thurstone put the issue as follows.

> *To be extremely intelligent is not the same as to be gifted in creative work. This may be taken as a hypothesis.*
>
> *It is a common observation in the universities that those students who have high intelligence, judged by available criteria, are not necessarily the ones who produce the most original ideas. All of us probably know a few men who are both creative and highly intelligent, but this combination is not the rule.*
>
> *The confusion between intelligence and creative talent is common. For example, Quiz Kids are often referred to as geniuses. They would undoubtedly score high in memory functions, including incidental memory and rote memory. But it is doubtful whether they are also fluent in producing original ideas.*

Nor is there anything inevitable about limiting the concept of giftedness to cognitive excellence alone, however defined. Although the question may be largely a semantic one, there is no doubt that many desirable qualities exist beyond those with an exclusively intellectual focus. Are there not some social qualities-say, moral character or psychological adjustment— which also might lead us to call an individual gifted, and might perhaps be reflected in superior school performance, to say nothing of excellence in other areas such as public service? Surely the study of such qualities might well be an adjunct to any general and systematic examination of giftedness.

The issues we have raised are, of course, not new or unique to us. The American Association for Gifted Children some time ago argued that qualities other than IQ be included in the conception of giftedness, and defined the gifted individual as "a person whose performance in any line of socially useful endeavor is consistently superior. This definition includes those talented in art, music, drama, and mathematics, as well as those who possess mechanical and social skills and those with high abstract verbal intelligence." " Despite such calls for freeing the concept of giftedness from its one-sided attachment to the IQ metric and for broadening the base for examining intellectual and social excellence in children, the essential point remains: in research as in educational practice, the IQ metric has continued to be the predominant and often exclusive criterion of giftedness. Accordingly, we undertook to examine empirically the consequences of applying other conceptions of giftedness as well as "high IQ" to the study of children.

Our preliminary efforts may briefly be summarized as follows. We began by collecting all the positive statements made about children, that is, statements like "He is an excellent student," "She is beautiful," "He is about the most trustworthy child I know," "She has a lot of pep and energy," "He is a fine athlete." Each statement suggested that if a child had such quality in an outstanding degree, he would be called in some way "gifted." After coinpiling a long list of such statements, we grouped them into a manageable number of categories. For example, statements dealing with "honesty," "trustworthiness," "character," and the like, were combined into the category "morality." This procedure led to thirteen categories which, so far as we could tell, appropriately included all the qualities characteristically used to describe children in laudatory terms. The categories were: intelligence, school achievement, social skills, athletic ability, personal appearance, physical health, energy level, sense of humor, creativity, morality, goal directedness, breadth of interests, psychological adjustment.

We proceeded to examine the nature of and interrelation among these qualities by asking groups of teachers and parents to evaluate the categories. Which of the categories were most indicative of "giftedness" in children? Which were most prognostic of "adult success?" Which qualities were most favored by teachers? Which by parents? The specific findings from this aspect of the study will be referred to in some detail in an ensuing chapter. What is important at the moment is that these preliminary studies indicated to us the advantages— although if we are not careful, certain disadvantages as well— of expanding the conception of giftedness to include a number of cognitive and psychosocial qualities in addition to the IQ. Furthermore, many of the common assumptions about the reactions of teachers and parents to the concept of giftedness—assumptions based on studies using only the IQ criterion of giftedness— were brought into serious question by our findings, tentative though these were. We discovered, for example, that although both teachers and parents defined the gifted child in the same cognitive terms, teachers preferred such gifted children in the classroom, but parents did not prefer them in the family. Or again, the relationship between the qualities defining giftedness in children and the qualities believed essential for adult success was *nil* for teachers and somewhat higher but still low for parents. In any case, this exploratory work encouraged us to begin with these thirteen categories at least as a tentative framework for studying giftedness in children.

We selected as the setting for the study a Midwestern private school, a choice predicated by the need for extensive data from children, parents, and teachers. The school in question had detailed cumulative records, and in addition was willing to accommodate its program to our work over a period of some weeks in a way that was not possible in the typical public school. The risk of dealing with an atypical population seemed to us to be outweighed by the advantages of having the cumulative records and the full cooperation of the children, their parents, and the teachers.

The primary critical technical problem was developing procedures for assessing the qualities represented by each of the categories. For several of the categories there already existed widely accepted assessment techniques; for the greater number, however, we were faced with the task of constructing our own instruments. For testing intelligence we could rely on the already available individual and group IQ tests. Where such variables as creativity or morality were concerned, we had to use tests that were still in the experimental stage, including some that were devised especially for this study. We need hardly add that although for some categories we felt our procedures were very satisfactory indeed, for others we did only the best we could, and hoped that others will do better on the basis of our failures.

After examining the data obtained, we decided that certain results were of greater theoretical and practical significance than others – the categories of intelligence and psychological health, for example, were potentially more fruitful than athletics or appearance. Although we used all the data in describing and classifying the subjects, we chose for continued examination: intelligence, psychological adjustment, creativity, breadth of interest, morality, and buoyancy, the last an empirically derived category combining the qualities humor and energy. The breadth of interest and buoyancy groups included so few subjects that we decided to limit our major effort to the four groups of gifted students representing *creativity, intelligence, morality,* and *psychological adjustment* – groups that seemed to be of central theoretical and practical significance, and of pre-eminent relevance to the issues we had raised. The focus of the present work then is on the following.

1. The identification of two groups of students each exhibiting as its salient characteristic a different type of cognitive excellence – the one high in intelligence but not concomitantly high in creativity, the other high in creativity but not concomitantly high in intelligence.
2. The identification of two groups of students each exhibiting as its salient characteristic a different type of psychosocial excellence-the one high in morality but not concomitantly high in psychological adjustment, the other high in psychological adjustment but not concomitantly high in morality.

3. The intensive study of each pair of groups.

   a. What is the nature of their behavior in school? For example, do they do equally well on tests of scholastic achievement? Are they perceived as equally desirable by their classroom teachers? Do they attach the same meaning to their educational experiences?

   b. What is the nature of their value orientations? For example, do they aspire to similar career goals? Do they hold similar views of the "good life?" More especially, with respect to the highly intelligent and the highly creative groups, what is the character of their fantasies and imaginative productions?

   c. What is the nature of their family environment? For example, do the parents of the two groups perceive their children in similar ways? Are there differences in the physical aspects of their homes? Are there differences in the patterns of parental control and dominance?

The account of what we did and what we found is divided into four sections. We present first the procedures and results for the cognitive variables. Then since the findings with respect to cognition, and more specifically creativity, are of central interest, we consider several theoretical formulations in this area, the intent being to illuminate our results in the light of varying conceptions of productive thinking and possibly to illuminate the conceptions in the light of our results. We next turn rather briefly and illustratively to the psychosocial groups. Finally, we present a number of case studies designed to give flesh and blood to the abstractions of the experimental and theoretical studies, and to provide specific qualifications to the quantitative conclusions, which tend unavoidably to be stated in general terms.

2

Highly Intelligent and Highly Creative Adolescent: Cognitive Giftedness

Cognition is the process whereby an organism becomes aware or obtains knowledge of an object, a quality, or an idea. That this process is complex in the extreme hardly needs exposition. Consider for a moment the problem of knowing about the universe, or a flower, of learning about colors or numbers, or the conjugation of *amo*, of understanding the second law of thermodynamics, of remembering your telephone number, or of gaining appreciation of the Spenserian sonnet. It is the process by which on person thinks of the language he has been using all his life as "the means through which we communicate with others," and another person as "the window through which we see experience." It is the process involved when a very young child looked at oil spilled on a wet pavement and said, "Oh, look Mommy, see a rainbow in the gutter," and the process by which her mother said, "That's not a rainbow, that's a dirty oil slick."

Guilford has suggested that there are about fifty known factors of the intellect, and there may be many more as yet unknown. For analytic purposes, however, in order to make the various factors more manageable, it is possible to begin by identifying two basic cognitive or intellective modes. The one mode tends toward retaining the known, learning the predetermined, and conserving what is. The second mode tends toward revising the known, exploring the undetermined, and constructing what might be. A person for whom the first mode or process is primary tends toward the *usual and expected.* A person for whom the second mode is primary tends toward the *novel and speculative.* The one favors certainty, the other risk. Both processes are found in all persons, but in varying proportions. The issue is not one of better or worse, or of more useful or less useful. Both have their place, and both must be recognized for their differences, commonalties, interactions, and distinctive functions in the individual's psychic economy.

Various terms have been used to describe the two processes. Guilford has suggested "convergent thinking" and "divergent thinking"; Rogers uses "defensiveness" and "openness"; Maslow "safety" and "growth." Whatever terms are used, it is clear that one process represents intellectual acquisitiveness and conformity, the other, intellectual inventiveness and innovation. One focuses on knowing what is already discovered, the other focuses on discovering what is yet to be known.

The most widely used technique for evaluating cognition or intellectual functioning is the intelligence test. English and English in their dictionary of psychological terms define the instrument as follows. "The test is a sample of the cognitive-function tasks that are usual and expected italics theirs in any large cultural group or subgroup." The conventional IQ test requires that the subject know the common association to a stimulus and the accepted solution to a problem. In many of these tests the subject must respond to a stimulus for which only one "unique" answer is correct. He is not asked to innovate, to speculate, to invent, to, as it were, come up with an emergent answer. Indeed, if the answer is "novel" it is likely to be scored wrong. In short, the conventional IQ test tends toward the evaluation of those cognitive processes that have been called convergent, retentive, conservative, more than those processes that have been called divergent, innovative, and constructive. It may be that the two processes are so related that it would be impossible to identify individuals who are high in one and not concomitantly high in the other. But if this is the assumption, it is an assumption well worth putting to the proof.

Highly Intelligent and the Highly Creative Adolescent: an Attempt at Differentiation

The first step in examining the foregoing assumption was to select subjects who do indeed exhibit these different types of cognitive excellence. Accordingly, we attempted to identify two groups of individuals, the one group high in intelligence as represented by the conventional IQ metric but not as high in the cognitive functions represented by tests of creativity, the other group high in the cognitive functions represented by the same tests of creativity but not as high in intelligence as represented by the conventional IQ metric.

Except for the pilot investigations needed to test the new instruments, the setting for the study was a private school in the Chicago area. The greatest proportion of students come from middle and upper middle class families residing in the immediate neighborhood. Many of the parents are connected with a large university, either as faculty, staff, or graduate students. Others occupy professional, managerial, and white-collar positions. A great many are college graduates and a sizable percentage hold advanced degrees. A negligible number of the parents are in semiskilled or unskilled occupations.

Admission to the school, above the kindergarten and primary grade level, is based on past academic performance, scores on entrance tests and interviews with both the child and the parents. The grade grouping of the school is similar to that of public schools in the area except that a single grade— the pre-freshman-replaces the traditional seventh and eighth grades; thus the students in the high school are one year advanced as compared with public school students. The mean IQ of the school is very high; for our subjects it was 132 with a standard deviation of 15.

All students from the sixth grade through the senior year of high school (292 boys; 241 girls) participated in the major testing phase of the study. Approximately forty test scores were obtained for each student. The total testing time required was about 20 hours spread over a period of several weeks. Additional data were secured from the school's records office, parent questionnaires, and parent interviews. Students for whom relatively complete data were available served as the sample from which the experimental groups were drawn (245 boys; 204 girls). This sample did not differ in any significant respect from the population.

The two experimental groups — one high in intelligence but not concomitantly high in creativity, the other high in creativity but not concomitantly high in intelligence — were composed on the basis of the following instruments.

Intelligence tests: Intelligence test data were supplied by the records office of the school. Either a Binet or a Henmon-Nelson IQ was available for each student, although perhaps a dozen were WISC scores. All scores were converted by regression equation to comparable Binet IQ's.

Creativity tests: As it is used in this study, the term "creativity" refers to a fairly specific type of cognitive ability reflected in performance on a series of paper-and-pencil tests. Unlike the popular definition, our use of the term does not assume that this type of intellective ability is characteristic only of persons judged to be creative in the artistic and scientific sense. Application of the popular criterion would of course make the empirical study of creative thinking in children almost impossible. Rather, we shall start with the assumption that these creative thinking abilities are found to some extent in all persons-children and adults, sculptors and astronomers, architects and artisans. As we shall see, the abilities (and the tasks used to assess them) seem to be logically related to the more common definition of creativity, and ultimately may perhaps be empirically related to it.

Stated in somewhat different language, our research interest focuses on "creative potential" in the same way that a music instructor is interested in assessing the musical potential of a child. Just as all children who possess fine tone discrimination or a highly developed sense of rhythm do not achieve distinction in music, so all children who possess outstanding creative thinking abilities, in our sense, may not become creative artists or scientists. Nonetheless, the absence of these abilities might lead to a prognosis of probable failure in creative accomplishment. In general, our tests of creativity involved the ability to deal inventively with verbal and numerical symbol systems and with object-space relations. What most of these tests had in common was that the score depended not on a single predetermined correct response as is most often the case with the common intelligence test, but on the number, novelty, and variety of adaptive responses to a given stimulus task. For example, one instrument called for varied verbal associations to stimulus words; another called for the ability to structure an incomplete or distorted perceptual stimulus; another for the ability to see many and different problems, given a single set of numerical data; still another required remote, or clever, or original responses to complex verbal situations. Since it was anticipated that the absolute level of these abilities might be different for boys and girls and for the several age grades in our sample, separate scoring norms were established by age and sex, thus assuring a relatively equal distribution of boys and girls and of age levels in our experimental groups. There were five creativity measures. These were taken or adapted from other tests, or constructed especially for the study as follow:

1. **Word Association:** The subject was asked to give as many definitions as possible to fairly common stimulus words (e.g. "bolt," "bark," "sack"). His score depended on the absolute number of definitions and the number of different categories into which these definitions could be put. For example, a student obtaining a low score on this instrument might reply to the stimulus word "bolt" by saying, "To fasten down; to secure; bolt a door; bolt a hatch on a ship." A student obtaining a high score might say in response to the same stimulus, "To fasten down; to run away quickly; to eat food rapidly; a bolt of cloth; a horse bolts; a bolt of lightning."
2. **Uses for Things:** The idea for this test derives from a description of two similar tests used by J. P. Guilford in his factor analytic studies of cognitive ability. The subject was required to give as many uses as he could for objects that customarily have a stereotyped function attached to them, for example, "brick," "paper-clip," "toothpick." His score depended on the number and originality of the uses he mentioned. A student obtaining a low score on this test might reply to the object "brick" by saying, "Bricks can be used for

building purposes. You can build a wall with brick, or you can build a sidewalk or a fireplace with a brick." A student obtaining a high score might say to the same item, "Bricks can be used for building. You can also use a brick as a paperweight. Use it as a doorstop. You can heat a brick and use it as a bed warmer. You can throw a brick as a weapon. You can hollow out the center of a brick and make an ashtray." Whereas the number of responses to the Word Association Test is restricted by the universe of meanings commonly attached to the given word, the number of responses that can be given to the Uses Test is almost limitless, depending only on the respondent's ingenuity and inventiveness.

3. **Hidden Shapes:** This test is part (G37) of Cattell's Objective Analytic Test Battery and consists of eighteen simple geometric figures each of which is followed by four complex figures. The subject was required to find the geometric figure that was hidden in the more complex form or pattern.
4. **Fables:** The subject was presented with four fables in which the last lines were missing. He was required to compose three different endings for each fable: a "moralistic," a "humorous," and a "sad" ending. Here is one of the fables.

The Mischievous Dog

A rascally dog used to run quietly to the heels of every passerby and bite them without warning. So his master was obliged to tie a bell around the cur's neck that he might give notice wherever he went. This the dog thought very fine indeed, and he went about tinkling it in pride all over town.

But an old hound said.

The subject's score depended on the number, appropriateness, and originality of the endings. Here are sample moralistic, humorous, and sad endings that received credit: "Pride cometh before a fall," "This is your plight, you dogs that bite," "That the dog would soon go insane from the constant tinkling." Here are endings in the same categories that did not receive credit: "Now you cannot bite as you've done before," "Now people can keep out of your way," "Well it looks like he won't bite any more people."

5. Make-up Problems: The subject was presented with four complex paragraphs each containing many numerical statements. He was required to make up as many mathematical problems as he could with the information given. He himself did not have to solve the problems or know how to solve them. The point of the task was t be able to see varied and new problems and relationships in a single set of data. Here is one of the situations.

Mr. Smith decided to purchase a house whose cost was $15,000. He made a down payment of $5000, and agreed to pay the rest with monthly payments. Each monthly payment included a portion of the principal, and interest charge computed at the rate of 5 per cent per year, plus a charge for insurance which cost $129.50 per year.

Mr. Smith found by talking to the former owner that it cost an average of $20 per month to heat the house. After he had owned the house for two years, he received $3000 through an uncle's will which he applied to what he still owed on the house. A year later he purchased a new stove and refrigerator on time payments which added $35 a month to his expenses. At the same time he added insulation to the house which dost him an additional $30 a month for 18 months, but which the contractor who installed it guaranteed would reduce his heating costs by 15 per cent. Given this information, set up as many problems as you can involving Mr. Smith's expenses in connection with the purchase and operation of his home.

The subject's score depended on the number, appropriateness, complexity, and originality of the problems. For example, the question, "How long will it be before Mr. Smith had saved enough on heating costs to make up for what he had paid for insulating the house?" received more credit than did the question, "How much did Mr. Smith still owe after his down payment?"

It must be remembered that this is a sample with a very high mean IQ, and some of the attenuation may be due to this factor. But, as we shall see, there are replications of these findings with other, less extreme groups. On the basis of the IQ measure and a summated score on the five creativity instruments, the two experimental groups were formed as follows.

1. **The High Creativity Group:** These were subjects in the top 20 per cent on the creativity measures when compared to students of the same age and sex, but *below* the top 20 per cent in IQ (N = 26: 15 boys, 11 girls).
2. **The High Intelligence Group:** These were subjects in the top 20 per cent in IQ when compared with students of the same age and sex, but *below* the top 20 per cent on the creativity measures (N = 28: 17 boys, 11 girls).

Table 2.1. Inter correlation among creativity and intelligence tests

		Boys (above diagonal) N = 292 *Variable Number*					
Variable Number	*Test*	*1*	2	3	4	5	6
1	Word Association		369	344	303	420	378
2	Uses	371		206	222	175	186
3	Hidden Shapes	351	197		159	414	366
4	Fables	320	276	153		220	131
5	Make-up Problems	488	279	525	269		246
6	Intelligence Quotient	371	147	303	115	393	
		Girls (below diagonal) N = 241					

The members of the high IQ group possess the demonstrated ability to perform with excellence in the type of problem-solving tasks common to the conventional intelligence test. They do not apparently possess the ability to perform with the same excellence on the type of cognitive tasks included in the "creativity" instruments. They may be able to define the word "homunculus" with ease or to supply quickly the "unique" missing digit in a number series, but they have less facility with problems requiring them to think of several novel uses for a stereotyped object like a brick or a new ending to a familiar fable.

The reverse is true for the members of the high creativity group. They do not do as well as the high IQ subjects on the intelligence test problems. But their performance is very striking indeed on tasks calling for inventiveness and originality. Although they may not be able to give the meaning of the word "homunculus" or to complete a number series with the same precision and rapidity as the high IQ's, they are able to think with surprising facility of using a brick as a bed warmer, a weapon, or if necessary as a paperweight, and they are able to create novel twists to fables almost at will.

Description of the two groups on the basis of test scores alone neglects certain significant qualitative differences, but these will emerge in other sections of this chapter and in the case studies. It must be emphasized that the qualitative differences are as important as the quantitative ones, and indeed the concept of style of cognitive functioning is much more central to the objectives of this study than any linear notion of "more or less" intellective ability or even the concept of "level" of cognitive functioning. We recognize that our experimental groups are composed of children who are unusual in the statistical sense. But the essential point for us is that they permit us to examine in almost type-case form the kinds of cognitive style they represent in such striking degree. And having said that our subjects are unusual children from a selective private school, we must add that children of the same types can be found in large numbers in other less selective schools as well.

The crucial question in studying the two groups of adolescents is not which is better, or which is more desirable, or which is of greater potential worth to society. Talent in all its forms is admirable and worthy of encouragement. There is no intent here to derogate the IQ metric as such, for it remains one of the best predictors of academic achievement we have. It "selects in," as it is supposed to do, many students who are likely to achieve better than the average. But at the same time— and this is the immediate point— it tends to "select out" some students who are also likely to achieve better than the average. These latter students are in many cases the kind represented by our High Creativity Group. The question for us is not the relative worth of different types of cognitive functioning nor the relative effectiveness of different types of instruments to assess cognitive ability. The crucial issue is how to increase our understanding of all the forms of cognition and human excellence, and of the forces that help to produce them.

With this goal in mind, we may approach the analysis of our highly intelligent and our highly creative adolescents by referring to the research questions posed in the first chapter. As these questions suggest, we are interested in examining these adolescents within three broad contexts: (1) as *students*, that is, what is their performance in school, how do their teachers perceive them, what is their motivation for achievement; (2) as *individuals*, that is, what are their personal values and attitudes, what is the nature of their fantasy-life, what are their ultimate career aspirations; (3) as *members of their family group*, that is, what is the character of the family and home environments in which these adolescents were born, developed, and are presently interacting.

Highly Intelligent and the Highly Creative Adolescents as Students: School Performance, Need: Achievement, and Perception by Teachers

In general the behavior of these adolescents in school may be specified in three separate questions. How do they perform on standardized achievement tests? What is their motivation or need for achievement? How do their teachers view them as students?

Scholastic achievement

The evaluation of scholastic achievement was based on standardized achievement test scores provided by the records office of the school. Two scores were obtained for each student, one in verbal achievement and one in numerical achievement.

In order to secure as stable and comprehensive an estimate of verbal achievement as possible, an average score was computed for all the standardized achievement test data relevant to the English curriculum at each grade level. At the sixth grade level, for example, the average score was based on four tests: Cooperative English Test C1, Reading Comprehension, Form Y; Iowa Language Test C, Basic Language Skills, Advanced Form *M*; Iowa Work Study Test *B*, Work Study Skills, Advanced Form *C*; Stanford Spelling Test, Form *F*. At the high school junior grade level, the average score was based on the Cooperative Literary Comprehension and Appreciation Test Form *T*, and the Cooperative English Test, C2, Reading

Comprehension, Form *T*, Upper Level. Similarly, for numerical achievement, at the sixth grade level, the score was based on the Iowa Every pupil Arithmetic Test, Advanced Form C. At the high school junior grade level, the score was based on the Cooperative Geometry Test, Form 2. All scores were transformed to standard scores, and a mean was obtained for each student to represent his achievement.

Table 2.2. Means and standard deviations of IQ and school achievement for total student population and experimental groups

		Total Population? (*N* = 449)	*High IQ* (*N* = 28)	*High Creative†* (*N* = 24)
IQ	$\bar{x}$+	132.00	150.00‡	127.00
	s	15.07	6.64	10.58
School	$\bar{x}$+	49.91	55.00‡	56.27‡
Achievement	*s*	7.36	5.95	7.90

? For purposes of comparison, the scores of each experimental group were extracted from the total population before "*t*" tests were computed.

† Two subjects were omitted from the sample of 26 high creative because they failed to furnish data on the McClelland Need: Achievement instrument which becomes relevant for the next experimental comparison.

‡ Differs significantly from the total population at the .001 level.

The achievement test performance of the high IQ students is significantly above that of the population from which they were drawn. In view of the traditional positive relationship between IQ and school performance, this finding is not at all surprising. But what now about the high creativity group? We observe that they *too* are significantly superior to the school population, and this is quite surprising, for they are below the school average in IQ. It will be recalled that students in the top 20 per cent in IQ were by definition excluded from this group. Indeed, despite the 23-point difference in mean IQ between the high Creative and the high IQ's, the achievement scores of the two groups are equally superior to the achievement scores of the school population as a whole. It seems evident that the cognitive abilities assessed by our creativity instruments account for a significant portion of the variance in school achievement.

Furthermore, the correlation between certain of the creativity tests and school achievement for our whole school population equal in size— and in some instances appreciably exceed-the correlation between IQ and school achievement.

The data with regard to verbal achievement are particularly noteworthy. For both boys and girls the correlation between verbal achievement and three of the creativity tests— Word Association, Hidden Shapes, and Make-up Problems— are as great as or greater than that between IQ and verbal achievement. When it is recalled that the students generally finished the three creativity tests in 15 minutes, 3 ½ minutes, and 30 minutes respectively, the comparison between these correlation and that obtained with the IQ test becomes all the more striking, and surely begs further study.

Table 2.3. Correlation between school achievement and tests of creativity and Intelligence for total sample

	Verbal Achievement		*Numerical Achievement*	
Cognitive Test	*Boys* (N = 292)	*Girls* (N = 241)	*Boys* (N = 292)	*Girls* (N = 241)
Word Association	549	538	406	344
Uses for Things	191	229	215	238
Hidden Shapes	474	420	363	306
Fables	205	330	092	177
Make-up Problems	524	604	302	407
Intelligence Quotient	377	408	401	259

Thus the two first and essential findings were: (1) a relatively low relationship between the IQ metric and measures of creativity, at least at the IQ level of our subjects, and (2) perhaps more significantly and surely more unexpectedly, despite the 23-point difference in IQ, the equal superiority of the high IQ and the high creativity groups in scholastic performance as measured by standardized achievement tests. In view of the nature of these findings and the singularity of the sample on which they were based, a crucial question became: would the same relationships between intelligence, creativity, and achievement be found with other samples?

As part of his studies of children's cognition, E. Paul Torrance undertook to replicate these two aspects of our work with eight different samples, including a selective school similar to the one we used, four elementary schools including a parochial school and a rural school, a public high school, and two samples of graduate students. The mean correlation between creativity measures and various IQ measures were: .16 and .17 with the Stanford-Binet; .32 with the Otis Quick Scoring; .26 with the Kuhlman-Anderson; .24 with the California Test of Mental Maturity;-.02 with the Miller Analogies for one graduate group, and .11 for the other graduate group. Using the same methods that we had used for selecting high IQ and high creativity students, he also compared the scholastic achievement of the two groups in each of his samples. In six of the schools he found the same results that we did: despite sizable differences in IQ, the two groups were equally superior in achievement to the population from which they were drawn. Only in the parochial school and the rural school were there contraindications.

The point we wish to make here is that although there are variations in the relationship between creativity and achievement as a consequence of certain school, pupil, and subject matter characteristics (just as there are in the case of the IQ), a positive and hitherto undisclosed relationship between performance on tests of creativity and on tests of scholastic achievement does seem to hold in a variety of situations. It is not merely an idiosyncrasy of the situation in which we happened to do our study. Let us be clear. We are not saying there is no relationship between IQ and creative thinking. Obviously the feeble-minded by IQ standards are not going to be creative. But at the high average level of intelligence and above, the two are sufficiently independent to warrant differentiation.

We might say a word here about the educational implications of these findings, a subject to which we shall return in the context of other observations. Since our creative students were not in the top of their class in IQ, their superiority in scholastic achievement places them, as such phenomena are handled today, not in the category of "gifted children" but rather in the pejorative category of "overachievers." This dubious classification implies that an IQ-Achievement discrepancy in favor of achievement is a function of emotional or "motivational" (as opposed to "cognitive") variables. It is assumed that the IQ metric does in fact represent the full and true measure of the subject's intellective abilities, and that motivational factors are "pushing" the "overachieving" child to outdo himself, as it were. Moreover, these presumed motivational factors are frequently linked in varying degree to social-psychological malfunctioning, and such children are sometimes sent to the counseling office to reduce their achievement to a level more in line with their IQ. It is noteworthy that the observed discrepancies between IQ and achievement are most usually not accounted for by saying that the test may be *overestimating* or *underestimating*, that is, that the fault is in the test, but that the student is *overachieving* or *underachieving*, that is, that the fault is in the child.

In view of the present data, we would raise the specific issue of whether it is emotional or motivational pathology, or distinctive intellectual ability that accounts for the superior scholastic ability of our creative students, despite their relatively lower IQ. And we may well raise the more general issue of whether so-called over achievement may not at least in some cases be related to excellence in cognitive functions not sampled by the conventional IQ metric rather than inevitably to psychopathology. Indeed, we wonder whether current studies in intellective processes other than those assessed by standard intelligence tests do not underscore the need for re-examining the entire concept of "over achievement." As a matter of fact, as will be seen in later data, students in our high creativity group who would by conventional criteria be labeled "overachievers" actually are less inclined toward "greasy grinding" for good grades (just for the sake of good grades) than are other students.

As it now stands, the concept of over achievement rests on what appears to be a logical dilemma. If, as is frequently said, measures of intelligence reflect general capacity (or potential), it is difficult to see how an individual's performance can exceed his potential or "capacity" to perform. That is, how can an individual do more than he is able to do? One alternative is to assume that academic performance is a function of intellectual capacity plus some motivational variables. This view, however, in no way reduces the dilemma, since the impossibility of exceeding our capacity remains.

A second alternative is to question the meaning of the concept of "capacity" and the instruments used to assess it. If we believe-as seems reasonable— that present measurements of intellectual functioning sample only a small portion of a person's intellectual resources, then the discovery that those who possess cognitive abilities not included in the IQ also do well in school achievement loses some of its mystery, and recourse to some all-explanatory extraneous principle becomes less necessary. The variance in the relationship between intelligence and learning left unexplained by the customary correlation of .50 is now most often attributed exclusively to emotional factors. On the basis of the present data, preliminary as it is, we would raise the general question whether part of this unexplained variance may not be attributable to cognitive functions of the type sampled in our creativity battery but not included in the IQ metric. Having said this, and perhaps sounding more abrupt than we intend, we need hardly add that our animadversion about the nature of the cognitive abilities sampled by the IQ test, the concept of over achievement as it is presently applied, and the use of an all-encompassing principle of motivation to account for over- and underachievement, in no way implies that emotional and motivational factors are not operative in cognition and learning. On the contrary, as we shall make clear, *general cognitive style and general motivational structure* are inextricably related and can be separated only for analytic purposes.

Motivation for Achievement

The question as to whether there *are* differences between our experimental groups in the specific motive "need for achievement" requires examination for at least two reasons. First, the issue is of interest in its own right— do the two groups differ in need: achievement? Second, and perhaps of greater relevance in the immediate context, could the equally superior scholastic achievement of the group with the lower IQ and the group with the higher IQ be accounted for by greater motivation to achieve on the part of one group over the other?

Two instruments were used to examine the achievement motivation of our subjects: McClelland's widely applied need: achievement measure and Strodtbeck's V-score, which is less familiar but has recently been used with good results in a study of adolescent achievement.

The McClelland instrument consists of six pictures to which the students are required to respond by writing short stories. The stories are then scored for the presence or absence of achievement themes. A story about a boy working hard to succeed in college would receive a higher need: achievement score than would a story about a boy coming home from school and taking a nap. The Strodtbeck instrument consists of eight items designed to assess the student's interest in planning for the future and his willingness to break away from home and family ties, if necessary, in order to attain achievement goals. Here are two illustrative items. "Nowadays with world conditions as they are, the wise person lives for today and lets tomorrow take care of itself," "Nothing in life is worth the sacrifice of moving away from your parents." A subject's score is determined by the number of times he indicates a desire to achieve and a willingness to break family ties.

Table 2.4. Means and standard deviations of total student population and experimental groups on need: achievement measure and Strodtbeck's V-score

		Total Population	*High IQ (N = 28)*	*High Creative*[?] *(N = 24)*
McClelland's need: achievement (T-scores)	x+	49.81	49.00	50.04
	s	9.49	7.97	8.39
Strodtbeck's V-scores	x+	6.11	6.28	6.42
	s	1.18	1.13	1.69

? Two subjects were omitted from the sample of 26 high creative because they failed to furnish data on the need: achievement instrument.

The results for the need: achievement and V-score variables are given in Table 2.4 . On these two measures of motivation to acnieve, the two experimental groups do not differ from each other, nor do they differ from the total student body. Although it should not be assumed that the two measures successfully assess all the motivational factors that might be linked to achievement behavior, the absence of any differences on these instruments suggests that the apparent "over achievement" of the high creative cannot be quickly ascribed to motivational differences alone.

Perception by Teachers

The answer to one significant question about the behavior of our highly creative and our highly intelligent subjects as students seems quite clear. Despite a 23-point difference in IQ and no difference in achievement motivation, they achieve equally well. There is, however, a second question of no less significance: are they also perceived equally well by their classroom teachers?

To answer this question, we asked the teachers to rate all students in the school on the degree to which they enjoy having them in class. The criterion on which the teachers were to do the rating read as follows.

> *This is a student whom the teacher especially enjoys having in class. When asked what kind of person you prefer as a member of your class, this is the student who comes most readily to mind. He may or may not be the one who gets along best in the classroom situation, he may or may not be the brightest child in the class, and he may or may not be the one who gets the best grades. But he is liked by you and is the sort of person about whom you are most likely to say, "Of all the children in my class, this is the one I most enjoy."*

The teachers were required to place all their students on a 5-point scale so that categories 1 and 5 each contained one-twelfth of the students; categories 2 and 4 each contained one-fourth of the students; and category 3 contained one-third of the students. The values 5, 8, 10, 12, and 15 were assigned to the categories and were used in the quantitative analysis. Comparisons were then made of the ratings given the two groups and the ratings of the entire school population.

The data are quite clear-cut. The high IQ group stands out as being more desirable than the average student, the high creativity group does not. It is apparent that an adolescent's desirability as a student is not a function only of his academic achievement. Even though the scholastic performance is the same, the high IQ students are preferred over the average students by their teachers, the creativity students are not. This result is quite striking, for, if anything, the reverse should be true. Here is a student— the high IQ one— who is doing scholastically only what, can be expected

Table 2.5. Means and standard deviations of teacher ratings for total student population and experimental groups

Teacher Rating		*Total Population*? (N = 449)	*High IQ* (N = 28)	*High Creative* † (N = 24)
Desirability	$\bar{x}$	10.23	11.20‡	10.54
as a student	s	3.64	1.56	1.95

? For purposes of comparison, the scores of each experimental group were extracted from the total population before t tests were computed.

† Two subjects were omitted from the sample of twenty-six high creative because appropriate data were unavailable.

‡ Differs significantly from the total population at the .01 level.

This is a finding of considerable import, for it suggests that teachers distinguish among high achievers, favoring one group of achievers over the population of students but not another group. They favor high achievers who are high IQ's, but not high achievers who are high creative. Again this finding cannot be said to be a function of the atypical sample, the atypical school, and perhaps the atypical teacher. Indeed, our observation was that in this school creative children were more likely to be favored than in other schools. In any case, in the series of studies to which we have already referred, Torrance replicated this finding as well. On the basis of his work with a variety of similarly defined groups, he concluded, "Two of the most consistent findings are for the high IQ pupils to be better known by their teachers and to be considered more desirable as pupils than the highly creative subjects."

The reason for this difference in the teachers' reactions is not immediately apparent, but at least two explanations suggest themselves although there may be others. One reason may derive from the so-called "halo effect" hypothesis. There is probably no information about a child that is potentially more status-setting, especially in school, than is his intelligence quotient. Once the teacher is informed that John "has" an IQ of 165, say, it is difficult for her to behave as she did before his IQ became known. She seems almost duty-bound to admire him and all his works. But if this "halo effect" is helpful in understanding why teachers give better ratings to the high IQ students than to the high creativity students despite their equal superiority in achievement, it is probably at best only a partial explanation. For one thing, it is unlikely that all IQ's were known to the teachers; and for another, their judgment could as well have been influenced by the achievement scores, which, like the IQ's, were available to them on the students' records, and which were the *same* for both groups.

A second and more fundamental reason for the different reaction of the teachers to the two groups might lie not in the nature of the information held by the teachers (which is at best problematical) but in the nature of the students themselves— their personal values and attitudes, their fantasies, and their long-term aspirations. A study of these not only might help to explain the different effect of those students on their teachers, but also may help us to understand the children themselves as individuals, and consequently also as students. It is, then, to the study in some depth of the high creativity and the high IQ adolescents as individuals that we must turn.

Before we do this, we would like to say a word about the educational implications of the findings so far. We have already remarked at some length on so-called over achievement. The problem of identifying the creative student, and even of some bias against him at the secondary school level, is probably self-evident enough not to require elaboration here. There is, however, an issue regarding the further education of these creative students that is perhaps more subtle and does bear specific comment.

Achievement grades aside, the two most common criteria applied to a prospective college student are (1) scholastic aptitude measures of the intelligence test (IQ) type, and (2) school recommendations based on teacher evaluations of student characteristics. Both of these indices tend to penalize the high creativity student in favor of the high IQ student; his aptitude scores and his ratings by teachers are likely to be less promising. And of course the apparent discrepancy between his achievement and his aptitude in favor of achievement, that is, his so-called "over achievement," is not likely to be of help either. Indeed, it is just this discrepancy which might label him a "greasy-grind" or "middle-class striver," and mark his application for "sudden death" in the college admissions office. It is ironic that the very student who may potentially be most creative is also more likely than other students to be labeled a greasy-grind by current test criteria.

Highly Intelligent and the Highly Creative Adolescents as Individuals: Values, Fantasies, and Aspirations

Values

The data regarding the values of the two groups were provided by the Outstanding Traits Test. This instrument contains descriptions of thirteen hypothetical children, each description exemplifying a desirable personal quality or trait. One child is described as having the highest IQ in the entire school, another as being the best athlete, another as having the keenest sense of humor, another as being best looking, another as the most creative person in the school, and so on.

The subjects were required to rank these thirteen descriptions of children in three ways as follows: (1) on the degree to which they themselves would like to be like the children, the resulting data providing what might be called the "self-ideal" of our subjects; (2) on the degree to which they believe each of the children with these various qualities would succeed in adult life, the resulting data providing what might be called the "success image" of our subjects; (3) on the degree to which they believed their teachers would like each of the children, the resulting data providing what might be called the "teacher perception" of our subjects.

The entire population of the school almost without exception ranked "social skills" first as the quality in which they would like to be outstanding, and "good looks," "high energy level," "athletics," and "health" last. In view of this very high agreement, the responses were re-ranked omitting the uniformly ranked qualities, thus leaving as the significant variables: moral character, creativity, goal directedness, intelligence, superior school performance, wide range of interest, emotional stability, and sense of humor. The findings reported here are based on the re-ranked data.

Two questions regarding the two experimental groups may be dealt with summarily. Do they perceive the qualities required for success in adult life the same way? Do they perceive the qualities favored by teachers the same way? Answers to these questions are obtained by correlating the rankings given by the two groups, first for "success image" and then for "teacher perception," that is, the rankings given in response to directions 2 and 3 preceding.

Table 2.6. Rank order correlation between high creative and high IQ students on three sections of the Outstanding Traits Test

	Section of Test		
	Success Image	*Teacher Perception*	*Self-ideal*
Correlation	1.00	.98	.41

As is readily apparent, the ranking of both these categories is practically identical for the two groups. The high creative and the high IQ's agree on what qualities make for adult success in our society and on what qualities teachers prefer in their students. However, as compared with these correlation of 1.00 and .98 respectively, the correlation between the self-ideal rankings — the qualities the adolescents in the two groups want for themselves-is but .41. Although the two groups agree almost exactly on what makes for adult success and on what makes for teacher approval, there is considerable disagreement on what qualities they prefer for themselves.

Let us proceed to a finer, and we believe especially revealing, analysis of the rankings made by the two groups. By comparing "self-ideal" ranking with "success-image" ranking," we may elicit an answer to the question: how success-oriented are the students? Are the qualities they value highly for themselves the same as those they believe make for "success" as adults? And by comparing the "self-ideal" ranking with the "teacher-perception" ranking, we may in effect obtain an answer to the question: how teacher-oriented are the students? Are the qualities they value highly for themselves the same as those they believe teachers value in students?

Table 2.7. Rank order correlation among subsections of the Outstanding Traits Test

	Subjects	
Components of Correlation	*High IQ* (N = 28)	*High Creative* (N = 26)
"Personal traits preferred for oneself" and "personal traits believed predictive of adult success"	.81	.10
"Personal traits preferred for oneself" and "personal traits believed favored by teachers"	.67	-.25

The results are again rather clear-cut. For the high IQ students the relationship between the qualities they value for themselves and those they believe lead to "success" as adults is quite close. That is, these students appear to be highly success oriented. For the high creativity students the relationship between the qualities *they* value and those they believe lead to "success" as adults is virtually *nil.* These students appear *not* to be highly success oriented (at least not by conventional standards of adult success).

The findings with respect to the teacher orientation of the two groups are equally suggestive. Again, for the high IQ students there is a fairly close relationship between the qualities they would like for themselves and the qualities they believe teachers like in students. Although the relationship is by no means perfect, it nonetheless suggests that high IQ students tend to be at least moderately teacher oriented. For the high creativity students the comparison shows little or no relationship. They are not teacher-oriented; if anything, there is apparently a tendency for the creative students to place the highest personal value on qualities which they feel teachers value least.

The data regarding the personal values of the two groups as reflected in their responses to the Outstanding Traits Test suggest that whereas both groups agree on the qualities that lead to adult success as commonly defined and on the qualities teachers favor in their students, the high IQ student wants for himself the qualities he believes make for adult success and which are similar to those he believes teachers like. In contrast, the high creativity student wants for himself qualities having no relationship to those he believes make for adult success and which are dissimilar to those he believes his teachers like. In effect, the high IQ is saying, "I know what makes for success and what teachers like, and I want these qualities too"; the high creative is saying, "I know as well as the high IQ what makes for conventional success and what teachers like, but these are not necessarily the qualities I want for myself."

These findings bear directly on the answers to two earlier questions— that on teacher ratings and that on the relationship between creativity and school achievement. If the desirability of students in the classroom is related to the congruence or discrepancy between their values and their teachers' values, in the light of the present data it is hardly surprising that our high IQ students are more favored by teachers than are our creative students. The high IQ students value and disvalue the same objects and ideals as they believe their teachers do; the high creativity students do not. And if the motivational impetus represented by a concern with adult success and a desire to emulate their teachers is absent or weak among the high creativity students, the observed relationship between creativity and school achievement becomes all the more significant. The result cannot be attributed to some special kind of motivation like "striving for good grades or success" which it is said leads to so-called "over achievement."

The question of what accounts for the differences in the success orientation and teacher orientation of the two groups is, in effect, the question of how the groups differ in their rankings of specific qualities in the self-ideal section of the Outstanding Traits Test. What qualities do the one group desire for themselves that the other group do not? When the data are examined with this question in mind, one quality stands out above all others. It is described in the Outstanding Traits Test quite simply as follows. *Here is the student with the best sense of humor in the school.* In their self ideal rankings the creative students place this quality third out of the thirteen (second of the eight re-ranked qualities used in the preceding analysis). The only qualities they give a higher rank are "getting along with others" (which the entire population ranked first) and "emotional stability."

"High marks," "high IQ," "goal directedness" are all ranked lower. In contrast the high IQ students, in *their* self-ideal rankings, place "sense of humor" *ninth* out of the thirteen qualities (eighth of the eight re-ranked qualities). "High marks," "high IQ," "goal directedness" are all ranked higher. *Both* groups *equally* rank "sense of humor" *ninth* among the qualities they believe teachers would like to see in children, and *tenth* among the qualities they believe will lead to success in adult life. (If we compare the self-ideal rankings of the two groups to those of the total student population, the self-ideal ratings of the high creativity group correlate .04 and .54 with boys and girls respectively. The corresponding correlation for the high IQ group are .74 and .94.)

The prominence of sense of humor in the self-ideal of the creative adolescent as compared with the high IQ adolescent is very striking, and indeed for no other group that we have studied does sense of humor attain a ranking higher than 7.5. But the saliency of humor for the high creatives is not only a matter of self-report or choice -- of wishful thinking, perhaps -- as might be possible on an instrument like the Outstanding Traits Test. Humor pervades all their free-response protocols, to which we shall refer later and as we shall see directly in the fantasy material.

Fantasy: Verbal and Nonverbal Imaginative Productions

We shall not enter here into the current controversy as to whether fantasy as elicited by projective techniques is or is not the "royal road to the unconscious," and hence to the deeper and more stable aspects of personality. We take the position that fantasy or imaginative production as observed in story telling and picture drawing is legitimate data for analysis, and that it does have certain advantages: it is not as readily under the "conscious" control of the individual as other assessment data, and it cannot as readily be manipulated as self-report data may be in line with the real or presumed criteria of the examiner. Moreover, story telling and picture drawing are, in effect, creative processes and, in the context of the present study, have special merits for observing possible distinctive characteristics of our highly intelligent and our highly creative adolescents. With respect to the fantasy material, then, we shall pose two interrelated general questions. (1) How do the two groups handle a problem requiring them to create something in the verbal realm as represented by a story, and in the nonverbal realm as represented by a picture, that is, what is the *process* of the constructive activity? (2) What is the content of the fantasy or imaginative production, that is, what is the *substance* of the constructive activity?

First, the verbal fantasy material. In addition to scoring the need: achievement protocols conventionally for the single achievement theme, the results of which have already been presented, we analyzed the *total* stories. We first sorted "blind" forty-seven protocols written by creative and noncreative subjects. The blind sorting resulted in only seven misplacements. Using categories suggested by this sorting, we then systematically analyzed the protocols of the two experimental groups. The analysis showed striking differences. The high creative adolescents were significantly higher than the high IQ adolescents in *stimulus-free themes, unexpected endings, humor, incongruities, and playfulness,* and showed a marked tendency toward more violence in their stories.

Here, for example, in response to the picture stimulus perceived most often as a man sitting in an airplane reclining seat on his return from a business trip or professional conference, are case-type stories given by a high IQ subject and a high creative subject.

Table 2.8. Categorization of fantasy productions of high IQ and high creative groups

	High IQ (N = 28)		*High Creative? (N = 24)*		*X2*
Content Analysis Categories	*Freq-uency †*	*Per cent*	*Freq-uency †*	*Per cent*	
Stimulus-free theme	11	39	18	75	5.31 ‡§
Unexpected ending	17	61	22	92	5.05 §
Presence of humor	7	25	17	71	9.16**
Presence of incongruity	10	36	17	71	5.06§

	High IQ (N = 28)		High Creative? (N = 24)		X2
Content Analysis Categories	*Freq-uency †*	*Per cent*	*Freq-uency †*	*Per cent*	
Presence of violence	13	46	13	75	3.27
Playful attitude toward theme	9	32	21	89	14.04**

? Two subjects were omitted from the sample of twenty-six high creative because they failed to furnish data on the McClelland need: achievement instruments.

† Numbers in the frequency column represent the subjects whose fantasy productions fit the corresponding categories.

‡ Yates correction was applied in the computation of chi squares in this table and in all other tables where chi square is used in this volume.

§ Significant at the .05 level.

** Significant at the .01 level.

The high IQ subject:

Mr. Smith is on his way home from a successful business trip. He is very happy and he is thinking about his wonderful family and how glad he will be to see them again. He can picture it, about an hour from now, his plane landing at the airport and Mrs. Smith and their three children all there welcoming him home again.

The high creative subject:

This man is flying back from Reno where he has just won a divorce from his wife. He couldn't stand to live with her anymore, he told the judge, because she wore so much cold cream on her face at night that her head would skid across the pillow and hit him in the head. He is now contemplating a new skid-proof face cream.

Or another, in response to the stimulus picture most often perceived as a man working late (or very early) in an office.

The high IQ subject:

There's ambitious Bob, down at the office at 6:30 in the morning. Every morning it's the same. He's trying to show his boss how energetic he is. Now, thinks Bob, maybe the boss will give me a raise for all my extra work. The trouble is that Bob has been doing this for the last three years, and the boss still hasn't given him a raise. He'll come in at 9: 00, not even noticing that Bob had been there so long, and poor Bob won't get his raise.

The high creative subject:

This man has just broken into this office of a new cereal company. He is a private eye employed by a competitor firm to find out the formula that makes the cereal bend, sag, and sway. After a thorough search of the office he comes upon what he thinks is the current formula. He is now copying it. It turns out that it is the wrong formula and the competitor's factory blows up. Poetic justice!

These stories were written in group sessions, often more than a hundred adolescents in the same room, with the maximum writing time 4 minutes per story. "Skid-proof face cream!" "Cereal that will bend, sag, and sway!" It is this ability to restructure stereotyped objects with case and rapidity — almost "naturally" — that seems to us to be the characteristic mark of our high creative as against our high IQ subjects.

The high creativity stories are of course not only humorous. Many of their productions deal with highly imaginative themes. Here, for example, to a picture typically seen as an executive working in his office is a story by one of the high creative.

This man is working on a time machine. In five minutes he will look up at the clock. It has not moved. His own thoughts have stopped time. He goes into the street. A man is getting onto a bus. His foot is on the step. He is not moving. Nothing moves. He tries to forget the equations. Slowly the figures start moving, like the sound of a record turned. He succeeds and has the first mental time machine.

Others of the high creativity stories express quite directly the wish to be creative, or the greater value of artistic or inventive production over other kinds of work. Here, for example, to a picture seen quite often as the rewrite room of a newspaper is a story by one of the high creatives.

This man just had an inspiration for a poem and as he can only work at his desk in the rewrite department of the daily newspaper he dashed to the office. His poem is very modern, about the city, and will be published in the very next issue of the paper. This man will become famous for this poem and others will soon leave the newspaper business to take up creative writing as a career. We wish him luck.

There is one other characteristic that is well illustrated by a number of the stories. This is a certain mocking attitude on the part of the creatives toward conformity and toward conventional "success" as represented by what they call the Average Boy — a theme that is almost never mentioned by the high IQ's. Here, for example, are two responses to the stimulus picture most often perceived as a high-school student doing his homework.

The high IQ subject:

John is a college student who posed for the picture doing his homework. It is an average day with the usual amount of work to do. John took a short break from his studies to pose for the pictures, but he will get back to his work immediately after. He has been working for an hour already and he has an hour's more work to go. After he finishes he will read a book and then go to bed. This work which he is doing is not especially hard but it has to be done.

The high creative subject:

The boy's name is Jack Evans and he is a senior in school who gets C's and B's, hates soccer, does not revolt against convention and has a girl friend named Lois who is a typical sorority fake. He is studying when someone entered the room whom he likes. He has a dull life in terms of anything that is not average. His parents are pleased because they have a red-blooded American boy. Actually, he is horribly average. He will go to college, take over his dad's business, marry a girl, and do absolutely nothing in the long run.

Here is another story by a high creativity adolescent characteristically mocking the "nice" boy, his family-derived ambition, and the triteness of his conventional success.

Freddie Jones was a nice boy. If you don't believe it just ask him. Freddie came from a theatrical family and wanted to be in show business somehow. However, the only talent he had was a nice smile. He posed for toothpaste ads on T.V. You may think this is kind of low brow, but I see nothing wrong with it. Freddie wanted to satisfy an ambition and he did it the best way in which he could. Freddie will never amount to much but he will be happy. How are you doing?

Answers to our two questions about the process and the content of the imaginative productions of the two groups may be summarized as follows.

1. With respect to process, the high creative tend to free themselves from the stimulus, using it largely as a point of departure for self-expression; the high IQ's tend to focus on the stimulus, using it as the invariant for communication. For the high IQ, the issue is essentially one of conserving what others give to him. If the picture stimulus is of a man in an airplane, he must tell a story about travel; if the picture stimulus is of a man in an office, he must tell a story about work. For the high creative, the issue is essentially one of constructing what he wants to give. The picture stimulus may be of a man in an airplane, but the story he wants to tell is about a divorce; the picture stimulus may be of a man alone in an office, but the story he wants to tell is of a private eye in a cereal factory.
2. With respect to the content (and of course the distinction between process and content being made here is only for analytic purposes), the fantasies of the high creativity adolescents contain at once more wit and more violence. They seem more expressive of impulses from within that are frequently inhibited, and descriptive of experiences from without that are often denied. The high creativity adolescent has a more playful— or if you will, more experimental— attitude toward conventional ideas, objects, and qualities. Rather than dealing only in predetermined categories, as the high IQ adolescent is likely to do, he tends to use categories that he himself originates. Cereal does not only snap, crackle, and pop, it can also bend, sag, and sway. Face cream does not only skid, it can also be skid-proof. The attainment of an ambition can mean not only success, it can also be Viewed in other sense.

In view of the striking differences between the two groups in their *verbal* imaginative productions, it seemed appropriate to examine the nature of their *nonverbal* imaginative productions. The data relevant to this issue were provided by drawings produced by the two groups. The test instrument was a sheet of paper with a printed single-lined border approximately 5½ by 7½ inches for framing a picture. Under the border was the title "Playing Tag in the School Yard." At the top of the paper above the border were the following directions. "In the space below, draw a picture appropriate to the title 'Playing Tag in the School Yard.' You may draw any picture you like— whatever you may imagine for this theme." The paper was distributed with other test materials and the subjects were told they could work on their drawings whenever they wished in the free time between the administration of the several other tests, or if they preferred at the end of the testing period.

Even a cursory look through the drawings of the two groups showed unmistakable and compelling differences. Here was a picture drawn by one of the high creative portraying a prison yard with guards apparently chasing ("playing tag with") the prisoners. Here was another, again by one of the high creative, apparently portraying a school of fantastic fish or space objects following one another. There was yet a third picture, a quite elaborate one, which seems to be a play on the word "tag" — ghosts are tagging the school building with various signs and slogans. Numerous other similar productions used the directions to "draw a picture appropriate to the title 'Playing Tag in the School Yard' " to serve as a point of playful departure rather than a point of conventional focus for the child's drawing— or sometimes lack of drawing. One of the creative subjects, for example, handed back what seemed at first glance only the blank sheet of paper— until one noticed that some words had been added to the title. The space within the picture frame had indeed been left as white as it had been, but the title had been changed to "Playing Tag in the School Yard— *During a Blizzard*."

Very few, perhaps three or four, of the drawings of the high IQ's had the same non-literal quality. Instead they stayed close to the directions, or perhaps better to that part of the directions which said "draw a picture appropriate to the title 'Playing Tag in the School Yard' " and neglected the part which said "You may draw any picture you like— whatever you imagine for this theme."

Table 2.9. Stimulus-free *vs.* stimulus-bound drawings by the high IQ and the high creative groups

	High IQ (N = 28)	*High Creative (N = 26)*	X^2	P
Stimulus-free	4	13	6.40	.02
Stimulus-bound	24	13		

Table2.9 does not adequately represent a number of the more subtle differences in the drawings of the two groups. It was not difficult to categorize the pictures of the high IQ group as 4 stimulus-free and 24 stimulus-bound. There was considerable difficulty in categorizing the pictures of the high creative group, for even the apparently stimulus-bound pictures were not quite as clearly in this category as were the similar pictures of the high IQ group. Many of the high creativity pictures, although following the directions quite closely, still tended not to be just straight representation. Among the stimulus-free drawings, the "blizzard" picture is an obvious attempt at humor, and the "ghost" picture an obvious pun on the word "tag." But many of the more stimulus-bound drawings of the high creative also have this same humorous "twist." For example, one individual is chasing another in what is obviously a playground, but the individual being chased seems to be held back by an "I Like Ike" sign dragging at his feet; or again, a dog seems to be chasing a child who is in turn chasing another child. When the pictures are classified into "humor-present" and "humor-absent" categories, the relationship between the high IQ and the high creativity drawings may be summarized as in Table 2.10.

Table 2.10. Humor-present *vs.* humor-absent in the drawings of the high IQ and the high creative groups

	High IQ (N = 28)	*High Creative (N = 26)*	X^2	P
Humor-present	5	14	6.16	.02
Humor-absent	23	12		

In addition to the differences in "freedom" and in "humor" in the pictures of the two groups, a third significant difference to be noted is the more frequent expression of aggression and violence in the drawings of the high creative as compared with the high IQ's. The data are presented in Table 2.11 .

Table 2.11. Violence-present vs. violence-absent drawings of the high 10 and the high creative groups

	High IQ (N = 28)	*High Creative (N = 26)*	X^2	*P*
Violence-present	1	9	6.68	.01
Violence-absent	27	17		

Two other trends in the data, though not statistically significant, are sufficiently consistent and strong to be worth observing. The representation of the space as a school yard by including or failing to include the concrete details of a conventional school yard or playground, that is, jungle gyms, see-saws, flagpole, slides, etc., has already been mentioned. Pictures without such objects may be called "detail-free"; pictures with such objects "detail-bound."

Table 2.12. Detail-free vs. detail-bound drawings of the high IQ and the high creative groups

	High IQ (N = 28)	*High Creative (N = 26)*	X^2	*P*
Detail-free	11	16	1.85	.20
Detail-bound	17	10		

The same trend toward a greater "concern with details" or "concreteness of representation" on the part of the high IQ's as compared with the high creatives is obtained by observing the number of drawings in which the building is specifically labeled a school, a kindergarten, or some such. The data are presented in Table 2.13 .

In summary, it seems clear that there are at least three global differences between the nonverbal imaginative productions of the high IQ and those of the high creativity adolescents.

Table 2.13. Building-labeled vs. building-unlabeled drawings of the high IQ and the high creative groups

	High IQ (*N* = 28)	*High Creative* (*N* = 26)	X^2	*P*
Building-labeled	11	5	1.73	.20
Building-unlabeled	17	21		

(1) The high creative are more stimulus-free. They tend to structure the task in their own terms, rather than merely to comply with it in the terms given. As a corollary, they are less bound by the specific details of the instructions. They do not, for example, feel compelled, as the high IQ's do, to include the conventional playthings of a school yard or to label the building a school, just because the title is "Playing Tag in the School Yard." It is as if the high IQ's were unable or at least unwilling to risk the possibility of error or of being misunderstood. The high Creative did not seem to worry about such risks. They seemed instead to be using their own imagination, and to be willing to leave something to the imagination of others.

(2) The high creative tend to be more fanciful and humorous. Indeed, some of their pictures seem to be rather esoteric fantasies or elaborate pictorial puns, apparently intended as much for their own enjoyment as anyone else's.

(3) The high creatives tend to express more aggression and violence. In this connection, it is not merely the presence or absence of violence that should be noted but that whereas the pictures of the high creatives seem to have personal meaning the pictures of the high IQ's seem only superficial representations. Clearly, there are very real and striking differences in the verbal and nonverbal imaginative productions of the two groups-differences that may be understood both in cognitive and motivational terms.

In the context of cognitive theory, for instance, Guilford's factors of convergent and divergent thinking are highly relevant to an understanding of our subjects. Discussing the production of tests to assess these factors, he states:

> *In tests of convergent thinking there is almost always one conclusion or answer that is regarded as unique, and thinking is to be channeled or controlled in the direction of that answer. In divergent thinking, on the other hand, there is much searching about or going off in various directions. Divergent thinking is characterized as being less goal-bound. There is freedom to go off in different directions. Rejecting the old solution and striking out in some new direction is necessary, and the resourceful organism will more probably succeed.*

Obviously in these terms our high IQ adolescents tend to favor "convergent" modes of thinking, and our high creativity adolescents to favor "divergent" modes of thinking.

In the context of motivational theory, Maslow's formulations of "defense" and "growth," for example, are similarly relevant to the present issues. He writes:

> *Every human being has both sets of forces within him. One set clings to safety and defensiveness out of fear, tending to regress, hanging on to the past afraid to take chances, afraid to jeopardize what he already has, afraid of independence, freedom, separation. The other set of forces impels him forward toward wholeness of self and uniqueness of self, toward full functioning of all his capacities, toward confidence in the face of the external world at the same time that he can accept his deepest, real unconscious Self. This basic dilemma or conflict between the defensive forces and the growth trends I conceive to be existential, imbedded in the deepest nature of the human being, now and forever into the future.*
>
> *Therefore we can consider the process of healthy growth to be a never-ending series of free choice situations, confronting each individual at every point throughout his life, in which he must choose between the delights of safety and growth, dependence and independence. Safety has both anxieties and delights; growth has both anxieties and delights.*

It is again apparent that in these terms our high IQ adolescents tend to favor the anxieties and delights of "safety," whereas our high creativity adolescents tend to favor the anxieties and delights of "growth."

Whether we assume the cognitive or the motivational stance, adopt for our use the one set of concepts or the other, or whether we attempt what seems the more fruitful procedure of seeing the two formulations as referring to similar processes in merely different terms, it seems to us that the essence of the performance of the high creativity adolescents lay in their ability to produce new forms, to risk conjoining elements that are customarily thought of as independent and dissimilar, to "go off in new directions." The creative adolescent seemed to need to free himself from the usual, to diverge from the customary behavior; he seemed to enjoy the risk and uncertainty of the *untried* and the *unknown*. In contrast, the high IQ adolescent seemed to possess to a high degree the ability and the need to focus on the usual and to be "channeled and controlled" in the direction of the "right" answer, the socially accepted solution. He appeared to shy away from the risk and uncertainty of the unknown and to seek the safety and security of the already *established* and the *known*.

A third formulation developed by Rogers is similar to Guilford's and Maslow's but emphasizes yet another aspect of the differences we found. Rogers identifies three qualities which seem to him characteristic of a potentially creative person.

1. *Openness to experience:* extensionality. This is the opposite of psychological defensiveness, when to protect the organization of the self certain experiences are prevented from coming into awareness except in distorted fashion. In a person who is open to experience each stimulus is freely relayed through the nervous system, without being distorted by any process of defensiveness. This means that instead of perceiving in predetermined categories (trees are green; college education is good; modern art is silly) the individual is aware of the existential moment as it is, thus being alive to many experiences which fall outside the usual categories (*this* tree is lavender; this college education is damaging; *this* modern sculpture has a powerful effect on me).
2. *An internal locus of evaluation.* Perhaps the most fundamental condition of creativity is that the source or locus of evaluative judgment is internal. The value of his product is, for the creative person, established not by the praise or criticism of others, but

by himself. Have I created something satisfying to *me*? Does it express a part of me— my feeling or my thought, my pain or my ecstasy? These are the only questions which really matter to the creative person, or to any person when he is being creative.

3. *The ability to toy with elements and concepts.* Associated with the openness and lack of rigidity described under 1 is the ability to play spontaneously with ideas, colors, shapes, relationships— to juggle elements into impossible juxtapositions, to shape wild hypotheses, to make the given problematic, to express the ridiculous, to translate from one form to another, to transform into improbable equivalents. It is from this spontaneous toying and exploration that there arises the hunch, the creative seeing of life in a new and significant way.

Each of these qualities, it seems to us, is reflected in the differences in the imaginative productions of the two groups. The high creatives are more stimulus-free and less categorical. As we have already observed, cereal *can* "bend, sag, and sway," as well as "snap, crackle, and pop," "tag" *can* mean "label" even in a school yard. And their imaginative productions contain elements of fantasy, such as incongruous associations, aggression, violence, which might not appear if their defensiveness were high. The high creatives' more "internal locus of evaluation" is also clearly apparent. Many of their productions are quite esoteric. Unlike the high IQ's, they do not bother with the conventional signs assuring immediate communication, and they seem relatively unconcerned whether their "message" will be understood by everyone. It is almost as if their own enjoyment or evaluation of their response to a stimulus is sufficient; and whereas the high IQ's are intent on *communicating to others,* the high creatives seem bent on expressing themselves. The same "internal locus of evaluation" is characteristic of the attitudes and value choices of the high creatives— their attitudes and values are quite different from those they believe necessary for standard adult success or those they believe their teachers favor, and they do not seem to care that they do differ.

Finally, there is probably no quality that more sharply differentiates our high creativity and our high IQ adolescents than the former's "ability to toy with elements and concepts," "to make the given problematic," "to express the ridiculous." It is in this "playfulness" with "givens," with "conventions," and with "predetermined categories" – in the ability to think of a brick as at once a part of a house and a paperweight, of Freddie Jones as at once attaining success but not amounting to much, of face cream that is at once slippery and skid-proof, and of tag that is at once a game and a label – that the freshness, vitality, and uniqueness, if not for some of us peculiarity, of the high creatives' response to the world is most clearly manifest.

One question might very well be asked here. To what extent do these characteristics of the imaginative productions carry over into products where the children are required to be more realistic as, say, in the writing of an autobiography? We shall deal with the nature of the autobiographies written by the two groups in greater detail Here we wish to say only that the imaginative qualities do carry over. We may illustrate the character of the differences in the autobiographies by citing a few first paragraphs. The following are samples by high creativity upper- and lower-grade students, respectively, and by high IQ upper- and lower-grade students.

Career Aspirations

We have so far examined certain aspects of our highly creative and our highly intelligent adolescents' achievement in school, their motivation for achievement, their effect on teachers, their values and attitudes, their fantasy life, and their imaginative productions. To round out the portraits, we need also to gain some insight into their ultimate goals and aspirations, at least as represented by their occupational and career choices.

The relevant data were obtained from the responses to three instruments, the first two administered to the students themselves, the third to their parents.

The two student instruments were the direct and the indirect forms of the Sentence-Completion Test. The direct form consisted of sixty open-ended sentence items among which were such career preference item stubs as "If the choice of a permanent career were left up to me, I would choose. ", "When I grow up I want to become an.", "I always wanted to be an." The subjects were required to respond "directly" to these items by completing each sentence stub so as to "reflect your own preference." The indirect form was exactly parallel to the direct form except that the sentence stubs were written in the third person using boys' names for the male subjects and girls' names for the female subjects— for example "If the choice of a permanent occupation were left up to him (her), Ken (Kate) would choose." , "When Stan (Jean) grows up, he (she) wants to become an." The subjects were required to respond "projectively" by completing the stubs as a "verbal speed test." The responses of the two groups to the two forms were analyzed for the number and kind of occupations mentioned. The parent instrument was the Parent Questionnaire, which included two items regarding their children's occupational goals as follows: "Has the pupil expressed interest in a particular career? If yes, specify." These responses were also analyzed for the number and kind of occupations mentioned.

Table 2.14. Quantity and quality of occupations mentioned by the experimental groups on direct and indirect sentence completion tests

		Number of Occupations Mentioned			*Unusual Occupations*	
Test	*Group*	*Total*	X	*s*	*Number mentioned*	*Number of subjects mentioning*
Direct	High IQ (N = 28)	51	1.82?	1.09	6	5 †
	High creative (N = 26)	68	2.61?	1.41	24	16 †
Indirect	High IQ (N = 28)	100	3.57 †	1.81	12	10?
	High creative (N = 26)	130	5.00 †	1.80	29	17?

t used to test differences between means in column 2.

X^2 used to test differences between frequencies in column 5.

? Significant at .10 level.

† Significant at .0 1 level.

The data from the Sentence Completion Tests are presented in Table 2.14. Differences between the two groups appear both in the *quantity* and *quality* of occupational goals. The *quantity* of occupational possibilities mentioned is significantly greater for the high creatives than for the high IQ's, the latter group mentioning an average of 1.82 different occupations on the Direct Sentence Completion Test and 3.57 on the Indirect Test, the former group mentioning an average of 2.61 and 5.00 on the respective instruments. The *quality* of the different occupations mentioned as possibilities is also significantly different for the two groups. When the occupations mentioned are analyzed into conventional (lawyer, doctor, professor) and unconventional (adventurer, inventor, writer) categories, it is found that the high creatives give a significantly greater proportion of unconventional occupations than do the high IQ's. For example, on the Direct Sentence Completion Test, 16 per cent of the high IQ's mention an unconventional occupation, 62 per cent of the high creatives mention at least one such occupation as a possibility.

The preceding findings based on the reports of the adolescents themselves are supported by the data from the Parent Questionnaire. Parents of twenty-four of the high IQ children and of twenty-four of the high creativity children responded to the Questionnaire. Sixteen of the high IQ parents and twenty of the high creativity parents reported that their children had expressed an interest in some career. What is most noteworthy in these reports is that twelve or 75 per cent of the high IQ parents mention occupations falling into but *five* career categories: engineering and architecture, science, medicine, law, and teaching; only seven or 35 per cent of the high creativity parents mention career choices falling exclusively into these five categories ($X2 = 4.21$, $p < .05$). Instead, the high creativity parents tend to mention such rather unconventional occupations as "veterinary" or "entertainer," such unresolved combinations as "law or music," "teaching or art," and such expressive professions as "writing" or "dancing," none of these latter being mentioned as possibilities by the parents of the high IQ children.

In short, with respect to the *quantity* of occupations considered, it may be said that the high creativity adolescents as compared with the high IQ adolescents are more "diffuse" in occupational goals or, depending on the point of view, that they are "more able and willing to deal with a greater range of career possibilities." With respect to the *quality* of occupations considered it may be said, again depending on the point of view, that high creativity adolescents are more "eccentric" in their occupational goals, or that they are "more able and willing to deal with career risks, that is, to take greater liberties with accepted standards of adult success." In connection with this last, we may recall the previously reported Outstanding Traits values data. There it was the high IQ group that was more conventionally success-oriented in its personal values, and the high creativity group that was less so. This proportion of unconventional occupations than do the high IQ's. For example, on the Direct Sentence Completion Test, 16 per cent of the high IQ's mention an unconventional occupation, 62 per cent of the high creatives mention at least one such occupation as a possibility.

Career Study in India

In India survey is conducted by major companies in various parts of the country. They generally conduct talent search programme across the schools and colleges for the search of highly intelligent students. It is drawn from their studies it is drawn from the survey of these companies the student of India are basically looking for the career in 5 streams:

- Engineering and architecture,
- Science,
- Medicine,
- Law, and
- Teaching

Instead a highly creative parents ten to make their ward career in the following streams:

- Veterinary (or entertainer)
- Law or Music
- Teaching or Art
- Writing or Dancing

The highly intelligent students have more career options has compared to low IQ students. In the direct completion test 16 per cent of the highly intelligent prefer an unconventional occupation where as 62 per cent of the highly creative prefer at least one such occupation of their preference.

One feature of these occupational data, although it is tangential to the immediate problem of the distinctive career aspirations of the two groups, seems to us of considerable theoretical significance, or at least suggestiveness. The high creatives give *essentially* the *same* number of unusual occupations in their "direct" (self-report) and their "indirect" (projective) responses, whereas the high IQ's give *twice as many* unusual occupations in their "indirect" responses as they do in their "direct" responses. Sixteen of the highly creative adolescents give unconventional occupations on the direct instrument, and seventeen on the indirect instrument; only five of the high IQ adolescents give any unconventional occupations on the direct instrument, but ten give unconventional occupations on the indirect instrument.

These empirical findings are in line with the psychoanalytic proposition by Kubie, among others, pointing to greater "flux" or movement of preconscious material into the conscious expression of the creative person, and the relative restriction of such movement in the more highly "intellectualized" person. The data are also in line with the observation by Rogers that the creative person is more "open" in his self-expression than the noncreative person, who, to protect the organization of the self and his relation to others, may resort to "defensiveness." And finally, the data are consistent with our own findings of greater acceptance and expression of impulse in the fantasy and imaginative productions of the highly creative than in those of the highly intelligent adolescents.

Indeed, a striking consistency— or at least interrelatedness— in the different kinds and levels of data obtained from the two groups is apparent. We have noted, for example, the greater personal orientation of the high IQ's than of the high creatives toward the "values that make for adult success," along with the more frequent choice of conventional careers (such as doctor or lawyer) by the high IQ's. Similarly, there is greater personal orientation of the high IQ's than of the high creatives toward the "values they believe favored by their teachers," and greater acceptance by the teachers themselves of the high IQ's as against the high creatives.

An even more direct consistency is the greater valuation placed on sense of humor by the highly creative group than by the highly intelligent group, and the more frequent appearance of humor in the fantasies of the one as compared with the other. In this connection, it is perhaps worth noting again the consistency between the verbal and the nonverbal imaginative productions of the two groups. And we have just seen the consistency between the impulse expression in the imaginative production of the high creatives and the homogeneity of their "self-report" and "projective" career aspirations, and the consistency between the impulse inhibition in the imaginative productions of the high IQ's and the heterogeneity of their "self-report" and "projective" career aspirations. We shall return to the implications of these consistencies and our overall results in due course. Here we want only to summarize briefly the findings up to this point.

1. On the basis of measures of so-called "intelligence" and so called "creativity," we were able to identify two groups of adolescents representing two types of cognitive giftedness, the one group very high in "intelligence" but lower in "creativity," the other very high in "creativity" but lower in "intelligence."
2. When they were so differentiated, despite a variation of 23 points in average IQ, the two groups were found to be equally superior in scholastic achievement to the population from which they were drawn, but they themselves differed significantly in a number of social-personal variables including perception by their teachers, their values and attitudes, their fantasies and imaginative productions, and their career aspirations.
3. The data with respect to both cognitively-oriented and socially-oriented behavior were found to be consistent, and the characteristics that describe the one describe the other. The high IQ's tend to converge on stereotyped meanings, to perceive personal success by conventional standards, to move

toward the model provided by teachers, to seek out careers that conform to what is expected of them. The high creatives tend to diverge from stereotyped meanings, to move away from the model provided by teachers, to seek out careers that do not conform to what is expected of them.

So far as the intent of the basic inquiry is concerned – that is, (1) the possibility of identifying two groups of adolescents differing significantly in type of cognitive giftedness as represented by the conventional IQ metric on the one hand and creativity measures on the other and (2) observing the concomitant distinctive characteristics of the two groups so differentiated – the findings seem clearly relevant and responsive. But we could not leave the general problem without inquiring, however tentatively, into the developmental background of our highly intelligent and our highly creative adolescents. Accordingly, irrespective of the possible role of genetic factors, we set ourselves the third issue for investigation, which we may now put as follows. Given the systematic differences in the cognitive and social-psychological functioning of the highly intelligent and the highly creative adolescents, do the two groups also vary systematically in the nature of their family environments?

Highly Intelligent and the Highly Creative Adolescent as Members of the Family Group: Selected Parental Variables

The data with respect to the family environment of the two groups were obtained from two sources. The Parent Questionnaire, a mailed check list and short-answer instrument, required parents to respond to certain specific questions (such as age and education) regarding themselves and their children. The Parent Interview, a 2-to 3-hour free-response conference, was held at home with the mother (except in one case where the mother was unavailable, the father consenting to serve instead). At the time of the interviews the parents of five other experimental groups were also being studied, with the interviewers not knowing to which of the seven groups any interviewee belonged. Interviews were obtained from approximately 80 per cent of the mothers of the highly intelligent and the highly creative adolescents. The analysis of the data may be discussed with reference to each of the following family variables.

1. Education and occupation of the parents.
2. Age of the parents.
3. Mother's recollection of her own family situation when she was her child's age.
4. Reading interests of the family, at least as represented by the number and type of magazines taken.
5. Parental satisfaction and dissatisfaction with the child and his school.
6. Parental satisfaction and dissatisfaction with their own child rearing practices.
7. Mother's description of the kinds of friends preferred for her child.

Education and Occupation of Parents

Educational data were available for the parents of twenty-four of the twenty-eight high IQ's and for twenty-four of the twenty six high creatives. When these data were analyzed by simply dichotomizing "college graduates" versus "others," the result obtained could be summarized as in Table 2.15 . When the data

Table 2.15. Number of college graduates among fathers and mothers of the two experimental groups

	Number of College Graduates			
	High IQ (N = 24)	*High Creative (N = 24)*	X^2	P?
Father	21	15	2.78	.10
Mother	16	12	.77	NS.

? Because of the exploratory nature of this phase of the research, many of the comparisons presented here were derived from the obtained data. Therefore, the probability values attached to the chi-squares in this and the following tables must be viewed with caution.

were analyzed by dichotomizing "with graduate training" versus "others," the result obtained could be summarized as in Table 2.16.

The children in the school under study came in large part from families that are in the employ of an urban university, or from families that although not employed by the university prefer to reside in or near the university community. As Tables 2.15 and 2.16 indicate, whichever analysis is undertaken the parents of the high IQ child tend to have a somewhat higher educational status than the parents of the high creativity child. But what is perhaps more noteworthy is the greater specialized training of both the mother and the father of the high IQ's.

Table 2.16. Number of parents having some graduate training

	Parents Having Graduate Training			
	High IQ (N = 24)	*High Creative* (N = 24)	X^2	P?
Father	19	13	2.34	.20
Mother	13	5	4.36	.05

The essential difference is probably not so much in the general level of cultivation, which is very high for both groups when compared to the general population, but in the significantly greater specialization of training, or, if you will, "professionalization of education" of the IQ group.

Table 2.17. Occupational status of the fathers of the two experimental groups

Occupational status	*High IQ* (N = 24)	*High Creative* (N = 24)	X^2	P
University teaching, Research, Editing	15	7	4.56	.05
Business	4	11		
Medicine, Law	5	6		

It appears that we are dealing not only with two different types of children but possibly with two different types of parents. A greater proportion of the high IQ fathers than of the high creativity fathers are found in the academic or educational occupations. But, despite their greater professional training, a somewhat greater proportion of the mothers of the high IQ children than of the high creativity children are exclusively housewives and do not hold other full or part-time jobs. It would seem that the mothers of the high IQ subjects have more time to devote to their children than do the mothers of the high creative subjects. In this connection, it will be shown that the high IQ mothers are in fact likely to be more vigilant about the "correct" upbringing of their children than are the high creativity mothers.

Table 2.18. Occupational status of the mothers of the two experimental groups

Occupational status	*High IQ* (N = 24)	*High Creative* (N = 24)	X^2	*P*
Housewife only	18	11	3.14	.10
Full or part-time employment	6	13		

Age of Parents

The mean age was almost exactly the same for the two groups of mothers, and although the age of the fathers tended to be slightly greater for the high IQ group than for the high creativity group, it was not significantly so. The significant difference between the two groups was in the discrepancy or congruence between the age of the father and the mother. If the data are dichotomized as 1 year or less age difference and 2 years or more age difference, the results may be summarized as in Table 2.19 .

We may only conjecture at this time about the reasons for the age discrepancies or similarities between the parents of the present sample, and about the effects of these age factors on the family environment. But two reasons for a number of the discrepancies seem relevant: waiting to finish advanced academic training before risking marital responsibilities, and waiting to be satisfactorily "settled" to maintain a family in the "right" style. Both reasons suggest an apparently greater insecurity among the high IQ parents than among the high creativity parents, a suggestion that is supported by subsequent interview data.

Table 2.19. Age difference between parents for the two experimental groups

Occupational status	*High IQ* (N = 24)	*High Creative* (N = 24)	X^2	P
0-1 years	4	13	5.83	.02
2 or more years	20	11		

Mother's Memories of Own Home

An important issue in the relationship we are exploring is the personality structure of the parents. The preferred procedure would have been to do a full-scale assessment of the parents, but for obvious reasons this was not feasible. Nonetheless, a 2-hour conversation does provide impressions, and answers to certain of the questions in the interview schedule do give at least hints and glimpses of the information it would have been desirable to have in more systematic form. Our overall impression was that the two groups of mothers were quite different, the mothers of the high IQ adolescents being less secure and at ease with themselves and the world than were the mothers of the high creative adolescents. This overall difference is most clearly shown in the two relevant case studies, but even the discrete responses to specific questions of the interview provide similar and perhaps more rigorous data. When, for example, one group of mothers tends to talk about the financial status and hardships of their own childhood, and under the same circumstances another group does not, this is a suggestive datum worth noting, for behavior of the present is surely not cut off from memories of the past.

The relevant interview question was: how would you describe the home you lived in as a child? The responses were long and detailed; the mothers seemed to enjoy relating their own real or imagined childhood experiences to their children's present situation. Here is a fairly typical response by one of the IQ mothers.

> *It was as typically Midwestern middle class American as one could find. Neither rich nor poor. The family belonged to a group of people important in town. Father was the principal of the school – active in church and in the literary group.*

The problem of quantifying this kind of material is of course formidable. Many differences that one "feels" as he reads the complete sets of interviews "wash out" as he attempts to categorize. Nonetheless, certain categorical differences may be noted. For example, seven of the twenty-two IQ mothers for whom interview material is available say specifically of their home that it was "middle class," whereas only one of the eighteen Creative mothers says this; only eight of the twenty-two IQ mothers describe their family in rather global-emotional terms, whereas twelve of the eighteen creative mothers tend to do this. That is, the IQ mothers are more stereotypic" in their descriptions (they tend to put themselves in "classes"); the creative mothers attempt more rounded descriptions.

But perhaps a more important categorical difference in the present context lies in the reference to the financial status of the home and childhood. As the data in Table 2.20 show, the high IQ parents tend not only to mention finances more often than the high creativity parents, but also to emphasize financial hardship more often.

Table 2.20. Mention of financial status and of poverty in descriptions of own home life by mothers of the two experimental groups

	High IQ (N = 22)	*High Creative* (N = 18)	X^2	P
Mention of finances	16	7	3.36	.10
Emphasis on poverty, financial hardship	9	1	4.84	.05

Whatever else these responses may imply about the different remembrance of things past and the areas of latest concern, they tend to support the suggestion of greater insecurity among the parents of the high IQ children than among the parents of the high creativity children.

Reading Interests in the Home

It is almost impossible to obtain an exact measure of the reading habits of a family. Nonetheless, an attempt toward a partial assessment was made by asking the following interview questions. What magazines and newspapers do you subscribe to or buy regularly? What magazines do you read just once in a while?

In the analysis, professional or scholarly journals, which would have increased the count for the high IQ parents, were omitted. Despite this, the difference in the number of magazines coming into the homes of the high IQ and the high creativity subjects is quite illuminating.

The twenty-two high IQ families reported reading "regularly" a total of 125 magazines, and "sometimes" 54 magazines. The eighteen high creative families reported reading "regularly" a total of 107 magazines, and "sometimes" 30 magazines. If the families are divided into those mentioning 6 or fewer and those mentioning 7 or more magazines, we get the relationship shown in Table 2.21.

Table 2.21. Number of magazines "taken" or read in homes of the two experimental groups

Number of Magazines	*High IQ (N = 22)*	*High Creative (N = 18)*	X^2	*P*
6 or fewer	7	12	3.52	.10
7 or more	15	6		

There are also some noteworthy qualitative trends in the data. For example, twenty-one of the twenty-two high IQ mothers report taking or reading 50 "mass media magazines". This is about 28 per cent of their total. Sixteen of the eighteen high creative mothers report taking or reading 27 "mass media magazines," which is about 19 per cent of their total. Conversely, five of the twenty-two high IQ mothers mention 7 "magazines of liberal political comment" — that is, about 3 per cent of their total-but seven of the eighteen high creative mothers mention 10 magazines in this category — that is, about 7 per cent of their total. Perhaps the most salient difference is in the number of children's magazines mentioned by the two groups.

Ten of the twenty two high IQ mothers mention 17 such magazines, three of the eighteen high creativity mothers mention 5 such magazines.

We hardly need comment that to observe the greater number of magazines and the greater number of children's magazines in the one home as against the other is not in any way to imply an immediate cause and effect relationship between type of family reading material and the type of cognitive functioning of the children. Yet it is by no means farfetched to suggest that the relationship between the function of the magazines and the cognitive styles is not merely accidental. We do not wish to enter here into any complex speculations about what the quantity and kind of journals taken into the home imply about the character of the parents or the environment they are providing for their children. Suffice it to say that the greater number of mass media journals and children's magazines tends to support three of our general impressions about the high IQ homes: greater conformity to conventional standards, greater child-centeredness, and greater implicit if not explicit pressure for the child to do well scholastically.

Parental Satisfaction and Dissatisfaction with the Child and His School

One aspect of the relation between family environment and type of cognitive excellence we are exploring may be posed more directly as follows. What are the attitudes of the two groups of parents toward their children and toward what they are learning? More specifically, we may ask: what are the reactions of the mothers to any unusual qualities in the child and to the type of education the child is getting? The two relevant interview questions were the following.

1. During your child's earliest years in school, did the teachers call to your attention or did you yourself notice anything unusual about him and school?
2. As far as the present school is concerned, what are the things you like best about the education your child is getting? Is there anything about your child's education at this school that you are not satisfied with?

Although the high IQ and the high creativity parents report the same number of total observations and the same number of favorable and unfavorable qualities in their children as seen by *teachers,* the high IQ parents report both a greater number of total observations (59 against 31) and a greater number of unfavorable qualities as seen by *themselves.* When the latter are dichotomized into "not more than one unfavorable quality" and "more than one unfavorable quality," the resulting relationship may be presented as in Table 2.22 .

Table 2.22. Number of unfavorable qualities observed in their children by mothers of the two groups

Number of Unfavourable Qualities Observed	*High IQ (N = 23)*	*High Creative (N = 19)*	X^2	*P*
Not more than one	13	17	4.04	.05
More than one	10	2		

What stands out in these data is the greater "vigilance" a "critical" or at least "less accepting" attitude of the high IQ mothers- they both observe *more* about their children and they observe a greater number of *objectionable* qualities. It is as if they were on the lookout for things to improve about their children.

No significant difference appeared in the kinds of satisfactions and dissatisfactions mentioned by the two groups, but there were two interesting trends in the data. One was for the high IQ mothers to express dissatisfaction with the school, even before they were asked-a trend that will become more marked, as we shall see, in their responses to the direct question on how they feel about the education their children are getting. The other trend was for the high creativity mother to mention a dissatisfaction with her child, and then to add spontaneously that she did not really care— she was willing to let the child go his own way.

The relative "vigilance" and critical attitude of the high IQ parents is seen again in their attitudes toward the school their children are attending. The high IQ parents report a greater number of total observations (138 against 95), and a greater number of dissatisfactions.

Table 2.23. Number of unfavorable school qualities observed by mothers of the two experimental groups

Number of Unfavourable Qualities Observed	*High IQ* (N = 23)	*High Creative* (N = 19)	X^2	P
Not more than one	7	12	3.27	.10
More than one	16	7		

The actual number of dissatisfactions mentioned by the high IQ mothers was 61, or 44 per cent of their total comments; the number mentioned by the high creativity mothers was 28, or 29 per cent of their total. The two groups tend to differ also in what they found worthy of comment in their children's school experience, and in the objects of their satisfaction and dissatisfaction. Although the frequencies in the different categories become rather small, and any generalization must be treated with caution, certain of the trends are of considerable interest. For example, 21 or 15 per cent of all the comments by the high IQ mothers are about the characteristics of the *teachers* in the school (e.g. "the teachers are excellent," "most of the teachers are vague and uncertain," "Mr.-is just no good at all," etc.); 6 or 6 per cent of the comments by the high creativity mothers are in this category. Conversely, 20 or 21 per cent of the comments by the high creativity mothers are about the characteristics of the *students* and their extracurricular activities (e.g. "there is a wide variety of students," "they don't have enough social life in the school," "there are too many upper class kids in the school," etc.); 16 or 12 per cent of the comments of the high IQ mothers are in this category.

The groups tend to differ in the *kind* of satisfactions and dissatisfactions. For example, there are 9 high IQ comments-all favorable– on the Enriched Program in the school, or as one of the high IQ mothers put it, "the opportunity to do more than is required." There are no comments here at all by the high creativity mothers. Or, to cite one more instance, a category of responses which we labeled Comparisons with the Traditional School comprised such statements as "the school should do more in the three R's," "there is not enough drill," "there are too many experimental ideas," "we need more *Shakespeare* and less *Diary of Anne Frank*." Twenty-nine or 21 per cent of the total comments by the high IQ mothers and 10 or

11 per cent of the total comments by the high creativity mothers fell into this category. Of the 29 high IQ comments, 23 or 79 per cent were "dissatisfied," that is, "there was not enough drill," "not enough enforcement and control," "not enough teaching in the three R's." Of the 10 high creativity comments, only 4 were "dissatisfied" in this respect.

Parental Satisfaction with their Child-Rearing Practices

Despite the apparent greater misgiving and uncertainty of the high IQ mother toward her child and toward the school, she expresses fewer misgivings and uncertainties than does the high creative mother regarding her own child-training practices. The relevant interview question was: as you look back on the ways you have tried to make your child responsible to you as far as bedtime, playing outside, leaving the house, homework, and so forth were concerned, would you say you were too lenient, not lenient enough, or what? The results are presented in Table 2.24.

Table 2.24. Mothers' satisfaction and dissatisfaction with their own child-training practices

Opinion of Own Child-Training Practice	*High IQ (N = 23)*	*High Creative (N = 19)*	X^2	*P*
Satisfied	17	8	3.15	.10
Dissatisfied	6	11		

It is almost as if the high IQ mother were critical of others but not about herself. From one point of view she has a right to be self-satisfied. If her object was to rear children who do well in school, who are well-liked by teachers, who accept the conventional values, and who aspire to careers in the prestige professions, she has of course succeeded.

Kinds of Friends Preferred for their Children

One final set of data rounds out the differences between the family environment of the high IQ and the high creativity families, at least as represented by the mothers' attitudes. The interview question was: what qualities do you like to see in your child's friends? There were two reasons for asking this question. The first and obvious one was that the responses would provide information about the friends the parents want their children to have. Second and no less important, in giving the qualities they would like to see in their children's friends the parents would also indirectly and therefore less defensively be providing information about the characteristics they would like to see in their own children as well.

Again, the high IQ mothers had somewhat more to say. But the striking finding was the difference in what they said. When the qualities mentioned are divided into two categories, the one relating to "external" characteristics (e.g. "good family," "good manners," "studious"), the other to "internal" characteristics (e.g. "sense of values," "interest in something," "openness — not secretive"), the resulting relationship may be summarized as in Table 25.

Table 2.25. Characteristics preferred for children's friends by mothers of the two groups

	High IQ (N = 23)		*High Creative (N = 19)*			
Characteristics	*X*[?]	*s*	*X*	*s*	*t*	*P*
External—specific e.g. good family, manners, studious	2.48	1.20	1.58	1.07	2.56	.02
Internal—general e.g. sense of values, interests, openness	.91	1.12	1.79	1.47	2.13	.05

? These means refer to the average number of characteristics mentioned.

A few sample responses may give some greater substance to these tabular differences. Here two high IQ mothers describe the qualities they would like to see in their child's friends. (1) "Sunday school children, religious, go to Church every Sunday, of parents whose standards are ours. Honest, sincere, clean-minded and mouthed. Studious." (2) "Right between the eyes — aware of my own inadequacies. Intelligence is certainly foremost— admit to my snobism. Kind of cultural background— not money. A level of family. What I don't like— wild kid who doesn't know how to behave in a house— dirty talk— I've put up with it— a certain amount is acceptable— outside can use up energies. Neither extroverted nor introverted."

Two high creativity mothers describe the qualities they would like to see in their child's friends. (1) "Like what I want to see in E (her child)— it's the same thing. Valid sense of values what a person is rather than what he appears to be. Satisfaction in creative constructive activity. Balance and maturity in interpersonal relations. Interest and enthusiasm for learning and reaching out beyond it to greater understanding." (2) "Openness— not secretive that old folks won't understand. Interest in something to do— not bored expression. Temperate in manners and habits. Frankness and honesty. Interest in living." It is here in the projections of desirable traits for their children's friends that we may perhaps see the most honest aspirations for their own children-as the high creative mother says, "It's the same thing."

It is clear that our two groups of parents tend to differ in their basic orientations toward themselves and their children. They differ in the recollection of their childhood experiences, in the kind of education they have obtained, in the career lines they have chosen, and in the kind of intellectual environment they provide in their homes. They also differ in their attitudes toward their children, toward the education the children are getting, and as to the qualities they would like their children to have. Again irrespective of the possible role of genetic factors, we would maintain that the differences between the two groups of children have their source not only in immediate school experiences but in the family environment in which they grew up. Schachtel's formulation of the pressures on the developing child to accept the "givens," the "codes," and "predetermined categories" of his culture seem to us very relevant here. He writes:

> *In everybody's life one can observe the effect of the pressure of society, as represented by parents, teachers, peers, toward the formation of a more or less definite, closed view of life and the world, a certain code of behavior as well as often very definite*

> *views about things and people and what they are there for. These views may be explicit or implicit. The parents answer the child's endless questions and their answers usually transmit the labels of the culture, the names of things, whether they are useful or useless, good or bad, etc. Inasmuch as the child looks upon the parent as all-knowing, or with fear, he accepts these views and with them very often the implicit assumption that these answers contain all there is to the subject. Obviously, there are great variations in parents with regard to the wish, or the absence of it, to impose their views as the only ones on the child or to further the child's own explorative curiosity; with regard to their own awareness of, and readiness to admit, the limited nature of their knowledge or, on the contrary, their wish to appear as omniscient or as the ones who always know best. The same holds true for teachers. Parents and teachers, in transmitting the current socio-cultural views of the world to the child, can help both to open and to close the world for the child. Even if they mostly want to open it, they cannot help but also close it, in some ways, because there is no man who is not to a considerable extent embedded in the culture in which he grew up, the language of his culture, etc.*
>
> *In addition to the closure of the world which results from the transmission of a familial and/or cultural viewpoint, parental curbing of the child's exploratory drive can also be a factor that interferes with the world-openness of the child and often leads to a more or less powerful strengthening of the tendency to avoid the unknown and remain embedded in the familiar.* The more worried the parents are about the dangers of the world, the more likely are they to impart this view to the child.

The family environments of our subjects, at least as portrayed in the mothers' interviews, are consonant with these formulations. It is the parents of the high IQ's rather than the parents of the high creatives who seem to be, in Schachtel's phrase, "more worried about the dangers of the world." It is they who more frequently recall financial insecurity during their own childhood, and presumably this may still be at least a latent concern. It is the high IQ parents who are more "vigilant" about their children's behavior and academic performance. They tend to be more critical of their children and of the education the school is providing. Nor is their vigilance limited only to concerns about their children's educational progress. They are vigilant too about their children's friends. The qualities they would like to see in these friends, which may be conceived of as projections of the qualities they are the most concerned with in their own children, focus on such conventional and immediately visible virtues as "cleanliness," "good manners," and "studiousness." In contrast, the parents of the high creativity adolescents focus on such less conventional qualities as the child's openness to experience," his "values," and his "interests and enthusiasm for life."

When these differences in the parents' attitudes and concerns are combined with the differences in educational specialization, the age discrepancy between father and mother, and the kind of reading material available in the home, the overall impression of the high IQ family is that it is one in which individual divergence is limited and risks minimized, and the overall impression of the high creativity family is that it is one in which individual divergence is permitted and risks are accepted. Thus not only Schachtel's formulation but Maslow's concepts of "defense" and "growth," which were used earlier to distinguish the high IQ adolescent and the high creativity adolescent, seem useful in distinguishing the family environments of the two groups.

Three qualifying remarks seem in order with respect to the parent data and the children themselves. First, in discussing the greater "vigilance" of the parents of the high IQ adolescents, we do not intend to give support to the current unfortunate dichotomy between "bad" authoritarianism and "good" permissiveness. The issue is not all-or-none, either-or, but is appropriate emphasis. Second, in adducing evidence for the greater "specialized education" and "bookishness" of the parents of the high IQ children as against the parents of the high creativity children, we do not intend to suggest that the presence of books or specialized knowledge fir the family leads inevitably to high IQ, or the absence to high creativity. It is not the presence or absence of books or specialized knowledge but their use and meaning in the home that is significant. Third, in putting the high IQ's and the high creatives in the family context, we may have seemed unqualifiedly to favor "divergent thinking" and "constructive cognition" over "convergent thinking" and "conservative cognition." As we have already said— and want to make it clear again — both high intelligence and high creativity are valuable, and we do not wish to give the impression of one group as somehow representing "good guys" and the other "bad guys." The distinction we are making between modes of cognitive giftedness is analytic and not necessarily evaluative. Both the "conservative," and the "constructive" aspects of cognition and social behavior are socially valuable.

3

Identification of Exceptional Ability

Introduction

If ability could be developed simply by exposing the able to opportunity in a rich environment, there would be little need to fret about identifying high potential. Ability being present could seize upon opportunity and flower accordingly in time. In such a situation schools would have only to offer a wealth of challenge and a variety of stimulating learning experiences. The able youngsters would do the rest.

Unfortunately, this automatic development of talent is mere wishful thinking. We are concerned about potential that is not realized, about high level ability wasted in low level pursuits, about drab lives spreading out before people who might live more richly, and about unfilled needs in a society demanding more top level competences than are apparently at hand. One of the keys to the problem lies in early identification of young people with talents so that they may move ahead with the arduous preparation required in high level careers. Early identification may provide the motivation necessary for strenuous effort. Perhaps it can be used to level obstacles of a cultural, educational, or financial nature as well.

The efforts to identify and deal differently with gifted individuals in school runs counter to the American folklore of equality and brotherhood, at least on the surface. In our assertions that all men are equal, we often overlook the fact that all men are also different. Failure to identify young people with bidden but genuine potential may result in denying them the opportunity which is equal in its challenge to less demanding opportunities presented to less able contemporaries.

The democratic ethos does not require foregoing efforts to identify ability. It requires that we look below the surface and give full value to ability that may be submerged in unequal environments. The Rockefeller Brothers Fund report on *The Pursuit of Excellence* states well the issue of democracy in the identification of students with exceptional ability:

> *First, we must not make the mistake of adopting a narrow or constricting view of excellence.* Our conception of excellence must enhance many kinds of achievement at many levels.
>
> *Second, we must not assume that native capacity is the sole ingredient in superior performance...a product of ability and motivation and character....*
>
> *Finally, we must recognize that judgments of difference in talent are not judgments of differences in human worth.*
>
> *To sum up, it is possible for us to cultivate the ideal of excellence while retaining the moral values of equality.*

Using Intelligence Tests Intelligently

Preceding chapters have set forth the values and limitations of intelligence testing, and the characteristics of gifted persons have been described in some detail because identification is dependent upon a combination of testing and recognition of the characteristics of unusual ability. The intelligence quotient is one index of intellectual ability. Other instruments are necessary because of occasional inadequacy, inaccuracy, or inappropriateness of the IQ score. On the basis of his exhaustive search for high intelligence subjects in California, Terman estimated that he had uncovered 80 per cent, possibly 90 per cent of the children in the top percentile of intellectual performance. The remainder, he assumed, were not discoverable because their superior ability was hidden by shyness, laziness, inferior adaptability, or slow school progress. Our problem today continues to be one of seeking out the 10 or 20 per cent who are hard to find. We have also to refine techniques in order to recognize those comparable to Terman's sample, and we need to inquire whether the Terman technique was broad enough to include the full breadth of talents that comprise giftedness.

With all these qualifications on the use of intelligence tests in mind, we may look at circumstances in which they are used or may be used. So long as schools are restricted to budgets requiring large group procedures, group intelligence tests will continue to serve as a primary screening device. In some schools children with high scores on the group test are subsequently given an individual test. In a few schools all children are given the individual test. Because of the expense of administering individual tests, some school systems try to replace it with an average of two or more group tests.

Teacher Observation

Because of the limitations noted in intelligence testing, other mechanisms are an obvious need. Most easily available, of course, are teacher judgments and, after a few years of schooling, teacher ratings. While Terman reported with some discouragement that teachers were right only half the time in selecting children of high mental endowment (as tested by the Stanford-Binet), he was gratified with the 50 per cent that he could include in his roster. Since that time (the early 1920's), efforts have been made to provide teachers with clues to help them identify exceptional pupils. Many school districts and professional associations have published lists of characteristics that may serve as keys.

One of the most systematic efforts to locate special talents has been that of the Quincy Youth Development Project. Starting in 1951, the project set out to explore the resource-potential inherent in a community to develop exceptional ability in its children and to remedy the maladjustment of handicapped children. The Quincy Youth Development Commission was established to cooperate with a research team from the University of Chicago. Tests were administered to an experimental group in the fourth grade and a control group in the sixth grade with the purpose of identifying talent and handicaps, and noting the effects of a planned program over the course of ten years.

The Quincy Project sought to identify gifts in the following areas: intellectual ability, scientific ability, leadership ability, creative ability, artistic talent, writing talent, dramatic talent, musical talent, mechanical skills and physical skills. Teachers were provided with a handbook that described a number of characteristic behaviors of each of these abilities. They were then given "ability rosters" for each gift. All children in the class were listed on the roster. The teacher was instructed to utilize one behavior and to consider how well each child met the description. Children outstanding in this regard— about 10 per cent was suggested— were to be scored "1" for the behavior. The teacher was then asked to take the next behavior and rate all children for this category. After considering all of the characteristic behaviors for a given ability, the teacher added up the "1's" given to each child, entered the total and noted the behaviors on which the child scored high. These lists of behavior represent an excellent guide for teacher observation.

It is of interest that teacher analysis of observed behavior precedes other recommended techniques that are included in the Quincy study. For general intelligence, both general intelligence tests and differential mental ability scales are recommended. In addition, informal analysis through tests and games is suggested (see section below on work samples). In science, observation is supplemented by use of cumulative records, standardized achievement and interest tests. To assess leadership potential various types of sociometric devices round out teacher observation. Work samples play an important part in creativity, art, writing, music, and mechanical skills.

Piekarz suggests that the teacher look for certain distinguishing characteristics in the early childhood program. In group activities gifted children show leadership in solving problems, foreseeing difficulties, and anticipating outcomes. They are resourceful in overcoming difficulties. They show unusual command of language and a large vocabulary. They are self-confident and unafraid to try new things. What they do in their spare time they follow through to completion, and they find distant goals motivating, not discouraging. In observing the child by himself the teacher should look for a show of independence and initiative. The kinds of books he selects to read, or to have read to him, and his interest in reading may be revealing. Hobbies after the age of seven or eight may also give some clue to unusual interest or ability. The teacher may be able to judge his work qualitatively by looking for attention to details and attempts at refinement. "Insatiable curiosity" is one of the characteristic attributes of the gifted child.

As the child grows older, Calhoun notes these characteristics of the bright child in the intermediate grades: a wide vocabulary, more scope in social relationships, a greater range and intensity of interests than is normally seen, and creative expression in music and art. He suggests the use of "situational tests" in identifying ability. Many children participate in the following, but greater interest and more effective work is shown by the gifted pupil in making scrap books, museum field trips, voluntary reading, bulletin board displays, selection of radio and television programs, creative writing, dramatics, writing music, reading poetry aloud, making maps, independent research, and responsiveness to humor .At the secondary level the North Central Association in its Superior and Talented Student Project suggests the following behavior characteristics to help teachers screen their students:

1. The student learns rapidly and easily.
2. He uses a great deal of common sense and practical knowledge.
3. He reasons things out, thinks clearly, recognizes relationships, and comprehends meanings.
4. He retains what he has heard or read without much rote drill.
5. He knows about many things of which most students are unaware.
6. He has a large vocabulary, which he uses easily and accurately.
7. He can read books that are one or more years in advance of the rest of the class.
8. He performs difficult mental tasks.
9. He asks many questions and has a wide range of interests.

10. He does some academic work one or more years in advance of the class.
11. He is original in his thinking, uses good but unusual methods.
12. He is alert, keenly observant, and responds quickly.

Many of the characteristics that identify able learners elude currently available aptitude and achievement tests and the quantitative measures which they produce. For example, Getzels urges consideration of the following "intellectual characteristics of the able learners":

1. He has greater curiosity and is not content with mere rote repetition.
2. He is more exploratory and is likely to want to go beyond the limits of a particular problem or the arbitrary restrictions of a particular lesson unit.
3. He is more autonomous and is likely to want to work out problems independently.
4. He is more abstract in his thinking and is likely to want to generalize from particulars to principles.
5. He is more creative and is likely to be impelled to add something original or imaginative of his own to a given problem or classroom project.

Numerous checklists are available for teachers. All require subjective, qualitative ratings. All require highly relative judgments. The ability to learn and remember new things is always stressed. Seeing relationships, being able to work with abstractions, and high verbal ability as expressed in speech and reading are other characteristics that alert the teacher to the possible presence of intellectual giftedness. Because of the nature of school programs the teacher is in a rare position to see such signs as no one else can.

Pitfalls in Teacher Observation

Certain pitfalls, however, have to be avoided as the teacher seeks to ascertain particular ability on the part of any child. Working with thirty or more children in a group, the teacher can easily assume giftedness where only glibness exists. The child who has an attractive personality sometimes wins the teacher over to the extent that the personality assessment influences the evaluation of ability. The amenable, obliging, docile child also has cards stacked in his favor. Conformity to teacher patterns and demands is more welcome in a crowded room than a continuous display of rebelliousness. It is much easier to recognize talent in the well-behaved, obliging, attractive, verbal child than in the non-conforming, rebellious, unprepossessing, withdrawing child. Small wonder, then, that Getzels and Jackson should find that teachers much preferred the high IQ group with conforming tendencies to the high creative group who were more independent and sometimes cynical.

Other factors that obstruct identification also cloud the perception of the teacher. The teacher generally sees the child, not his background. Frequently, however, the teacher is evaluating the effects of his background and not the child's native ability. The child from the culturally rich home needs relatively little ability to outshine the youngster from the home that is on the wrong side of the cultural tracks. In addition, the teacher often has no way of distinguishing between the youngster's own ability and drive and the extent to which the child is achieving as a result of Mother or Dad's coaching or pressure. To a certain point assistance may not matter, since ultimately we are interested in how well the individual employs his gifts. However, there are numerous cases where the early bloom fades inexplicably or where early promise settles into underachievement or resentment. If genuine ability is not present, at some point, parental assistance and pressure cease to help and the child who has been mistakenly selected for more complex intellectual tasks finds himself lost and frustrated. Sometimes, unfortunately, genuine ability rebels when the child becomes aware that he is merely an alter ego for an ambitious parent seeking to lead a second life. This awareness often comes in adolescence with an awakening sense of self, and the adolescent asserts a rejection of his parents' values. Repudiating the academic values of an ambitious parent can result in serious underachievement.

Past Achievement

At the high school and college level no single index gives as high a correlation with later academic performance as school grades. School grades share with achievement tests the advantage of including a builtin measure of persistence, drive, and study skills. While there are fundamental differences between elementary school and secondary school, between high school and college, it is also true that there are many basic similarities in the over-all educational process. For similar reasons the publishers of the Scholastic Aptitude Tests regard their tests as indicators of *developed* ability. Motivational factors are therein tested in their effects. The advantage of the school grades over the aptitude tests lies in the fact that they reflect a teacher's experience with a given student over an extended period – a semester, a year, or more. The aptitude test may have the advantage of standardization and objective scoring but is always a more limited sample of the individual's performance and experience. Two more types of evidence that are valuable in identification, therefore, are the child's accumulated school performance and the scores of standardized achievement tests.

Of all academic achievements, the most generally useful in predicting later performance is reading skill. There are various reasons why this should be true. Conventional definitions of intelligence lean heavily on verbal, abstract, symbolic, relational items. All of these are involved in reading. Considerable overlapping is to be found between some definitions of intelligence and the components of reading skill. Moreover, since the usual way of validating intelligence and aptitude tests is to judge their predictive value in scholastic performance, it is not strange that reading should be of paramount importance since it is the basic means to success in the upper academic reaches. While it is true that not all good readers do well in college, poor readers find it difficult simply to survive there.

One caution must also be observed. The success of using reading scores in predicting academic success carries with it its own limitation. So long as we limit intelligence to verbal types of behavior we find a high correlation with reading ability. So long as we define giftedness as success in verbal undertakings dependent upon reading, we find a high correlation between performance and reading ability. If, however, we broaden our concept of intelligence to include such things as creativity, social leadership, spatial perception, numerical concepts, and computation, reading skills play a somewhat less central role. Also, if we use as our criterion successful vocational application, personal development, social responsibility, and emotional adjustment, correlation with reading skills are also likely to be rather low.

The same conclusion is to be found here as in the employment of intelligence tests. The scores reported are helpful indices but they relate to limited facets of giftedness. The child with the unusual reading score must certainly be considered for inclusion in any intellectually gifted group. But the failure to achieve a high reading score is not necessarily a sign that other intellectual abilities are absent.

Children and Parents as Sources

A number of other methods are also of value in seeking to identify gifted boys and girls. Children reveal themselves in many contexts. In addition to the school environment, interaction with other children and activities in the home provides a reservoir of information. Sometimes teachers are surprised to note realistic appraisals of children by their friends. For some time, sociometry has depended for information about social interaction upon children's choice and rejection of each other. The familiar sociogram gives us an interesting picture of social leadership. In intellectual fields children are also able at times to spot superior ability. The "grind" may not be the star in a sociogram but he is often the center of attraction when homework has to be done— or when correct answers are sought surreptitiously during a test.

Among the members of a highly selected group, however, rank order is not always apparent to the children. Brumbaugh secured some interesting but inaccurate responses from eleven-year-olds in the Hunter College Elementary School (all children above 135 IQ; median 150) when she asked them, "What is an IQ?" She obtained results that were still more startling when the pupils were asked to guess which children in the class had the highest IQ's. In most cases there was little accurate perception of relative brightness in the classes she interviewed.

With more mature perspective, parents may be in a better position to judge exceptional ability although consanguineity may not be the best guarantee of objectivity. Parents may not be expected to give a dispassionate appraisal, but their efforts may be given some direction through use of checklists to indicate the kinds of activities their children engage in. Brumbaugh and Roshco have developed the following checklist for parents. It may also be used as the basis for a conference between parent and teacher:

1. Did your child walk and talk earlier than most other children of his age and sex?
2. Did he show a comparatively early interest in words?
3. Does he have an exceptionally large vocabulary for his age?
4. Did he show an early interest in reading?
5. Did he show an early interest in clocks, calendars, jigsaw puzzles?
6. Did he show an early interest in numbers?
7. Does he express curiosity about many things?
8. Does he have more stamina and strength than other children of his age and sex?
9. Does he tend to associate with children older than himself?
10. Does he act as a leader among children of his own age?
11. Does he have a good memory?
12. Does he show unusual reasoning power?
13. Does he have an unusual capacity for planning and organizing?
14. Does he relate information gained in the past to new knowledge that he acquires?
15. Does he show more interest in creative effort and new activities than in routine and repetitive tasks?
16. Does he try to excel in almost everything he does?
17. Does he concentrate on a single activity for a prolonged period without getting bored?
18. Does he usually have a number of interests that keep him busy?
19. Does he persist in his efforts in the face of unexpected difficulties?
20. Does he figure out his own solutions to problems and show uncommon "common sense?"
21. Does he have a sense of humor that is advanced for his age?

22. Does he show sensitivity to the feelings of others?
23. Does he show a comparatively early interest in God, religion, and questions of right and wrong?
24. Does he make collections that are more advanced or unusual than those of others in his age group?
25. Does he show an intense interest in some artistic activity, such as drawing, singing, dancing, writing, playing a musical instrument?
26. Does he make up stories that are vivid and dramatic or relate his experiences with a great deal of exact detail?
27. Does he like puzzles and various kinds of "problem" games?
28. Does he have exceptional ability in mathematics?
29. Does he show an unusual interest in science or mechanics?
30. Does he show awareness of things that are new or novel?

Looking for Hidden Potential

Identification procedures must be viewed in the light of purposes to be served by the search for special ability. Test scores generally indicate which young people have *already* "arrived" or which young people are well on their way. These individuals do not represent a problem of identification. In addition, being easily found, they are readily served. The problem lies in those children and youth who *ought* to be on the way but who are prevented by personal, cultural, or educational handicaps. If the purpose of identification is to group together children who are already reading better than their classmates, the reading test is an effective instrument. If the purpose is to find those youngsters who ought to be reading well, the reading test by itself proves to be too limited.

A second determinant of identification procedures is the nature of the program for which children are being selected. If the purpose is to establish classes which will be taking farther flights into academic areas with verbal material, achievement and intelligence tests as now constituted represent a viable approach. On the basis of past success, future achievement in comparable activities can be predicted. If the aim, however, is to stimulate creative abilities and to encourage originality, the conventional tests yield few valid clues. Again, we return to the Chicago and Minnesota findings that high intelligence (as defined by scores on existing tests) and high creativity are not synonymous.

The important jobs in identification— finding potential that has not yet been nourished, and discovering talents that do not necessarily correlate strongly with school achievement— remain a challenge. Attention to the purposes of identification and to the nature of the school program that makes identification necessary may prevent wasting resources on inappropriate procedures and instruments.

Degree of Ability and Range of Talents

One may seek individuals more than three standard deviations above the mean of intellectual ability— the top one-half of 1 per cent— and be assured that those included will do extremely well academically with few exceptions. But at the same time one must recognize that so narrow a selection will exclude a very large number of extremely capable individuals because of (1) the standard error of the instrument employed, (2) qualitative inadequacies of all existing tests, (3) personal differences among subjects not related to intellectual ability alone but affecting scores on tests, (4) cultural differences among subjects which contaminate the scores on aptitude and achievement tests. In very large communities, a highly selective criterion (top one-half or 1 per cent, top 2 or 3 per cent) is frequently used, with the rationalization that able children who are excluded still have the opportunity to learn in a rich program offered to all students in the school system. Their chief loss, it is claimed, is in exclusion from association with bright children only which is effected by grouping. Moreover, there is research that questions the academic value of grouping itself.

In all but the largest communities selection of the very exceptional group is not even a matter of choice but is simply not feasible. One-half of 1 per cent yields only fifteen children in a school district of three thousand pupils. Even 3 per cent gives a group of only 90 scholars in all 12 grades. A large high school of one thousand pupils normally enrolls but 30 students with IQ's over 130 (to take the simplest distinction). Unless a community is large enough to bring together children from more than one school it is rarely possible to assemble as many as 25 students for a class of the top one-half per cent or even top 3 per cent in ability. But organizational reasons are not the only rationale for widening the range of ability to be identified. In terms of intellectually gifted students the primary aim of education in the common schools is preparation for college. While some students survive in college with average intelligence, by and large, students who do well in college average above 115 IQ. This fact justifies many school districts in including in their "gifted" group the top fifth of the intelligence distribution. This is substantially the recommendation of James Conant in his report, *The American High School.* It should be apparent, however, that a school program geared to very exceptional ability may be too rigorous for the top fifth, and that teachers planning work for the top fifth may not adequately involve the top half-per cent if all youngsters in the class are treated as a group.

Not only is the range of abilities at issue; there is also the problem of the range of talents that ought to be included. The facile assumption that all students of superior *general* ability ought to be identified ignores the fact that a large number of individuals might be added who show special promise in any *one* field — science, mathematics, linguistics, writing, dramatics, speech, music, art, industrial arts, retail selling, bookkeeping, typewriting, etc., — but whose general ability is undistinguished. Conversely, students may be found who do very well in general but who have no outstanding talent in any one field. In the past we have generally taken the student with the high general average and excluded the student with unusual special ability if limited to a single field. This may merely indicate unwillingness to accept the specialized nature of our times and occupations.

Issues in Identifying Talent

McClelland takes a critical view of the whole of identification procedures as currently employed. He feels that not enough objective information has been accumulated on a scientific basis. He sets forth a number of issues in identification of talent whereon research is needed. One problem arises from our assumption that abilities are static — that a talent discovered at age ten will be constant ten, twenty, thirty years later. Actually the problem of prediction is complicated because potential varies over a period of time in proportion to opportunity for development and use. Second, McClelland points out that we have few functional analyses of superior performance in any walk of life. If we had these analyses we could recognize the components that are necessary for success and use them in identifying potential superiority. Without them, we remain very much in the dark.

For the most part we employ measures that have a high correlation with success in school. While this kind of instrument predicts success in school and college relatively well, unfortunately the correlation with success in life is not encouraging. This is true simply because there is "a lack of fit between performance in school and later life".

Third, a normal way of identifying characteristics necessary for success is to analyze the life and performance of persons eminent in their field. Such analysis is made after these persons have attained their position. Did these persons show the same characteristics and behave in the same manner prior to their achievement of success? Not what they are now, but what they were in the early period is necessary for us to know if we are to identify potential achievers at a future time. Again the information for early identification is not available.

Fourth, McClelland raises an interesting question which is shared by others. "What evidence," he asks, "is there that intelligence is not a threshold type of variable; that once a person has a certain minimal level of intelligence his performance beyond that point is uncorrelated with his ability? Several studies suggest that if such a minimal level is set fairly high, ability may no longer play a crucial role in success". This question is reinforced by observation that virtuosi in various fields may show high, but not exceptional intelligence. Brandwein, in *The Gifted Student as a Future Scientist*, suggests that selection of science potential begins with a somewhat higher-than-average intelligence but must be reinforced by spatial perception and a strong interest in science.

All of these uncertainties led McClelland to the conclusion that we are barking up the wrong tree in seeking to identify talent with our crude methods. We should shift, he suggests, "to studying the process by which talent becomes actual, by which it develops". Failing to do so, we place emphasis on talent potential as the fixed attribute of a very small number of people. Were we to learn more about the process of developing talents we might include many more people in our efforts and we might bring many and greater gifts to fruition. Anne Hoppock, speaking for the Association for Childhood Education, expresses a similar point of view. Tax-supported schools, she points out, are designed for all the children of all the people. Each parent has the right to expect the school will value his child and help him become his best self. "By seeking the undiscovered resources which lie within every child, we best assure the identification of very able children.... Perhaps the most effective way to find the creative potentialities of children is to put them in an environment which encourages them to behave creatively".

To assist in the development of a framework for research on the conditions and outcomes necessary for identification and development of superior ability. Research that fills in such a chart for eminent performance in specific fields such as medicine, law, or teaching is needed if competent identification is to be achieved.

Recognition of Special Abilities

Traditional concern with the "universal man," the "well-rounded individual," and "liberal education" often obscures the fact that people have special abilities and operate as specialists in their daily tasks. No one will quarrel with the lofty educational ideal expressed by the individual of broad culture and wide-ranging interests and abilities. No one will deny the desirability of broadly educated physicists and versatile humanists, but neither can society afford to reject the gifts that come from the narrow physicist who has but minor interest in society and the arts or from the linguist who is scientifically illiterate. Anderson notes, "We can say with some assurance that the human being possesses many special abilities which are uncorrelated, or correlated to such a slight degree that one cannot be predicted from the other".

What this signifies in identification of talent is the need to seek out special interests and abilities whether or not they are related to high general ability. If one accepts the factorial thesis, then one seeks to identify individuals showing high ability in those factors that are related to success in particular fields. For example, space perception correlates well with scientific training and performance. A high general intelligence score that omits space perception is not as helpful as it might be in predicting science aptitude. A high general score and a low space perception score do not augur well for success in science. A high space perception score, accompanied by other factors important in science, would be more promising than a general score alone. The discovery of low to moderate correlation among various factors on tests such as the CAVD and the Differential Aptitude Test batteries supports greater utilization of scores on individual factors than is now the case.

The multi-factor approach also questions the validity of various identification procedures in use in elementary and secondary schools. First the reliance upon single cumulative scores from general intelligence tests appear to be excessive. While high general intelligence is perhaps identified, no doubt many children are excluded who show moderate general ability but who have unusual talents in specific fields. Second, establishing high *average* grades as a screening device for special programs in the school or in particular subjects raises the same question. Honor schools often enroll many students in some special classes where they show only the barest interest. They are there because of general grade averages and aptitude scores. Third, admission to colleges and to special programs in colleges on the basis of general aptitude tests or high school averages is subject to the same criticism. A high general mediocrity may be pre-empting opportunity which should be afforded to high special abilities that are not also favored with high performance in non-related fields.

What is needed, therefore, is some means to identify special ability in particular fields. Having identified such ability, schools must then find some way of fully challenging this ability whether it is accompanied by superior general intelligence or not. The old assumption that everyone in secondary schools and colleges must be exposed to the same dose of the cultural heritage violates this point of view. Somehow we have to find academically respectable ways of exempting Einsteins, Edisons, and Churchills from requirements that have little meaning for them instead of subjecting them to regimes that prevent their potential from revealing itself.

Interest as a Sign of Potential

Ways of identifying special abilities attracted the efforts of a Science Study Group established at the University School at The Ohio State University in 1958. First the group adopted the following criteria by which they might select "manifestations of talents":

> *(1) they (manifestations of talent) should apply to talent of all kinds; (2) they should be specific enough for quantitative treatment...; (3) they should be discrete enough so that there is no confusion about what is meant; (4) they should be expressable in verbal terms — that is, be able to be described behaviorally; and (5) they should be few enough in number so that the full range can be held in mind.*

On this basis the group selected six manifestations which, by implication, "define talent as an intensity of interest along with the skills, understandings, and commitments that come when this intensity is long continued" (*Ibid.*). The six manifestations follow:

1. prolonged pursuit of an interest
2. great amount of time devoted to an interest
3. active search for information and ideas — that is, expanding to ever-broadened understandings
4. multiplicity of related interests in the field
5. degree of self-initiated interests or concerns
6. accumulation of an unusual degree of skill and understanding

The cardinal place of interest and self-selection by the individual is revealing. It confirms Brandwein's finding at Forest Hills High School in New York when he sought to identify students with special ability in science. Students were invited to apply for a special program if they were interested; in addition, teachers were asked to nominate students and records of school performance were examined. In 90 per cent of the cases students coming into the new program identified themselves. Only 10 per cent were added as a result of teacher nomination.

These two examples also serve to support arguments for avoiding restrictive identification procedures. These arguments assert our inability with available instruments to distinguish accurately young people of high promise. Instead, support is found for broadening the range of opportunity. In organization of special classes, the range of ability may be extended in order to include students showing unusual interest.

A second inference may also be drawn from the use of interest as a primary identifying factor. It is all good and well to utilize interest when children come from equally stimulating cultures into the school situation. What of the "mute, inglorious Miltons" who have never had the opportunity to develop an interest in the Muse? While certainly the school is helped by interests already developed, the school represents in many areas the only medium through which new interests may be awakened. Before it can assess potential, then, for many individuals and in many areas of study the school must first present rich opportunities for experience. On the basis of a fair chance in specific areas, pupils can develop and show interests which the school can evaluate for future promise. For "culturally deprived" populations the school has a particularly challenging— and socially responsible— task.

Individual Intellective Factors

How, then, does one proceed to identify these special factors in intelligence and other special abilities? One does not, of course, simply discard the general intelligence test, scores on the Binet and Wechsler-Bellevue scales, or the general results of group tests. One means of broadening procedures is to consider scores on non-verbal tests and on tests claiming to be "culture-fair." High scores on these tests may serve to increase the reservoir of exceptional potential. Second, one may attempt to devise tests such as the Hunter Aptitude Scales for Gifted Children to identify exceptional scores in factors for which one is looking in pre-reading age groups. With older children one may employ group tests to yield separate scores for individual factors. These include the Thorndike CAVD tests, the Differential Aptitude Tests, the California Tests of Mental Maturity, the Kuhlmann-Anderson Intelligence Tests, and the Terman-McNemar Test among others. Although total scores are available on these tests, attention should be focused on very high scores on any of the sub-tests or separate factors.

Achievement in Individual Areas

Achievement is a sign of ability motivated within a favorable, supporting environment. Accordingly, high scores in particular areas of achievement also identify special ability, although some children will be missed because of low motivation or cultural handicaps. High scores in any single area on the usual standardized achievement test may also be regarded as one sign of potential. These tests have the advantage of being free from human bias which may color any one teacher's evaluation of a given child's ability— for better or for worse! Here again, it is the high score on an individual test that we are looking for, not the high "profile."

Teacher Opinion

Teacher judgment and school grades also help to increase the size of a gifted population. The "human element" may affect judgment, but sympathetic observation often uncovers ability hidden by negative motivational or cultural effects. A perceptive teacher is often able to discern *interest* and *potential* that are more a promise than an actuality while the test is limited to performance in the present. Once again, it is more significant to learn that Jenny is a "whiz" in history than to discover that she is a very mediocre scholar in all other areas.

An interesting instance of teacher sensitivity to special talent is manifested in a study by Pegnato and Birch in a Pittsburgh junior high school enrolling 1,400 students. Teachers in the school were asked to name students whom they regarded as gifted. They selected the following:

154 as "gifted" (no further definition)
137 as outstanding in music (71) or art (66)
82 for leadership qualities (home room or student council officers)
179 as outstanding in mathematics

Of the nominees, 450 had IQ scores over 115; 334 had earned achievement test scores three or more grades above their grade placement. Of considerable interest is the fact that teachers named 781 individual children out of the total of 1,400 as gifted in one way or another.

Special Tests

Special tests are also helpful. The Watson-Glaser Critical-Thinking Appraisal does not correlate very highly with general intelligence test scores. It may therefore be looked to for identification of a group of students who would be ignored on an IQ basis alone. The Test of Critical Thinking in Social Science serves the same purpose. Burton, Kimball, and Wing list and annotate other tests that shed some light on critical thinking ability in general and critical analysis in literature, natural sciences and the social sciences. In such fields as music and art, tests that are truly predictive of later performance would meet a very real need. Some tests (Lewerenz Test of Fundamental Ability in Visual Art, Horn Art Aptitude Inventory, Seashore Measure of Music Talent, Drake Musical Memory Test, Kwalwasser-Ruch Test of Musical Accomplishment, Meier Art Judgment Test) are available and have been used more or less extensively for a number of years. Unfortunately, they give a rather rough estimate of success. To some extent they are affected by the fact that one may know a great deal *about* particular areas without being able to *do* anything oneself. One of the main values of these tests is the indication of interest that familiarity suggests. In testing for social leadership qualities the Quincy Youth Development Project devised a "Behavior Description Chart" to guide teachers in their observation. The chart is organized into eighteen sets of descriptive statements with five statements in each set. For each set the teacher is asked to mark the statement which is most and least descriptive of the child he is evaluating. As indicated in the example that follows, it is not obvious which statement represents maximum leadership:

A. Quarrelsome
B. Likes jobs which give him responsibility
C. Avoids games
D. Does his share, but does not seek leadership
E. Is usually courteous to other children

A more widely used method of identifying leadership is to utilize children's choices as expressed in sociograms. Asking children to name two or three classmates whom they would choose as friends, whom they would like to play particular games with, whom they would join on specified committees, whom they would want to work with on particular jobs, whom they would like to sit next to— such questions yield information on simple popularity or information on children's perceptions as to the helpfulness of other children. Recognizing that the responses may say as much about the child replying as about the children chosen, the questioner may in any case distill interesting information about leadership roles as perceived by a child's contemporaries.

Still another technique is that used by Gardner and Thompson working with college students at Syracuse University. In interviews students were asked to rank fraternity brothers in order to determine various social characteristics and their effect upon group morale and productivity. They were assisted (or "forced") in this process by being asked first to select the highest and lowest member with respect to a given attribute such as loyal friendship, and then to name another who would seem to be "just about average." The student was then asked to name another fraternity brother who ranked in between the top and the average member, and a fourth brother who ranked in between the bottom and the average member. This device served to set up four quartiles, and the student then ranked remaining members in order as being more or less loyal (the attribute in this example) than the five students selected as reference points by the respondent himself.

The four scales used in the Syracuse research are of interest in attempting to come to grips with the elusive elements that comprise social leadership. They were designated as Playmirth (members with whom the respondent enjoys spending an evening for fun), Succorance (persons he regards as helpful and sympathetic in an emergency), Achievement-recognition (persons whose company is valued as helping to secure recognition from others for purpose of achievement), and Affiliation (persons valued for their loyal friendship). The technique described for a college population, but variations may be worth exploring for use with younger students. This technique was employed as an improvement over the simple sociogram since it forced attention to all members of the group and was not limited only to those who came easily to mind. Nor was it limited to the most noticeable members (for good or ill) in the group.

Considerable experimentation is in process on the identification of social leaders, for in social, business, and political affairs it is often such a leader who secures action. No clear evidence is yet available which indicates predictive value of the devices being tested.

Identification in Individual Subject Areas

Specialists in each of the academic areas are concerned with predictive devices that may help identify potential in their areas. Accordingly, as one reads any of the professional journals devoted to a particular area one finds results of such efforts. One of the more helpful sources is the series of booklets being published by the Academically Talented Student Project of the National Education Association. Relevant sections are to be found in currently completed bulletins on English, Modern Foreign Languages, Social Studies, Mathematics, Science, Administration, Art, and Music. Specialists in most subject areas recommend employment of general intelligence tests, achievement tests in their own area, teacher grades, and teacher opinions. They urge consideration of items such as the following:

- Use and comprehension of a wide vocabulary
- Ability to learn easily and rapidly and an eagerness to do so
- Long attention span for difficult material
- Asking of meaningful questions and intellectual curiosity in general
- Broad interests high-lighted by intensive interest in a subject area or in careers related to the subject
- Ability in intellectual operations such as generalization, comparison, understanding relationships, handling abstractions and critical thinking
- Originality, creativity, and imagination
- Retention of learning
- Dislike of routine, drill or rote, memory exercises
- Ability to work independently
- Ability to work with others
- Power of self-appraisal and self-criticism and a self-motivating quality.

In addition, as might be expected, specialists ask for particular competences in areas related to their subject. These are considered in some detail in later chapters in this volume which deal with individual subject areas.

Work Samples

In many fields the only valid reflection of potential is through early expression of promise. While some tests exist in fields like music, art, and creative writing, auditions and examinations of sample products yield results that correlate much better with success. New York City maintains two special high schools dealing with some such fields, an academic high school called the High School of Music and Art, and a vocational high school called the High School of Performing Arts. These schools select their students partly by auditions in dramatics, dance, and musical performance (vocal or instrumental) and by evaluation of artistic creations. Judges are generally persons from the performing arts who voluntarily give their time to select young people who show promise of talent. Emphasis is not on the finished product but on the glimpses of originality, inventiveness, feeling, and creativeness that distinguish the artist of the future from the person who can turn in a well-trained but uninspired performance. New York City as a center for the arts is able to provide a milieu and personnel. Each community has to seek out professional and lay expertise that is available in order to supplement judgment of teachers with exceptional background and artistic taste.

The performance criterion has the merit of assessing motivation, persistence, and ability to learn, as well as aptitude. However, it suffers even more than most standardized tests in reflecting the opportunities and handicaps of the child's environment.

In academic areas also the work sample is important. Originality and creativity in writing are more likely to appear in a student's work than on a standardized test, although some general picture of creative perspective may be forthcoming from the ingenious measures recently tested in research projects at the University of Chicago, University of Minnesota, Hunter College, and a few other centers. Since there are signs that creativeness may often be particular rather than general, the work sample is a desirable supplement to the new tests. The sample shows creativeness in a specific application.

What is true in writing is true in regard to the way in which a student approaches a problem in mathematics or a social-political-economic situation which invites fresh insight.

It is of interest that performance is the best criterion that foreign language specialists can offer to identify exceptional ability in linguistic talent. Urging the initiation of foreign language in the third grade if at all possible, they recommend results of early learning as the measure of ability to proceed further.

One of the interesting assumptions underlying exhibits at science fairs and the project report in the Westinghouse Science Talent Search is the belief that a boy or girl will show potential and originality more in the projects he undertakes than in any other way. In industrial arts, vocational fields, and home economics the work sample again is a primary way of judging promise.

DeHaan and Kough suggest some interesting situations in which performance can be observed. Games testing memory, general information, and ability to reorient oneself are offered as informal means of checking general intelligence. Creativity is evidenced in listing quickly all the things that students may think of which share a particular quality (such as all things that are round), in imagining "what happens if" some peculiar event were to take place, in suggesting improvements in common objects, or in listing multiple uses for common objects. Identification of dramatic talent may be fostered by observing efforts at pantomime, at acting out a story, or at reading a play aloud. The Quincy Youth Development Project, to which DeHaan and Kough contributed, sought to locate art aptitude by rating four drawings that students submitted. One was a draw-a-man assignment with instructions carefully standardized. Other drawings were of a schoolroom, a scenic picture, and a favorite subject. The jury looked for representational ability, line technique, area technique, flexibility of objects, compositional unity, color, artistic movement (path of viewer's vision), creative liberty and communicativeness, rating each of these on a five-point scale. A parallel performance test was employed in identifying writing ability. Children were asked to write four papers and given a modified thematic apperception test. The four papers included narration of a "most exciting event," description of "the person I would like to be like," a letter to grandmother, and the weaving of a story around any four of some twenty word pictures (two-word phrases, like "magic pebble") presented to the children. The efforts were again given to a jury for analysis. A very important problem in the employment of work samples is establishing criteria for analysis. Unfortunately, the prize in some science fairs is awarded for nothing more inspired than a beautifully copied drawing from a textbook or other source. This is more likely to happen when judges are poorly instructed and the objectives of the fair are not clearly understood. More typical would be the performance of the artists evaluating applicants at New York's School for Performing Arts where signs of originality, insight, and professional sparkle take precedence over a polished performance alone. Suggested criteria follow:

1. Does the work show signs of fresh viewpoint or insight?
2. Does the technique indicate individuality and initiative in attempting to solve the problem undertaken?
3. Does the work show persistence in attempting to solve the problem? Is there effort to work out details as well as the broad pattern?
4. Is the subject imitative or does it show a fresh sensitivity to beauty, to problems in the area or to possibilities of the medium employed?
5. Is something of a "professional" verve foreshadowed?
6. Is nothing more evident than patient practice and conformity to a given model?
7. Is there any sign of "protest" against customary practices, procedures, solutions, or ideas?
8. Is there any sign that the work would have been accomplished without the external motivation of a contest?
9. Is there evidence of capacity for self-criticism, self-evaluation, and subsequent, independent improvement?

Summary

Where special programs can be offered to selected groups it will always be necessary to identify promise. To sum up ideas set forth in this chapter, the following procedure may be attempted:

1. Endeavor to identify intellective and personal factors necessary for high performance in the field under consideration. Establish a "threshold IQ" if possible and build upon this a percentile or score level for particular intellectual factors that appear necessary.
2. Administer intelligence tests that give both a general and special factor score.
3. Secure some measure of general creativity and attempt this with the group.
4. Invite volunteers to apply in order to secure an important measure of interest through self selection.
5. Secure teacher recommendations.
6. Consult student grades in the particular area and in related subjects.
7. Employ any special tests which give a measure of achievement, interest, or aptitude.
8. Seek out work samples in the particular area. If possible form a qualified jury to evaluate the samples.
9. Identify students who apparently have had no opportunity to develop interest or skill in the area. Expose these students to exploratory experiences. Include the top fifth(or tenth, or fiftieth, or whatever fraction school policy establishes) of the exploratory students in the special program on a tryout basis. Provide for volunteers from this group, too, after they have had a chance to "get their feet wet."
10. Keep the special group open for students who may later be identified, and permit students who feel they have made a mistake to withdraw.

Perhaps the most important conclusion to draw is that life and education are the best means of identification. Tests and other measures are only a very halting kind of shorthand. Anderson states this point of view effectively.

> *From the developmental point of view it is also clear that a good and universal program of education for children between the ages of five and seventeen years offers the best opportunity for the*

systematic exploration of talent because it covers substantial portions of the period of growth and permits children to find themselves through contact with stimulating materials and ideas. Hence from a developmental point of view, short-term tests and measures complement education rather than become the primary device for locating talent.

4

Creativity as an Aspect of Giftedness

Introduction

The appropriateness of such procedures, however, has to be measured against the aims of our culture and its schools. Academic achievement in the realm of the customary disciplines is certainly valuable, but there are some who would question this goal as the only value to be sought. Gardner Murphy, in his provocative volume, *Human Potentialities*, raises serious objection. He has little doubt of the ability of gifted youngsters to absorb the heritage. This, he says, is not the need of our times when civilization walks a tightrope between catastrophe and glory. We have a pressing need "to see in perspective where the major areas for fresh creations exist; in particular to discover those areas in which curiosity about the social order, eagerness to understand man's predicament, may be capable of highest development, in order that an educational process attuned to the need for full utilization of such a capacity may do its work while there is time".

More important than learning to apply the old is releasing man's potential to design the new. More important than slow progress by extrapolating into the future from the past is the rapid jump forward or the adoption of new directions in a creative process similar to a biological mutation. Murphy sees no hope in any tendencies now afoot for resolving the international tensions that have beset the world increasingly since the turn of the century. New and creative ideas, dramatically different and not continuous with our current thinking, will be needed to break existing stalemates. Murphy seems devoutly to believe that man has the necessary equipment, biological and social, continuously to develop such creative responses:

> *Because man has this rich potentiality for sensory, motor, intellectual experience, and has to combine all this in fresh acts of cultural creativeness, he is doing nothing more than realizing these potentialities when he writes* Macbeth *or flies a plane at Kitty Hawk. And it is not only human to invent oneself out of one world into another; it is also human to keep moving toward a destination which is not set within man's present nature but keeps changing as the nature of his environment changes.*

This point of view is shared by Sinnott who regards life itself as a creative process. In biological forms below man, Sinnott sees life as conservative and rigidly fixed in its genetic constitution. This rigidity is found in man's *physical* structure, too, but in the complexity of the human brain Sinnott finds infinite possibilities of new mental patterns. He regards imagination as the basic formative quality of life emerging from rigid physical limitations to express itself in high creativity.

Creativity, like Motherhood and Fatherland, will find few adversaries, but differences exist in the approach to its development and release. One argument is that creativeness is a function of adult performance, that in youth one gets ready. One needs experience, understanding, knowledge, and skill. One needs the tools of humankind as arms.

This is the basic justification for considering education as the transmission of the cultural heritage, for prescribing a curriculum determined by experts, for requiring more learning, and more "coverage" for the able. The counter-argument stems from a belief that creativeness is an aspect of personality and intelligence that stems from birth or early childhood, that creativeness is learned and therefore may be encouraged or inhibited by the environment. Such an argument justifies "progressive" school programs, permissive environments, student participation in establishing goals, and exploratory activities as part of an educational program for creativeness.

The release of creativity is thus argued on social grounds, on the needs of the world in time of crisis for original, "emergent" approaches rather than the extension of trends already established. The importance of the issue, however, lies not only in social need — the manpower concept — but also in individual self-realization — the development of man, as an ideal. Helping the gifted individual truly to realize his own gifts, his own being, depends upon release of unique and creative powers.

Creativity and Intellectual Giftedness

Implicit in the preceding statement and in the thoughts of many persons concerned with education of the gifted is the assumption that creativity is one aspect of giftedness. Taylor indicates that such an assumption depends upon the definition of intelligence that is employed. When high scores on current intelligence tests are taken as the criterion of giftedness, creative ability is not necessarily found among the population regarded as gifted. In such a case, the word *gifted* apparently is attached "to high academic performance in school like activities which are often not very creative in nature." As a result, Taylor suggests that we may more accurately posit the existence of numerous different types of giftedness, one of which is the high IQ. Different kinds of creativeness may make tip a whole class of other gifts, and still other types — such as planning, evaluation, decision making, communication — may also exist separately.

Guilford relates this shortcoming in intelligence tests to the history of psychological research on the theory of learning. Much research, he points out, has been done with lower animals in which signs of creativeness are almost non-existent. In addition, the effort to "scientize" and quantify resulted in developing learning theories formulated so as to cover phenomena that lend themselves to ordering in a logical scheme. Unfortunately, what may have proved feasible has not proved comprehensive as well, and it is time that learning theory take into consideration such matters as insight and creative activity. Guilford describes how Binet validated his tests against achievement in school subjects, primarily reading and arithmetic, subjects which are "not conspicuously demanding of creative talent. The content of intelligence tests reveals little of an obviously creative nature.".

This analysis may help explain the source of Leta Hollingworth puzzlement when she discovered that only one-third of her very high IQ subjects displayed any remarkable creativity. Most of Terman's thousand most gifted subjects also are apparently making their way effectively through life, but a disappointingly small number have distinguished themselves in creative performance. In more recent years efforts have been made to apply objective measures in order to compare the scores of individuals on intelligence and creativity tests. Getzels and Jackson found remarkably little overlapping between high intelligence (IQ) and high creativity groups when they tested the young people in a private high school with an intellectually superior population. Torrance, testing children in elementary schools, noted an overlapping of only 30 per cent of students who scored within the top 20 per cent on both IQ and creativity measures. On the other hand, Simpson and Martinson, studying gifted children in California, observe that "the IQ as an identification criterion locates individuals of great variety and virtuosity." They question the view that a high IQ is more a mark of conformity to the school and its academic demands than it is a sign of creativity.

Actually, an accommodation of the two views — that IQ does or does not correlate with creativeness — is possible. Barron indicates that the correlation of the two factors over the whole range of ability is approximately +.40, but that the correlation between intelligence and creativity among individuals with IQ's over 120 is only +.10. The Simpson Martinson study apparently covers creativity within the whole range of ability; Getzels and Jackson, Terman, and Hollingworth worked only within the narrow limits of high ability. MacKinnon computed a correlation for creative architests of-.08 between scores on Terman's Concept Mastery Test and tests of creativeness. For creative scientists, the correlation was-.07. Taken together, all these findings support the generalization that a moderately high level of intelligence is necessary for creative work, "but beyond that point being more or less intelligent does not crucially determine the level of a person's creativeness".

Taylor, Murphy, and others have long noted the relatively low creative component in school and college work. Intelligence tests have been validated against academic performance. A tight little circle has been closed in which intelligence and academic performance are equated and creativity excluded. Small wonder, then, that a low relationship exists between academic performance and adult success. To the extent that creativity may be needed in adult enterprise (and Taylor presents some evidence to bear this out) a solution may lie in greater recognition of creative ability and the revamping of academic programs so that creative behavior may be nurtured.

Defining Creativeness

In seeking to secure nominations of creative students from faculty members at the University of Nebraska, Drevdahl presented the following definition to his colleagues:

> *Creativity is the capacity of persons to produce compositions, products, or ideas of any sort which are essentially new or novel, and previously unknown to the producer. It can be imaginative activity, or thought synthesis, where the product is not mere summation. It may involve the forming of new patterns and combinations of information derived from past experience, and the transplanting of old relation ships to new situations, and may involve the generation of new correlates. It must be purposeful or goal directed, not mere idle fantasy – although it need not have immediate practical application or be a perfect and complete product. It may take the form of an artistic, literary or scientific production or may be of a procedural or methodological nature.*

A number of other definitions have been offered. Torrance sums up many of them by noting that almost all involve production of something new or original and a process that includes four elements: sensing some kind of deficiency, formulating ideas or hypotheses, testing hypotheses, and communicating results. In the Interdisciplinary Symposia on Creativity, Dow, Fromm, Maslow, Rogers, and May agree in addition on a greater emphasis on self-awareness, the sense of "I," "not primarily to discover something new, but to experience in such a way that the experience originates in me". Maslow appears to equate his concept of the "peak experience" with "self-actualizing creativeness." Rogers defines the creative process as "the emergence in action of a novel relational product growing out of the uniqueness of the individual on the one hand and the materials, events, people or circumstances of his life on the other." He finds the necessary motivation to creativity in the tendency of "man to actualize himself to become his potentialities," "the urge to expand, extend, develop, mature— the tendency to express and activate all the capacities of the organism."

In attempting to define creativity we shall find it useful to employ four perspectives suggested by Mooney. He points out that creativeness is variously considered in relation to (1) the product created, (2) the process of creating, (3) the person of the creator, and (4) the environment in which the creative work is done.

The Creative Product

Obviously, creativity must ultimately be manifested through performance or expression. To be sure, distinctions have to be made. A scientific discovery, for example, may be historically creative— like Salk's polio vaccine, or it may be personally creative— like the high school student's unaided discovery that the difference between squares of consecutive integers increases by 2. Russell draws the distinction well:

> *Home and school can consider creative thinking (a) as a discovery which is fresh for the child himself, involving self-realization, (b) as the production of ideas or materials which contribute to the pleasure or welfare of the group to which the child belongs, and (c) as a comparatively rare, original contribution to the culture, a contribution which only a few gifted individuals can make. Obviously, homes and schools are more concerned with the first two types of creative activity, but in so doing they may be paving the way for the third type of contribution.*

Distinctions between major and minor gifts in creativity must also be recognized, since failure to do so might eliminate all but works in the class of *Hamlet* and the "Mona Lisa." This may be carried to the opposite extreme where every learning act is regarded as creative. Such is Kilpatrick's claim that all learning is creative since in learning the child achieves some new insight or reorganizes his experience in a way that is new for him.

There is some merit in Kilpatrick's view because it makes the term less cabalistic, less the prerogative of the favored few. Burton, on the other hand, distinguishes between creativity and learning as the difference between what the child learns to create himself and the discovery of what others have learned. "Learning," he says, "is more the process of discovery than creation. Through discovery of what others have learned the child learns to create himself, but that learning is not necessarily creative". There are limitations, too, to a definition of creativity that becomes as broad as learning, for it ceases to be helpful in identifying a factor whose discovery is needed for maximum development.

Generally speaking, there is considerable agreement on the following attributes of the creative *product*:

> *Novelty or originality of contribution; either new for the individual or new for the culture; the contribution may represent a product, a method, or a new insight into a problem.*
>
> *Social value; since objective criteria are difficult to apply, the contribution has to merit acceptance by some group of people at some point in time*
>
> *An intellectual content and background, but not restricted to areas of intellectual endeavor; intelligence is viewed as a necessary but not a sufficient condition in itself.*

Creativity as a Process

A highly creative product ought to stem from a creative process. Teacher and parent are more likely to see the process in its early stages than they are to see an extraordinary product. If the process has its own characteristics and if these can be identified, it would behave the teacher or parent to assist in developing the process.

One form of the process is described as creative thinking. Russell places emphasis on self-discovery, perceptual and integrative factors in the chapter he devotes to creative thinking. Guilford distinguishes between convergent and divergent thinking on the basis of directedness in the process. Convergent thinking points toward the one acceptable solution. "Divergent thinking...(is) characterized...as being less goal bound. There is freedom to go off in different directions.... Rejecting the old solution and striking out in some new direction is necessary, and the resourceful organism will more probably succeed.". Working with Guilford's distinction, Getzels and Jackson define creative thought as "goal directed, easily flexible, manipulation of knowledge in a wide variety of novel or original ways." In the process they note such factors as adaptive flexibility, associational fluency, and perhaps most important, originality.

The nature of divergent thinking is to be found also in the mental activity we often call fantasy. Getzels and Jackson noted the greater use by their high-creative subjects of stimulus-free themes and unexpected endings. Their divergent thinking was further exemplified in humor, playfulness, and greater use of incongruities. They also noted: "The creative adolescent seems to possess the ability to free himself from the unusual, to 'diverge' from the customary. He seems to enjoy the risk and uncertainty of the unknown".

Crutchfield, on the other hand, declines to attribute all creativity to divergent thinking. He finds differences in the characteristics of the "so-called creative process" in accordance with the nature of the creative task involved. Divergent thinking is found in some, convergent thinking in others. Crutchfield insists that the creative process is not mysterious, that it is not a single unitary process with sharply defined or sequential stages, and that considerable analysis of the process is still needed.

Mooney identifies four elements in the creative process as he observes the individual in relation to (1) the extension of his experiencing, (2) the focussing of his experiencing, (3) the management of his actions during experiencing, and (4) the derivation of significance from his experiencing. As catchwords for these four aspects, Mooney suggests *openness, self-realization, control, and aesthetic evaluation*. The "openness" criterion is discussed later in this chapter. The second element involves, in Mooney's words "focus through self-differentiation and self realization," a willingness to be different about things, a persistent inquiry into the meaning of the individual's own life. "Control" involves a self-discipline but also a mastery of the materials and tools of one's work. Finally, Significance is derived in terms of aesthetics—harmony of form and function, pattern, order. Presumably these functions may characterize intellectual as well as artistic performance.

Leuba helps to throw some light on the question of why some people are more open to experience than others. He relates a factor of increased stimulation to creative effort. He questions the assumption that people do things to reduce such needs as curiosity and tension, but feels that much behavior arises in order to increase these stimulation. He formulates a "principle of optimal stimulation," "that those activities are strengthened and tend to predominate which raise stimulation from inadequate levels toward an optimal one." Accordingly, he notes that students "do not ordinarily seem to study in order to reduce drives, anxieties, or tensions; on the contrary, they seem to learn most effectively what is stimulating and exciting to them". One might assume from Leuba's hypothesis that the creative individuals are those with a maximum of curiosity, those who seek stimulation and develop a maximum of autonomous interest and activity because of the stimulation they find in the process.

There are various theories which throws light on gifted education. Some of these theories are explaining about the various thinkers which have their different perceptions and different theories. Fantasy as one of the exaple given above which explain about the mental activity.

The effort to identify observable factors in the creative process extends from relatively simple analyses to the more recent work of Guilford and his associates where 14 factors are identified and 53 tests employed to measure aspects of these factors. Guilford first hypothesis included sensitivity to problems, ideational fluency (fluidity of ideas), flexibility of set (ability to change tack, to shift from one frame of reference to another when "first guesses" do not work out), ideational novelty (fluidity of new ideas, new solutions), synthesizing ability, analyzing ability, reorganizing or redefining ability (rearranging materials and ideas in new ways to meet new needs), span of ideational structure and evaluating ability. At first, Guilford suggested these as possible factors in creative scientific work, but later study by his group has apparently established a conviction that these factors apply in other fields as well. The fourteen factors listed by the group as factors in creative thinking include such general abilities as verbal comprehension, numerical facility, perceptual speed, visualization, and general reasoning. Perhaps more specific to creativity are other factors they list: word fluency, associational fluency, ideational fluency, closure, originality, redefinition, adaptive flexibility, spontaneous flexibility, and sensitivity to problems. Viktor Lowenfeld and his associates sought independently at Pennsylvania State University to find measurable criteria responsible for creativeness. Focussing on art rather than science, Lowenfeld points out "that both investigations, after exploring numerous possible criteria, arrived at almost exactly the same eight criteria of creativity." "This would, then, as far as our data are concerned, establish that *creativeness in the arts has common attributes with creativeness in the sciences*" (*Ibid.*). Lowenfeld lists the following "eight attributes of creativity which significantly differentiate creative from less- or noncreative persons in both investigations":

- Sensitivity to problems
- Fluency of ideas (the number of different ideas which a person may have when thinking of using a single item, for example)
- Flexibility (the individual's ability to adjust quickly to new situations)
- Originality (uncommonness of verbal and sensory responses)
- Redefinition and the ability to rearrange (redefining a material by using it in a new way or by giving it a new meaning)
- Analysis or the ability to abstract (starting with the whole and arriving at details)
- Synthesis and closure (combining of several elements to form a new whole)

Coherence of organization ("that part of creativity most closely related to aesthetics, for aesthetic growth appears to be responsible for the changes from a chaos on the lower end of the continuum to the most complete harmonious organization on the upper end.

While noting the similarity between creativity in the arts and in the sciences, we should also do well to take note of MacKinnon distinction between the two areas. In the sciences, he indicates, the creative product is not related to the creator. The creator is a person who acts largely as a mediator between externally defined needs and goals. He operates on some aspect of the environment to produce a novel and appropriate product, but he adds little of himself as a result. By contrast, the artist develops a product that is clearly an expression of his inner states, of his needs, perceptions, and evaluations. Considering the polar distinction between internal and external, between self and environment, one cannot but wonder at the many similarities discovered both in the creative process and the creative personality in the two areas.

Stages in Creative Performance

Attention to the creative act itself has been focussed in an attempt to order various stages within the act. Using somewhat different terminology in order to express slightly different insights, several writers seem to agree on the following elements:

1. Sensitivity to a problem or to a theme for expression. Psychologists relate this to openness to experience, to adventurousness, to a willingness to explore in realms of the unknown. The willingness to extend experience is involved in the desire to understand both what is going on inside oneself and in the environment, and in interest in new ideas, fresh perspectives, and experimentation. Murphy refers to "sensitiveness, the presence of a need that satisfies itself and feeds upon more and more material of a certain type— color, space, relations, tone, rhythm. As satiation occurs, the need sets itself a bigger, more complex goal of the same type; and the individual *learns to create*". This sensitiveness may be perceptual, involving sensory qualities, but it may also be conceptual, concerned with relations that are interpersonal or abstract. The highly sensitive person becomes more and more involved in these experiences until he is inexorably driven to find new forms or ideas.

A period of "incubation", "accumulation" (Murphy), or "searching" follows the initial sensitivity or preparation. The individual adds to his background, centers his action for fulfillment, begins to order, organize, and refine his increasing store of experience.

2. A moment of creative insight (DeHaan) occurs which provides the necessary organization, the new form, the new ideas as if *de novo,* but actually as the culmination of subconscious processes that have all along been paralleling the conscious. Murphy and Wallas refer to this event as illumination:

Usually in a moment of excited self-direction toward the goal, an integration of the accumulated material takes place in which both conscious and subconscious storehouses of experience are drawn from. A whole that is the answer to the long quest is made manifest in a moment often characterized by *illumination.*

3. A period of confirmation (DeHaan), polishing (Murphy), or verification (Wallas) is necessary to complete the creative act. The new insight, idea, form, tone, composition, or solution needs testing, elaboration, or extension. "As the need and achievement are relived again and again, it becomes clear that the need is not perfectly fulfilled or that secondary needs are still frustrated and the work of art or of science is accordingly hammered out until it is more adequate."

Scepticism as to the ordering of elements in the creative act may indeed be appropriate. Certainly the occurrence of insight or illumination may appear at any point in the sequence; it may also characterize each of the four stages.

The imaginative burst of insight is the element that reflects a sense of mystery in the process. For this reason investigators are concerned with the role of fantasy in the creative process and the factor of fantasy in the personality structure of creative doers and thinkers.

Russell quotes Vinacke's attempt to analyze stages in imaginative thought. He defines four steps. The first is simple play and enjoyment of the activity; this is followed by interpretation and appreciation. Fantasy gives way to more serious efforts as "guidance of action" leads to anticipation and planning. Finally, constructive or creative thoughts ranging from fantasy to problem-solving may lead to closure.

Murphy has given considerable attention to "subliminal" fantasy and dream components in creative action. He quotes F. W.

H. Myers' phrase, "subliminal uprush," as defining the "process of being overwhelmed by accumulated unconscious or subliminal material. Exactly the right set, together with a vast fund of relevant material... may be touched off by a slight or even a subliminal cue, so that one reacts to many relevant phases of a problem at once. Murphy cites, too, Prince's concept of the coconscious, that material in the unconscious which has been building up simultaneously with material in the conscious mind is suddenly released or made available. He suggests that such a concept may explain what he calls elsewhere "dream creativeness" – the claim by Robert Louis Stevenson, Coleridge, and various other writers and scholars that their inspiration arrived in dreams while asleep. Murphy makes the following guess:

> *Partly because the outer world is not there to say no, partly because the senses can contribute only a few and feeble interferences, partly because none has at his disposal the entire material of his life, and partly because no critical standards, no acid test can be invoked, the dream typically reaches heights and spreads out over areas which the disciplined mind of the civilized adult would not dare to scan.*

Ghiselin provides a fascinating interpretation of the role of the unconscious and "self-surrender" to the inner promptings of imagination in his introduction to an anthology of accounts of the creative process at work by eminent scientists, authors, and scholars.

Working on a less poetic level, Crutchfield inquires into the conditions necessary for inception of the creative process. He insists that the task has to be the person's *own* problem, one that he experiences intensively as his concern, and not one assigned to him by others. He needs the freedom, thereafter, to discover, to select and to define elements for himself, with a sense that things as they are don't "fit." The creative process involves "some effective transformation or reorganization of cognitive elements." Then, Crutchfield cites these conditions as necessary for the transformation: that the elements be available, that they be selectively activated, contiguous, salient, free, and fitting.

The Creative Person

A third way to look at creativity is to study the creative person himself. This view starts from the assumption that the creative product is neither a happy accident nor simply the result of faithful pursuit of the proper methodology; creative work is seen as the expression of creative personality. The fact that few great men have been limited to a single contribution supports this point of view. Now, since the school can scarcely expect to help its immature clientele produce works of creative authority, conceivably its greatest contribution can be in the direction of fostering the development of creative personalities. One issue that arises is whether creativity is a unique phenomenon or a matter of degree. In the latter case a continuum would be assumed wherein some small amount of creativeness is found in even the least original of mortals. While admitting that the supreme heights of creative endeavor are scaled by few individuals in a century, Russell joins a large band who deny that only the bright child, only the genius can create. Creativity, he says, may be found at all levels of intelligence. The editors of New York City's *Curriculum and Materials* concur: "Creativity is widely distributed. It is not confined to one geographical area, the gifted, or any ethnic or social group". A democratic ethos based on the belief that a divine spark gives worth and dignity to every human being must start from such an assumption. From a practical point of view as well, the absence of established instruments for identifying creativeness at an early age argues in favor of assuming the existence of some creative ability in every pupil. Crutchfield also assumes that every human being is in some way creative. Despite wide individual differences, Crutchfield focusses on the pragmatic consideration that the actual creative performance of every person falls far short of his potential. Guilford agrees. He concedes that heredity may establish lines of development, but notes that individuals rarely realize their full development in any respect. He expresses faith that there is considerable room for improvement in creativity as well as in other native abilities, however limited by heredity. Factor analysis employed to describe creativity is utilized in describing the creative person as well. A number of studies have used some method of identifying creative persons and have then measured the distinctive characteristics of these subjects. Barron, for example, worked with a group of one hundred Air Force captains, administering a test of originality and then forming two groups for purposes of comparison on a basis of high and low scores on the originality measure. To justify his procedure he remarked, "There is good reason for believing...that originality is almost habitual with persons who produce a really singular insight". He defined originality as the capacity for producing adaptive responses which are original, and he found evidence to support the following hypotheses:

- That original persons prefer complexity and some degree of apparent imbalance in phenomena.
- That original persons are more complex psychodynamically and have greater personal scope.
- That original persons are more independent in their judgments.
- That original persons are more self-assertive and dominant.
- That original persons reject suppression as a mechanism for the control of impulses.

Drevdahl employed a population of undergraduate and graduate students at the University of Nebraska in order to compare personality characteristics, intelligence, and creativity ratings. Drevdahl then administered a number of tests to them and drew the following conclusions:

- Creative persons are superior in verbal facility, fluency, flexibility, and originality.
- Creative persons are more withdrawn and quiescent. Creative artists are somewhat more radical and self-sufficient than creative scientists or non-creatives.
- The art group are more sensitive emotionally, more bohemian.
- Individuality or non-conformity appear to be desirable for creativity.

Some studies of creative children and adolescents add perspective on the nature of creative personality. Getzels and Jackson discovered high academic achievement as one characteristic. Contrasting their high-creativity group of adolescents with the high intelligence (i.e., high IQ) group, they discovered that academic achievement was quite similar in the two groups despite an average difference of 23 points in IQ scores. Although they scored as high on standardized tests, the high creative were not rated as well as the high intelligence group, nor above the average for the school, when teachers expressed preferences for students in terms of the degree to which they would enjoy having individual students in their class. In rating qualities they would prefer for themselves— character, emotional stability, goal directedness, creativity, wide range of interests, high marks, high IQ, and sense of humor— the high IQ and high creative groups produced rankings which were very similar except for one significant difference. The high creative ranked a sense of humor second; the high IQ's ranked it last in the group of eight characteristics.

Correlation determined by Getzels and Jackson between the qualities that students prefer for themselves and those which they believe teachers to value are also provocative of conjecture. The high IQ's showed a positive correlation of .67 between their choices and their idea of teacher values. The high creatives showed a minus .25 correlation in this comparison. This may reflect the failure of the high creatives to win teacher approval to the same extent as the high IQ's. It may result either from rejection of the teacher's values or a feeling of rejection by the teacher.

Both the high-intelligence and the high creative groups seem to believe that their values are closer than are the teacher's to qualities needed for success in adult life. Correlation coefficients between qualities they desire for themselves and those they feel necessary for adult success follow:

High IQ	.91
High creatives	.10

The correlation for the creatives proves to be very low, indicating perhaps that they take themselves less seriously than the high IQ's, perhaps that they are in rebellion against adult values, or perhaps that they are both more idealistic and more cynical than the high IQ's.

One of the widely noted personality characteristics is regarded by some as eccentricity, by others as non-conformism. Griffin reports her analysis of "movement responses" in Rorschach tests of persons of established creative accomplishment. Such responses, according to the Rorschach manual, should indicate "more individualized intelligence, greater creative ability, more 'inner life,' stable affective reactions, less adaptability to reality, more intensive than extensive rapport." Griffin reports her concurrence with other investigators in finding creative individuals scoring low in this area and therefore not less adaptive to reality.

Russell rejects the view that creativity is related to revolt; he regards creative endeavor as representing progress along an indicated path rather than rebellion from it. Murphy admits that factors exist which involve nervous wear and tear for the highly creative individual. The craving for experience and expression is intense. The drive to achieve a solution for a particular problem may take the individual out of context with most of his environment. He may be so engrossed in himself that he considers himself above the normal conventions of health and society. He experiences inevitable frustrations in moving forward in new areas. Yet, "all of this does not in the least mean that most geniuses are abnormal; only that nervous wear and tear are not uncommonly associated with high creativeness" .

Murphy is quite consistent on this point, for he sees emotional well being as a product and a process in creative work:

> *It is, after all, realization of self that actualizes the potential that keeps hand and brain at work. Whatever incompleteness or frustration gnaws at the heart may give fire or fury to the effort – but* fulfillment, *rather than frustration, may also lead on to finer fulfillment. If the organized skills and the passion for experience are there, then, paradoxically, both defeat and victory may lead on to new victory.*

Drevdahl and Cattell , in testing a large number of established artists and scientists, attribute to them "what Riesman classifies as the autonomous person who both thinks and acts differently from the apparently unthinking average." Their analysis of 153 creative artists and writers indicated that they "differed from the normal population in being more intelligent, emotionally more mature (ego strength), dominant, adventurous, emotionally sensitive, bohemian, radical, self-sufficient and of a higher ergic-tension." On a test of sixteen personality factors devised by Cattell, the writer-artist group was found to be similar to a creative scientist population tested by Cattell and Drevdahl in another study. They do confirm, however, the contention that creative persons may hold themselves above customary conventions: "Conformity, concern for propriety, adherence to social standards and dictates are somewhat lacking in our experimental population". Additional studies by Fromm, Barron, MacKinnon, Gough, Crutchfield, Taylor, Drews, and Arnold serve to confirm the picture of the creative person already presented. A composite of these reports would reveal the following characteristics:

- A positive view of self, leading to freedom from defensiveness and toward a capacity for self-actualization; psychiatric stability which takes stress and turmoil in stride .
- A sense of commitment, of full involvement; a sense of destiny about oneself; a strong drive toward achievement for its own sake; a sense of strong personal goals and attendant direction of energy in their pursuit
- An openness to experience: in relation to the environment, to other people and to one's own inner life; a willingness to admit to consciousness aspects of inner experience that are denied by others, and a drive to express them; intuitive perception and thought
- Cognitive capacities of an extraordinary nature reflecting strong theoretical values, a preference for the complex, asymmetrical, and unordered; a capacity to entertain many ideas simultaneously; independence of judgment; unwillingness to accept any stage as final
- A balance between intellectuality and emotionality; strong aesthetic interests and orientation; freedom from excessive restraint of impulse; high aesthetic sensitivity
- Autonomy in the face of social pressure; an ability to maintain one's integrity reflecting limited concern for the reaction of others; achievement via independence rather than conformity; independence in thought and action; relative freedom from conventional restraints on interests.

The most ambitious effort to describe creative personality is found in Mooney "Indices of Creative Behavior". Mooney collected 266 criteria of this kind .He is aware of his own vitality"; No. 79;

"He is highly perceptive of some aspects of his environment.") and then classified them under headings related to his conceptual framework for identifying creative talent. He suggests two major rubrics: Self Orientation, and Orientation to Others. The following headings and sub-heads are used in his organization:

Part I. Self Orientation

- Openness for the reception and extension of experience: direct and spontaneous experiencing; openness to self, environment, life, growth and emergence, the unknown, and ideas.
- Movement toward the differentiation and realization of self: reaching beyond conformity, asserting independence, realizing uniqueness, creating self and world.
- Disciplined management of means to significant experience: selection of vital work, concentration of effort, conservation of energy, control of work, management of materials, self-management.
- Esthetic ordering of the forms of experience: reflective turn of mind, sensitivity to harmonies of relationships; feeling way through; structuring toward simplicity and unity; sensing of analogies; concern for vital forms; autonomy of ideas; acceptance and productive use of the unconscious; awareness of values, purposes, assumptions; positive, concrete, vivid, relative thought.

Part II. Orientation to Others

- Openness for the reception and extension of experience with others: openness in feeling toward others, openness in feeling of others toward him, protection of a system of openness in interpersonal relations, openness to learning about human nature.
- Disciplined management of means to significant experience with people: skills used in dealing with others, concepts underlying his dealings with others, self-management.

The indices that Mooney lists should be helpful as parents, teachers and other adults (1) seek to identify creative behavior, and

(2) work with young people in helping them develop behavior patterns that tend toward creative expression. These criteria certainly broaden the notion of creativity as commonly held and reinforce the assumption that creativeness, in varying degrees, may inhere in all or in most human beings. To this extent, they may serve as some of the more important goals in education.

Testing for Creativity

One of the interesting by-products of the effort to identify specific factors in creativeness has been the development of ingenious devices to measure hypothesized factors. Seeking evidence for as many as sixteen different factors, Guilford and his colleagues devised 53 separate tests and were satisfied that they had established fourteen of the sixteen factors. Cattell, Thurstone, Jackson, Getzels, Torrance, Wilson, and Barron are only some of the investigators who have developed measures for such factors as fluency, sensitivity to problems, closure (or redefinition), facility, humor, perceptual speed, and flexibility of set.

Getzels and Jackson utilized in their study a group of five measures of creativity, some of which were constructed by Guilford and Cattell. The five measures were: (1) word association, asking for as many definitions as possible of common stimulus words; (2) uses for common things, with responses scored according to the number and unusual quality of suggested uses for so common and versatile a thing as a brick; (3) hidden shapes, seeking for perception of a given geometric form concealed in a more complex form or pattern; (4) fables, seeking for cleverness in suggested endings (moralistic, humorous or sad) for uncompleted fables; (5) make-up problems, searching for variety in the number of problems that the subject could pose, given paragraphs with a number of numerical statements.

Barron used Guilford's unusual uses test and seven others in seeking to measure originality among his group of Air Force captains. A Consequences Test (write what would happen if certain changes were suddenly to take place in a given situation) and a Plot Title Test (provide titles for given stories) were also borrowed from Guilford to identify cleverness and novelty in approach. In addition, the Rorschach and Thematic Apperception Test were administered to measure originality of response. Anagrams were employed to measure both originality and correctness of solutions. Subjects used as many words as possible in a given list in making up a story as still another test of originality. Finally achromatic inkblots were presented, with high scores assigned to the more infrequent responses. All tests called for free responses in order to provide a maximum area of free operation, reflecting Torrance's scepticism as to the possibility of developing "multiple-choice or other objective-type tests which will take full account of individual differences in creative thinking". Ratings on six of the eight tests Barron employed correlated to a high degree with independent observers' ratings, but the Rorschach and the inkblots showed low correlation.

Guilford and his associates have probably been most assiduous in seeking to test for highly specific factors. Working with 410 Air Cadets and student officers, they designed their 53 separate tests. As an example of their procedure, the following were tests employed to measure ideational fluency, one of their fourteen factors: plot titles, consequences, common situations, brick uses, impossibilities, and sentence analysis.

Torrance and his group working at the University of Minnesota have attempted to adapt a number of tests to children of elementary school age and have also introduced a number of tests of their own. They discovered that they could successfully administer both to children in grades four to six and to college students adaptations of Guilford's tests of unusual uses (substituting a tin can for a brick), impossibilities, consequences, problems, improvements, and situations. They developed a battery in which children were asked to suggest improvements in certain toys so that they would be "more fun to play with." Torrance and Reading built an "Ask-and-Guess Test" showing a situation such as Tom, the Piper's Son, stealing a pig and being chased by some one. "The subject is asked to think of all the questions he can about what is happening, questions which cannot be answered by looking at the picture. Then he is asked to think of all of the possible things which could have caused the action and finally to list all of the possible consequences".

The Minnesota group also developed two non-verbal tests: (1) 120 presenting a geometrical figure and asking the subject to sketch objects using the figure as the main element in the design, and (2) looking for non-essential details which a child introduces in drawing a picture of a house, tree, or person (adaptation of Buck's H-T-P Test).

The tests have been used to secure scores on factors also sought by other investigators: ideational fluency, spontaneous flexibility, inventiveness (called "inventivlevel"), and constructiveness. Torrance indicates the group "had no intention of getting into the psychometric business" when they initiated their studies of creative thinking, but "are being seduced" into standardizing the "batteries of fairly promising measures" which they have thus far developed.

For the teacher in the classroom or even for the school administrator, many of these tests may not be available or practicable. One may expect that the same criticisms applied to various intelligence measures may be made of these tests: first, that the effort invested in identification of a few might better go into developing the potential of a higher number of students; second, that any test is subject to the effects of cultural background which may enhance the apparent creativity of some and hide the potential of others; third, that it is difficult to devise any test for which all subjects will be equally motivated. However, the tests serve a real purpose in rescuing creativity as a concept from the realm of mystery and miracles. The tests indicate that factors which may be identified are involved, and they suggest that that which may be measured may also be improved by schools and other social institutions.

Teachers, of course, may justifiably want to experiment with the tests described as giving more of an objective picture than observation alone provides. That identification of gifted youngsters still depends upon the teacher's role as an observer is indicated by the following suggestions given to teachers in New York City:

Creative Potential – Clues to Look For Children who show these characteristics have creative potential :

Satisfaction in activities which challenge and call for new and different approaches.

- Self-discipline, persistence, and sustained concentration.
- Ability to go beyond the facts and to discern new implications, to imagine and to speculate.

- Originality in going beyond what is now accepted and looking forward to what may be accepted later.
- Flexibility and spontaneity that are tied to a goal or purpose.
- Ability to enter wholeheartedly and personally into in experience.

Ability to find some unity in apparent diversity, to perceive structure or to create a new design, to discover similarities and to relate or connect things.

- Sensitive perception of some aspects of the world of nature and of man.
- Auditory imagery as vivid as actual tonal perception.
- High abstract and verbal intelligence, and inventiveness.
- Awareness of, and concern about, unsolved problems.
- Fluency of thought; capacity to evaluate the quality and logic of ideas.
- Ability to analyze, to abstract and to synthesize.
- Rugged mental health and stability.

The Creative Environment

A fourth perspective on creativity is the environment which fosters creative personality and behavior. This perspective is most meaningful to teachers and others who work with children because it is in enhancing the environment that they can make their greatest contribution to education for creativeness. The environment, of course, includes both the immediate influences that affect the child, and the creative artist and the culture itself as it encourages or inhibits creative behavior.

In "*Creativity and Culture,*" Stein develops a strong relationship between the two elements in his title. He takes what he calls a "bipolar view," assuming that an interaction between individual and environment is crucial to creative endeavor. "A creative work," he says, "is a novel work that is accepted as tenable or useful or satisfying *by a group in time.*" The "culture fosters creativity to the extent that it provides an individual with the opportunity to experience its many facets. A culture that limits the freedom of a person to study in one or a variety of areas cuts down his opportunity to pick out the gaps that exist in the culture and also keeps him from learning the necessary media of communicating his feelings or ideas.".

In an interesting inquiry into *"Environment and Creativity,"* Taylor looks into relationships between superior and subordinate, the effects of the group on the individual, the influence of "the organization," and the culture or *Zeitgeist*. For the working engineer or scientist, the relationship between superior and subordinate is regarded as the most important single factor in creative productivity. Creative effort depends upon an environment in which a man is free to make honest mistakes. While some studies of the group and its effect on the individual show greater productivity for the individual working alone, Taylor insists that the nature of the particular group is critical. In some instances, individuals may feel that they can be creative only when they work in the group with which they identify. In considering the effects on the individual of "the organization," Taylor draws on Simon and March's "law" that programmed activity tends to drive out unprogrammed activity. He makes the inference that the organization reduces time available for creative effort to the extent that it imposes increasing demands on the creative worker for programmed activities (assigned tasks). Finally, Taylor notes effects of the subculture as it operates through the socioeconomic class, and the influence of the larger culture through the *Zeitgeist* or spirit of the times.

For creativity to exist, says Stein, three things are essential: (1) a person who is sensitive to the gaps in his culture and who is able to develop solutions to close the gap; (2) means of communication which are available to that person; (3) an audience which will be receptive to him and to his solutions.

We find mingled pessimism and optimism concerning the availability of these solutions. A number of voices are being heard that bemoan an apparent tendency for creativity to be submerged in organization. Whytes' *Organization Man*, and Riesman's other-directed contemporaries are counterparts of fears expressed in the Rockefeller Brothers Fund report, *The Pursuit of Excellence*, and in the more scholarly formulations of Murphy and Mooney. Technological society means more than the standardization of mechanical parts. It seems to impose upon us a need to do as others do. The concentration of power, industry, and population which characterizes modern life seems to promote group enterprise, group methods, group discussion, sometimes at the expense of individual enterprise, thought, and invention. "Mass production and mass education," says Smith, tend to stifle individual thinking and individual expression." Mooney is troubled with obstacles to creative endeavor that arise from three sources. One is the interdependence in contemporary industrial society that makes being different, original, or dissident more difficult. A second is our "outside enemies" – imagined and real fears that enforce conformity upon us to protect us from such enemies as domestic and foreign adversaries in the Cold War, for example. A third is "inward inexperience," the fact that we are so unpracticed in taking a long, hard look at ourselves. We are so accustomed to our struggle with the outside environment that we do not know ourselves well enough to stand up as individuals so that each of us may dare to realize his unique potential.

Murphy, while recognizing the threats of group life, also contemplates its strengths. He finds a group or "corporate character" of the thinking process in all creative eras. He says we "need to understand both the forces underlying highly focused creative activity of a genius and forces underlying culture-wide creativity which has characterized some people for long periods.... Where there is a generation of creators...there is mutual stimulation and release through understanding". Perhaps Murphy is challenging us to forego romantic nostalgia, recognize the potential that exists at any time, and "be up and doing."

It seems obvious to recognize current emphases (but has it ever been different?) on what is correct, on good taste and on the "well-adjusted." Riesman implies greater freedom to be "self-differentiating" (Mooney's term) in a past era marked by greater inner-directedness. Yet the witch trials of Salem, the tyranny of the small town, and the pressures of pioneer life were all very powerful stimuli toward conformity in earlier times. Recent creative surges in nuclear physics, modern mathematics, architecture, and sculpture, to name but a few fields selected at random, seem to confirm Murphy's assertion of "culture-wide creativity" and the assumption of ever present creativity in fields that are given kudos by the culture.

School and Creative Growth

Among a host of community influences the school has a most important role to play in the development or inhibition of the creative disposition. The school (or any institution, for that matter) may serve to raise high barriers such as those mentioned. "Much more than a limited restraining effect" is feared by Murphy. "There is always the possibility of a critical interference with the integrative process by which the many free components in a free personality flow together at the time of the first great explorations in life". Accordingly, he advises provision in schools of special facilities for recognition and encouragment of highly creative persons. It is not enough to urge students to think creatively. They must be encouraged to associate freely with creative peers in fellowship with daring and inspired teachers. He describes a sequence: "First, support, a hand to hold; then a few steps alone; then a race against time to see how much a short life can yield".

Russell points out that young children are often creative in language, construction, play, graphic, and dramatic activities. These creative tendencies are associated with other characteristics such as ease of emotional response, lack of conventional knowledge, and comparative freedom to experiment. Creative thinking in children ranges from highly personal, imaginative productions to solutions of special problems in not unusual ways. The personal, autistic dimension decreases, however, in favor of more highly directed problem-solving as tasks are set by the school and these replace self-initiated and self-directed activity. The child is caught between demands of spontaneity and conformity. "Childhood and creativity often go together," Russell says. "One of the consequences of growing up is that people begin to behave in rubrics, to act in terms of stereotypes". Smith concurs: "An inhibited and restricted child learns to imitate and will soon content himself with following set patterns in life rather than to take the initiative to think through his problems for himself. To think creatively each child must identify himself with his own experiences. In fact, he must experience intensely himself". Torrance lists "a number of factors which appear to block the development of creative thinking abilities":

- Premature attempts to eliminate fantasy ("Many teachers and parents regard fantasies as something unhealthy and to be eliminated.")
- Restrictions on manipulativeness and curiosity ("a significant relationship between degree of manipulation and quality and quantity of inventive responses") Overemphasis on sex roles ("The high degree of sensitivity involved in creative thinking has a distinctly feminine character in our society; the independence and autonomy required has a distinctly masculine character.")
- Overemphasis on prevention of frustration
- Induction of fear and timidity ("We have been unable to evoke a maximum performance from some subjects because of their fear and timidity.")
- Emphasis on verbal skills ("The school's overemphasis on verbal skills and insufficient emphasis on problem solving..."

In a later publication, Torrance lists other "problems in maintaining creativity." Many of these problems arise from personal relationships with parents, teachers or classmates. Included are "sanctions against divergency" – the feeling of others that they are threatened when creative children express their uniqueness. Equally difficult for others to accept is the creative child's preference to learn on his own, to find his unique identity (in a sense, to be different), to attempt difficult tasks and dangerous activities. Torrance adds these factors together to speak of the "psychological estrangement of creative children."

The problem of recognition is mentioned by many writers. Henry is concerned with recognition because he believes that creativity, like other learning, needs to be reinforced. He makes the following hypotheses concerning "pre-creativity" in elementary school children:

- Creativity is probably associated with responses not customarily reinforced.
- Creativity is associated with heterogeneity of responses....
- Creativity is accidental (unplanned, unscheduled) behavior in a social organization.
- Creative responses are inadvertently reinforced.

Henry seems convinced that creativity has to fight against odds in asserting itself in childhood. "It would seem to be the nature of creativity and novelty in children that it begins as an accidental, customarily unreinforced, response, occurring in a matrix of standardized behavior, and that in the beginning it tends to survive by eluding the cultural controls, by appearing undetected amid the cultural stereotypes. One might say that *in the beginning creative activity is like a criminal eluding the police by losing himself in the crowd*". He regards the creative response as being in essence an error, a deviation from required homogeneity, which is rewarded. On the basis of this reinforcement, the deviation from the pattern tends to spread or generalize.

The school would seem to be caught on the horns of a dilemma. On one side is the matter of maximum free, independent growth, the attainment of which seems consonant with growth in creative power. On the other side are the needs to maintain a cultural heritage, to set learning assignments, to "acculturate" the individual. In this lie hazards of conformism and limiting creative growth and behavior.

To guide schools in fostering creative development, Drews suggests certain conditions which facilitate the burgeoning of talent, and these may be applied to creativity as well. The conditions include expectancy of original and superior work, encouragement, provision of models in school and community, giving of awards, freedom to develop, and psychological acceptance of originality and superior performance. Torrance puts emphasis on rewarding diverse contributions, developing minimum skills, utilizing opportunities, and developing values and purposes. In recognition of possible obstacles, he advocates reducing overemphasis on sex roles, avoiding equation of divergency with mental illness, reducing isolation, and helping youngsters to cope with anxieties or fears.

DeHaan and Havighurst, analyzing specific activities in schools provide a list of procedures that stifle activities and a second list which promote creative effort. On the negative side:

- High standards of achievement for low level work
- Inflexible assignments and methods of work
- Impatience of adults

- Conformity to group standards of mediocrity
- The teacher's attitude

On the positive side they suggest procedures to develop creativity:

- Encourage the gifted child to be productive.
- Make extra time available.
- Provide stimulation to produce and perform.
- Provide materials.
- Serve as an audience.
- Help children become more sensitive to their own inner needs and problems in the environment.
- Employ activities to stimulate creativity.
- Assist in extra-curricular activities.
- Inform parents of child's abilities.
- Refer child and parents to other agencies that can assist.
- Help find scholarships, contests, awards.

Other writers confirm or extend the preceding list of what the schools ought to do. Guilford believes we need more understanding of the nature of thinking. Upon such understanding we might build knowledge of what specific steps to take in order to teach students to think. Murphy looks for "a pattern of creative skills...which may be gained by persistent practice." The school should be able to help students discover and manipulate their sensory experience "so as to restructure their relations, to complicate them, and to improvise new ones." Russell suggests the school may help in the building of a background of related experiences and afford "accessibility of a variety of materials, time and a permissive atmosphere for creative work, and a teacher who has had experience in creative activities." He adduces evidence that appreciation as well as performance of a creative sort can also be encouraged in the classroom or other group situations.

Some suggestions are available for emphasis on specific skills, presumably involved in creative performance. Moreno sees a need for "spontaneity training" and advocates the use of psychodrama to release creativity in children and adolescents. He gives examples of such procedures in teaching communication skills, foreign languages, and even vocational skills.

Various authors have given attention to development of sensitivity, including both sense perception and intuitive perception. Carlson recommends such training at the early childhood level, and urges a balance between impression and expression. MacKinnon says frankly that we do not know how much educational method can do to foster the development of intuitive perception and intuitive thinking. However, he ventures the guess that rote learning, emphasis on various facts per se, and memorization reinforce sense perception, while other methods may contribute to strengthening intuitive perception and thinking. These methods include, he suggests, efforts to transfer from one subject to another, efforts to seek out common principles that relate facts in different disciplines, stress on analogies, metaphors and symbols, and exercises in "imaginative play."

In suggesting criteria for evaluation of programs aiming at creative development, Hilgard also prescribes a recipe for method. These criteria include the following:

1. *Initiation* of inquiry by students on their own
2. Opportunity to take responsibility for creative work, to exhibit it, and to take satisfaction even "in small evidences of creativity"
3. Judging the student's original work in terms of individual progress rather than group norms
4. Time for substantial involvement in "idiosyncratic specialization"
5. Evidence of yearly progress toward diversity of talent rather than conformity. Self-initiation, recognition and satisfaction, individual goals, time for "divergent" activity, and progress toward diversity are Hilgard's key words in growth toward creativeness.

Drews argues the merits of discovery as a way of learning and cites the work of Beberman in the University of Illinois Curriculum Studies in Mathematics. The "open-ended" experiment in science would be another illustration of this approach.

Torrance follows a similar track in underscoring the individual learning styles of different persons. In a study in four quite different school environments, Torrance compared how well creative subjects learned in situations exhibiting learning by memory as contrasted with situations where pupil initiative and discovery were presumably more in evidence. He noted that highly creative students learned as much as high IQ students, but not in all schools. "Apparently highly creative individuals prefer to learn creatively rather than by authority and when given an opportunity to learn in that way achieve as well as their more intelligent but less creative peers". With Torrance, Getzels and Jackson distinguish between IQ and creativeness, between remembering and discovering, between information and knowledge.

While there is a tendency to underscore process in learning rather than the subject-matter absorbed, MacKinnon indicates the need to have a large body of facts as well as reasoning skills in order to establish the widest possible set of relationships among facts. He notes the complementary nature of theoretical and aesthetic values held by creative persons and urges school attention both to the cognitive search for truth and the aesthetic search for beauty.

Taylor, writing on *"The Effects of Instructional Media on Creativity,"* offers some insights that spread from media to the whole realm of instruction. He starts from a general concern with the impression normally given in complex technological aids of omniscience, of a closed universe, and of single ways to do things. He seeks, instead, ways of using new media and instruction in general so that students develop a picture of an open universe where new questions are always possible, where solutions are not permanently fixed, and where individual learning styles and problem-solving strategies are encouraged. To do this, he would like discussion and recitation techniques to recognize bold, intuitive leaps as well as systematic steps forward. He wants all students to see that new ideas cannot be judged solely by present-day common-sense notions. He urges development of evaluative methods that don't "program" or fence students in, therein reducing their chances to be creative. Instruction should recognize the need for a rich inner life, for creative reception as well as creative expression, and for the development of a sense of genuine involvement on the part of students. On the surface teaching by television and programmed instruction threaten such goals. Taylor implies other, more creative possibilities in the use of the new technology if educators will establish and seek an objective of creativeness.

Concern for creative development necessitates fundamental rethinking in programs – even programs for the gifted – which have traditionally revolved about conventional definitions of intelligence and giftedness. Torrance indicates the sweeping nature of needed reforms. A program that really focussed on creativity would first of all have to reorient identification procedures so that measures of creativeness were added to conventional IQ scores. Second, there would have to be a rethinking of objectives of the curriculum and of particular courses so as to include creative thinking. For example, Torrance cites a study of social studies units in high schools in which the teachers classified their work as 70.7 per cent cognitive, 5.3 per cent memorizing, 18.7 per cent convergent thinking, 1.7 per cent divergent thinking, and 3.6 per cent evaluative. While the proportions may vary in other subjects, the small portion allowed for divergent thinking suggests the scope of reform necessary. Third, change is needed in the curriculum so that students may learn creatively much of what they now learn by authority. Fourth, new methods and materials must be developed to foster creative growth and to stimulate students to learn creatively. Fifth, new measures of achievement must be devised to include assessment of creative thinking in the year's learning performance. Finally, teacher-pupil relationships have to be reviewed to discover ways for rewarding creative thought.

Teacher and Creative Growth

Because of the impact of school climate, models and interpersonal relationships, the teacher would seem to play a large part in the encouragement or inhibition of creative tendencies. Carlson and Torrance prescribe a teacher who is himself a fully functioning, self-actualizing person. They seek a teacher who is sensitive, resourceful, flexible, willing to get off the beaten track. His view of himself must be so positive that he can relate constructively to others and particularly to creative students who may be so self-consciously different as to seem obnoxious at times. This positive view of self is probably necessary, moreover, to avoid regarding the unusual student as a threat. To inspire sensitivity and intuitive perception on the part of his proteges, the teacher must exhibit the openness to experience he is trying to foster in others. He must share the theoretical and aesthetic orientations of his gifted students if he is to be able to partake in their creative discourse.

Torrance is interested, too, in the teacher's function as a guide. He lists the following roles that the teacher plays: a "refuge" against the slings, woes, and criticism of the world, a sponsor or patron, a guide in understanding difference from other people, a listener for communing ideas, a resource for recognition of creative talent.

Rasey indicates the need for shift in role-concept on the part of teachers from that of "imparter of knowledge" to that of "creator." She sees the teacher as a stage manager and scene shifter leading the child into areas rich in experience.

Ministered in a uniform way, the child tends to abandon his heterogeneous (creative) behavior in order to obtain the affection of the teacher. Thus, he is likely to "stay in line" to satisfy his need for love— and it may be the teacher who is apparently giving greatest attention to children's needs who may serve most, though unintentionally, to stifle creativity.

Guidelines in School Approaches to Creativity

From the foregoing analyses of the creative process, creative product, creative personality, and environmental factors essential to creativity, a number of guidelines may be inferred to assist school personnel in fostering creative development.

One of the initial phases in creating has been identified as opening windows on experience. Lowenfeld seeks to encourage spontaneity of expression and resulting ability to take advantage of a given situation in developing new ones. The mind, he says, seems never to stand still, but maintains a "chain reaction" in response to the initial stimulus. In children the initial response may well be found in fantasy:

> *As soon as phantasy is translated into some form of expression through the intuitive power of the creator, it ceases to be mere phantasy. Educationally, this is of great significance because it answers the often placed question of how far we should go in stimulating the phantasy of children without "overstimulating" them. We cannot go far enough as long as the child uses it and turns it into concrete and factual material, such as his creations. It*

is the intuitive quality of the imagery of the gifts which does not stop without this great fulfillment.

Russell, too, believes that fantasy, wishes, and dreams are involved in imaginative thought. He raises the practical question as to the extent to which these can flourish in a busy classroom of 30 or 35 children. He suggests planning of certain quiet periods during the day with a chance for children to read, write, draw, or rest— and be open to the dream-fantasy-wish process.

Stimulation through a rich environment appears to be a universal recipe in the education for creative expression and interpretation of experience. The maintenance of spontaneity is part of this. If the first guideline is the maintenance of a rich environment, the second is freedom from a completely structured situation which gives the child little opportunity for creative endeavor. Patterning the responses of children, setting endless tasks for children to perform, asking for illustration rather than free expression in art forms: these leave the child little opportunity to explore his own world of imagination, dream, and aspiration.

A third guideline is recognition given to the creative child. The psychological principle of reinforcement through reward is applied here. School and home are advised to look at creativity in children as a process rather than as a product— to expect what is personally original to the child, not what is historically new to human civilization. The child should be helped to sense personal satisfaction in being creative.

A fourth guideline recognizes closure, redefinition, or reorganization of experience in creative behavior. Russell emphasizes the importance of both the perceptual and the integrative factors in creative thinking. To the teacher this may suggest the value of placing emphasis on helping youngsters see relationships, contrasts and sequences.

A fifth guideline counsels recognition of group contributions to individual creativity. While the group can exert tyrannical control that represses originality, it can also stimulate certain types of creative thinking. Both Murphy and Russell have pointed to the interpersonal stimulation that comes from groups working simultaneously on similar problems or similar media. The theoretical justification for the committee approach to problems is the expectation that new syntheses may appear as a result of group endeavor. These outcomes may be quite different from any of the ideas that the individuals in the group originally introduced.

Sixth guideline is recognition of the role of self-discovery in creativity. In expressing his own unique thoughts, the individual may be regarded as ultimately finding himself. Mooney describes this process as self-realization and self-differentiation. An inference that teachers and parents may draw is that a path to development of creative activity is assisting children to find themselves. Such discovery may come through creative play or dramatics or through any other activity that helps develop a sense of self. Hopkins declares, "Each child must be free to create the new meanings necessary to release and emerge himself. Children must understand through use of personal empirical observation the process of their own creativeness which is their own life fulfillment".

Seventh guideline underscores the importance of readiness as a factor in creativeness as in other human processes. Readiness is approached through environmental stimulation, but also through what Murphy calls "the inner logic of material and the inner logic of human personality in relation to the structure of material".

To Murphy creativeness represents a developmental process that follows the growth of the child. In the early years he sees childlike fantasy and the delight of the child in "sensory values, meanings, pursuit of curiosity, delight in uniformities and laws". As the child grows older he notes a "great burst of fresh enthusiasm which sweeps like wildfire through the minds of those boys and girls who want to know, to control, who want to get hold of meanings, who want to grow in and through this strange, exciting, challenging environment". With John Fiske, he points out that the gradual prolongation in our culture of infancy permits mankind a span of years for the enrichment of creative potentialities before the responsibilities of adulthood arrive. These adolescent years, with childish fantasy not far in the background, with enthusiasm at a fever pitch, are the years when one may hope for uniquely creative endeavor. The tragedy of the period is that adolescence is often wasted in drilling into young people "standardized information and skills— skills often picked up incidentally in adolescence much more easily if creative discovery has been fostered in the first years of the latency period [childhood]". To teachers and curriculum planners the significance of this point of view is strong. Emphasis on learning for college entrance, on skills for future use, may blot out a time in life which is uniquely adapted to initiating creative outlooks and endeavors.

Eighth, the importance of the community has to be recognized as a stimulus to creative effort and as an environment which reinforces or represses divergent thought and expression. The school which arrogates to itself the whole of educational planning and operation assumes a needlessly heavy burden of responsibility and closes the door on far richer resources than any school could ever have. Access must be had not only to the activities and facilities of the school, but also to communication with actively creating individuals in the community, farms, industry, libraries, museums, and the physical environment of the total milieu.

The teacher, of course, is the crucial figure in the school environment. Strang underlines the need for teachers "who maintain an attitude of inquiry, who do not know all the answers." She seeks the teacher who "is alert to creative sparks in his pupils. He watches, listens, and perceives potentialities, notices children who want to do the original thing, who put ideas together in new relations."

Comparable to the influence of the teacher is the atmosphere of the school and the classroom. Hopkins defines "creative climate" as involving: an atmosphere in which each person receives a maximum acceptance by direct empathy; ways of working which enable each child to remove fears that stem from authoritarian experiences, which help the child locate new areas of interest; freedom for the child to create new meaning necessary to release and further his own emergence as an individual. Strang seeks a school atmosphere which "demands order and discipline while it offers opportunities for initiative and originality." Such an atmosphere assures a quiet background for contemplation, exploration, and performance. It protects the child from the intrusions of disorder and from the inhibiting effects of prohibitions raised at every point by too strict a discipline.

Summary

In the education of gifted children there is probably no objective more important than the development of creative ability. From the perspective of the individual there is the need, challenge, opportunity, and responsibility to help each person become all that he possibly may. His essential individuality is to be found in his originality rather than his adaptation to a culture, his assimilation of the heritage, however desirable these may be as *means* to the end of individual development. From the perspective of society there is little point in concentrating attention on education of the gifted unless the very able are being helped to create something new, to add something to the culture, and not simply to maintain it as they have received it.

To assist in development of creativity, educators can draw upon a rapidly developing body of research. Perhaps the greatest contribution comes from an attitude that creativity is not so mysterious that it defies study and analysis. As a result, recent investigation appears to confirm the existence of specific, observable factors within the global concept of creativeness. Ingenious tests have been developed which measure these factors with some reliability, and these factors are found to undergird creative work in dissimilar fields. In addition to defining creativity as a personal characteristic, research has had some success in describing the creative process and in distinguishing stages in this process. Investigations into the nature of the creative personality have uncovered a body of information which may also assist educators in developing characteristics essential to the realization of creative potential.

Research on creativity has been performed in school situations also. Provocative evidence has already been gathered on relationships among creativeness, intelligence test scores, and school achievement. This research indicates a need to reevaluate reliance upon the IQ, even as a predictor of scholastic performance. Investigators are concerned about measured attitudes of teachers toward children with high creative potential. There is growing emphasis upon the impact of the school environment, methods and materials on children, and their attitude toward creativity.

The extent to which creative potential is released may well serve as a fundamental criterion in judging the effectiveness of any program that purports to promote giftedness. Against such a criterion one must evaluate all of the controversial proposals that are made. Does acceleration by shortening the period of formal school attendance hasten self-realization in the independence of adulthood and thereby enhance creative behavior? Or does acceleration place emphasis upon more rapid mastery of the heritage and thereby eliminate opportunities arising in a less hurried schedule for creative thought or playful fantasy? Does homogeneous grouping ensure the play of one creative mind against another? Or does homogeneous grouping promote conformity to teacher-imposed standards? Do suggestions to increase the academic load and homework of secondary school students enforce a richer and more stimulating environment? Or does the greater load preclude unstructured, independent, creative activities? Does a more rigidly prescriptive curriculum guarantee tools with which to work? Or does prescription violate principles of "controlled freedom" for creative talent?

Too often new proposals are made on a basis of what seemed to work in some mythically golden era in the past or on a basis of personal predilection or vested interest. In education of the gifted, as in other areas, objectives and criteria are of basic import. One such criterion is the contribution made by any proposal to development of individuals who will be creative in living their own lives and in facing the pressing needs of our times.

5

Language Arts for the Gifted Student

Introduction

The verbal nature of most school programs places primary focus on language development of the gifted. To some extent this focus simply reflects the bookish orientation of formal education. Perhaps more important is the continuing, and probably increasing, significance of verbal and symbolic factors both in scholarly and business endeavors. The growing demand for more formal education in many vocational and professional fields places increasing weight upon more effective language skills for the gifted. This chapter will consider aspects of language arts in elementary and secondary schools including the foreign language program.

Elementary School Programs

Reading

Many intellectually gifted children enter the first grade at six years of age already reading. Some are already reading when they enter kindergarten at five. Others who have the capacity for early reading are not doing so simply because the environment has not given them adequate motivation or opportunity. Still others, despite their general ability, will develop reading ability at a later date.

In no part of the school program is as much attention given to differential progress as in reading in the elementary school. Appropriate instruction in the primary grades should result in an individualized approach for bright children that dispenses with readiness programs for the early readers and curtails time spent in readiness for those showing ability to get on with actual reading. On the other hand, where the teacher suspects that genuine ability is disguised by cultural handicaps, definite need may be apparent for more time than usual on extending the pupil's background of experience. Grouping early readers together within the classroom may help them share their new-found skill with others, thus avoiding an unnecessary preparatory program.

Even more important is the availability of a wide range of materials to suit the interests and capabilities of the children. The problem of providing material at the children's interest level while respecting the limits of their reading vocabulary affects all children, but it is aggravated for the gifted. In the first few grades the speaking vocabulary and concepts that children use and understand far outstrip their reading vocabulary. While the authors of the standard reading series have done wonders in using limited sight vocabularies to tell stories that have some interest and humor, no textbook representative can seriously claim that the content of the readers stretches the intellect, imagination, or curiosity – except for reading skill – of the average six- and seven-year-old, let alone the gifted child. It is also true that the content of many stories prepared as "children's literature" is not up to the interest level of bright pupils.

The primitive reading ability of the young child can be supplemented by other means that bring him literature he can understand but which he cannot yet read. In the first two grades there remains good reason for the teacher to read to gifted children so that reading matter of all kinds can be used which meets their interests. In addition, a well-stocked classroom and school library should include more challenging material than that which is simply "at grade level." The reading lists prepared by the Association for Childhood Education, the National Council of Teachers of English, the American Library Association, and the annotations in the *Children's Catalogue* provide guidance in selecting books for library shelves. Many state departments of education and local school systems also publish valuable bibliographies.

The general aims in reading instruction have particular relevance in teaching the gifted. Basic is the development of strong and worthwhile interests in reading. For the gifted more than anyone else, reading represents the major avenue of learning and a fruitful source of enjoyment and enriched living. Second is the development of fundamental skills for independence in reading, such as word perception and recognition. Earlier independence can be expected of the gifted, and they can make more use of independence in reading. Third is the development of comprehension which is not limited to reading in a narrow sense but is a function of thinking in general. In order to read complex material or to read critically one must develop the ability to think critically and maintain attitudes necessary for clear thinking. A most important part of reading development for the gifted is building habits, skills, and attitudes that are part of thinking in general.

In all three of these aims the integral relationship between reading and other communication arts— writing, listening, speaking, and utilization of the mass media— is important. Coordinating these other aspects of communication with reading is especially rewarding when working with the gifted because of their greater scope in all verbal fields. For the gifted as well as for other children, reading is not to be taught in a vacuum; it is to be taught as part of a total communication program. Communication processes and products have value in themselves but they also facilitate learning in all subject areas. Accordingly, much reading instruction and growth will be done in conjunction with the teaching of social studies, science, mathematics, and other areas. When working with the gifted, teachers can take advantage of superior verbal powers to promote greater learning through independent reading of text, supplementary, and reference materials. They must also be prepared to teach special reading skills needed in these areas if children are to be successful in independent study efforts.

In the primary grades children with special ability should get off to a flying start in the enjoyment of reading, both from their own perusal of pre-primer, primer, and "easy reader" books, and from hearing the teacher read a host of interesting stories and informative paragraphs and articles. Teachers should bear in mind the devastating criticism of John Hersey and others concerning the content of basic readers as far as interest is concerned and should bring in as much other material as possible. Two provocative criticisms of the reading series are (1) the lack of masculine interest for the boys and (2) the middle class orientation of practically all series used in schools. Introduction of mechanical, scientific, sports, or cowboy motifs as found in many of the inexpensive little picture books prepared for children is one way of attacking the first problem. A number of authors have written stories about lower class backgrounds and minority ethnic groups in recent years; these may be found in listings such as the American Council on Education's *Reading Ladders for Human Relations*.

Reading Skills for the Gifted

As children build up impetus in striving for independence in reading, the teacher can be helpful in hastening introduction to various forms of word analysis. The rapid accumulation of sight vocabulary by the gifted warrants early exposure first to phonetic and second to structural analysis. It seems particularly wasteful not to give the gifted child these tools of independence as soon as their interest and sight vocabulary warrant. The use of context clues as an aid in perception is a normal concomitant of building the sight vocabulary even in pre-primers. Finally, the most sophisticated source of word analysis can be tapped with the gifted while they are still in elementary school. This is the recognition of words by their derivation from other languages. Slowly and gradually children can build a familiarity with the most important roots coming from Latin, Greek, and French. Where a foreign language is taught in elementary school, this approach has the greatest possibility of effective use. In the middle and upper grades specific study techniques enter the reading curriculum of bright children. These include the following:

1. Determining the purpose of reading a particular item and adapting one's method of reading to this purpose

2. Increasing ability to comprehend difficult material: finding the main idea, ordering ideas in sequence, relating details to the ideas they elaborate
3. Responding actively to reading materials: drawing inferences, seeing relationships, arriving at conclusions
4. Reacting critically to material: discriminating among sources, weighing the validity of information presented, selecting what is important and relevant, distinguishing fact from opinion, turning to other sources to check accuracy and significance of material read
5. Locating information: using table of contents and index in book; employment of dictionary, glossary, encyclopedia, atlas and other reference works; reading maps, charts, graphs, and tables; use of library tools such as the card catalogue and periodical guides
6. Note-taking in reading reference material and following discussions
7. Organizing material read or heard; outlining and writing summaries
8. Learning ways to remember important material: selecting facts worth remembering, practicing recall, reorganizing material in different ways, utilizing mnemonic devices

All of these skills have relevance for every child. Since they are related to superior verbal ability, they have a special future value and are more meaningful even in elementary grades for the intellectually gifted.

Improvement of Reading

It is a truism that one learns to read by reading. Part of the school's and the parents' responsibility is to implant the desire to read, to make reading rewarding, and to ensure that the pleasures derived from reading have at least an even chance in competition with the lures of television, the movies, and other time-consuming media. Availability of interesting and enriching reading material at home and in school is, of course, essential. The school library and the community library should be familiar haunts for the bright child, but they become so only as teachers and parents provide time and make the necessary arrangements. Reading, like other good habits, is "catching." Parents build their children's interest in reading when they select books for themselves on the family trip to the library while also helping the children make their own choices. The teacher can do the same when he takes his class or a few pupils to the school library. The teacher's occasional references to adult books and magazine articles which he has just read reinforce the growth of a positive attitude toward reading as a desirable and pleasurable activity.

There are other specific things that the teacher can do to stimulate interest in reading. A genuine stimulus can come through "outside" reading in class. Least enriching and most boring, however, is the book report for extra credit. It is far better to act out brief dramatizations when three or four children have read the same book or story. Children can also be arranged in small groups for sessions of shared story telling based on books most recently read. Art and construction activities can be related to books as well as to other themes. Children may be encouraged to do creative writing on a topic suggested by a book they have read. They may compile a list of favorite books recommended for Christmas or birthday gifts. The social instincts of children support the use of devices where individual reading can result in group activity and recognition.

There is general agreement that even gifted children benefit from a planned program of instruction as indicated above. Superior ability does not warrant a "just let them alone" approach, but rather promises greater achievement where instruction is provided. Independence, however, can be encouraged. Strang recommends that bright pupils be allowed to make reading plans of their own. The teacher provides access to materials of value and guides the child's reading according to the plan the pupil is following.

Some bright children, unfortunately, will be found who experience real difficulty in reading. In some cases particular school conditions or culturally inhibiting environments are at fault, but in most cases deep seated emotional causes are found to exist. A complicating factor lies in the fact that retardation in reading generally hides the existence of superior ability, since reading is taken as a sign of ability in its own right and since reading is often involved in other measures of talent. Where high ability is suspected despite poor reading achievement, the teacher should seek assistance in appraising both the child's real ability and the causes of his reading handicap.

Finally, there is a problem of balance in the life of the child. The stereotype of the bookworm is well known. Some bright children do find escape in books; some compensate for real or imagined inferiority in other fields by turning to reading; some simply become so engrossed in reading that they have time for little else. The teacher who is academically oriented by virtue of his training may unwittingly encourage pupils to neglect other aspects of their development. On the other hand, Strang notes that a much larger number of pupils find their reading time is usurped by other activities, and that this competition from other areas is greatest at age twelve or thirteen when reading activity might be at its maximum.

Of particular importance is the choice of books in the bright child's free reading. Larrick *A Teacher's Guide to Children's Books* clothes the bare bones of a book list with many readable suggestions for enhancing children's reading activities. "Acceleration," in the sense of reading adult books, is a poor solution for a twelve-year-old with eighteen-year-old reading ability. In deploring a diet of Hemingway, Dreiser, Faulkner, and O'Neill for fifth and sixth graders, Sattley notes "the lack of knowledge among parents and teachers of the wonderful world of books, existing today which are meaningful, challenging, and important to young people." She recognizes the appeal that some adult books will have for children, and she does not advocate forbidding these books to children. However, she feels that the girl who is immersed in *Gone with the Wind* and the boy who is entranced with *Moby Dick* ought not to be missing at the same time the books that have greater meaning for children of their own age. Mr. Popper, Mary Poppins, Dr. Doolittle, and Freddy, the Detective, are part of the social, as well as the literary, life of the fourth and fifth graders, she says. She suggests the following "principles of reading guidance" for the child:

> *To broaden and deepen boys' and girls' experiences through reading; to fit the book to the child, not the child to the book; to recognize that every age has its masterpieces, and to set the masterpieces of the present and of the past into reasonable*

perspective; to challenge but not push; to be wise and patient enough to wait for the child's own pattern of growth to unfold.

Other Language Arts

The general policy that undergirds the approach to reading is valid, too, in other phases of the language arts program. This policy involves acceleration of the learning sequence, enrichment of learning at all points of the sequence both in quality and quantity, use of more varied and more advanced materials, encouragement of creative leanings, and consideration of the probable academic orientation that practically all bright children will be taking until they are twenty years old or older.

Writing

The bright child generally enters the first grade able to write capital, and sometimes small, letters in manuscript. He is interested in doing more with his skill, but his muscular coordination is not likely to be much advanced over that of average children. While it is true that sight reading vocabulary is woefully behind the child's thought and speaking ability, his writing skills are even less developed. The teacher's first aid to bright kindergartners and first graders is service as an amanuensis, "printing" stories at the child's dictation, writing captions for pictures the child has drawn or painted, helping the children to compose and then to write down little poems. One teacher in a school for the gifted found it possible to hectograph a monthly magazine which included some contributions from each of the six-year-olds in her class.

Perhaps the most trying aspect of writing in the primary grades is the large gap between the child's creative ideas and the primitive state of his handwriting and spelling skills. Two apparently contradictory but actually supplementary approaches are suggested. The child bursting with ideas to express may be more easily persuaded of the value of handwriting skills and spelling knowledge. Necessary practice may accordingly be more easily motivated. On the other hand, the child's urge to express himself should not be dampened by discouraging insistence upon correctness for its own sake. Ultimately, of course, high standards of expression— both content and form – should be demanded of the capable student, but early efforts should be greeted with appreciation of what the child is trying to say rather than blue-penciling of the inevitable errors that reflect the discrepancy between the child's ideas and his expressive techniques.

Wyatt reports studies of various facets of creative writing. There is some agreement that children through grade nine write better on derived topics than from their personal experience. This may imply that children should not be expected to be "self-starters" before senior high school. Young children improve when the teacher reads aloud their compositions. They also show growth when they are able to read their own work to their classmates. For gifted children there is a positive correlation between the amount of reading done and the complexity of sentence structure they attempt. This complexity, however, presents problems since children are often not able to punctuate or capitalize properly, and sentence structure errors increase precisely in the years (upper elementary) when the desire for complex expression outruns ability to handle complex sentences on paper. Many errors seem to relate to sentence structure and general writing competence. As a result, isolated drills rarely improve the elementary pupil's writing. Wyatt suggests the need for a number of studies on creative writing, including evaluation of programs (1) where focus is placed on specific mechanisms needing improvement rather than on a general program for the whole class; (2) where emphasis is placed on increased writing rather than on drills; (3) where children are given more freedom to use their imagination in compositions, and (4) where grouping based on writing ability is employed experimentally.

Unfortunately, the elementary school teacher has to make a distinction between correctness in practice exercises and correctness in creative expression. As the child becomes more mature in his skills the distinction may gradually be blurred and eventually discarded. Some teachers are successful in making this transition by finding ways to "publish" the child's work and therefore by giving him incentive to perfect spelling and usage and to improve handwriting while still expressing himself creatively. Class magazines, letters to visitors, notes to parents and adult friends, and bulletin board displays are some common devices used.

Obviously sustained practice is needed to develop handwriting, whether manuscript or cursive, which is legible, attractive, and rapid enough not to discourage the writer. Recognizing the bright child's early impatience with drill, the teacher must seek varied applications that carry some meaning and immediate usefulness to the child. Understanding the part that knowledge of progress plays in learning, the teacher can help the child develop a system for himself of recording his own improvement. This can take the form of a portfolio with work samples, a table showing marks received or the number of errors noted, or a chart that indicates the time taken to write a given number of words. There is no reason to adopt for gifted children a different sequence in manuscript and cursive writing than is used with other children. Muscular coordination is not much advanced, and grade-for-grade, the gifted child may have poorer coordination since he is likely to be somewhat accelerated and therefore younger than other children in the same grade. There is a good argument to retain manuscript writing for several years so that the child need not make a change when he is at last developing some facility in writing down his ideas.

Teachers in special classes for the gifted find a primer size typewriter especially valuable for children in the primary grades, both for reading and writing. In the middle grades there is some research supporting the introduction of typewriting as a skill in itself and for the contribution that it apparently makes to academic progress. Few bright children will become typists or stenographers, but typewriting has become almost a necessity in college, and practically all children of high intellectual ability may be expected to enroll eventually. While children should not be encouraged to regard typewriting as an alternative to development of skill in handwriting, there is good reason to introduce typewriting as part of the enrichment program for gifted pupils.

Spelling

Much that is said of handwriting applies to spelling as well. Since English spelling is not strictly phonetic, spelling involves considerable memorization and drill as well as the application of rules and logic. A combination of phonetics, rules, and ratiocination through derivation can help to put spelling on a rational rather than on a memorative basis alone. Enrichment in spelling involves not only the introduction of more difficult words but also exploration into reasons why words are spelled as they are.

Good practice in teaching spelling to the gifted is comparable to good spelling practice in general. The keeping of individual word lists is an obvious necessity when one considers the futility of stress on any particular words beyond the three thousand in most frequent use. While the first three thousand appear in the spoken and written vocabulary of a large proportion of the people, any individual words beyond that may be used by only 1 or 2 per cent of the literate population. Horn declares that a "law of diminishing returns operates very markedly after a few hundred words have been taught," and suggests that only the three thousand words of highest frequency in his *Basic Writing Vocabulary* be taught formally. Instead of formal drills on established spelling lists— over and beyond the most frequently used words, and particularly the words most commonly misspelled, the "spelling demons"— emphasis should be placed on spelling words that the individual child uses or on new words that come up in connection with new subject matter. An important goal should be improved use of the dictionary as a resource in solving spelling problems.

Second, the futility of drill on words already spelled properly should be considered. The gifted, no more than the average, should not be wasting time copying five or ten times a word they have never misspelled. There is validity in the common use of spelling pre-tests by teachers and excusing pupils from practice on words they spell right initially.

Third, spelling should be integrated with word study, reading, and writing. New words encountered in reading or needed in writing should lead to the dictionary and then to use by pupils in their own speech and writing. Emphasis upon creative and colorful use of words may eliminate elements of drudgery in word study and spelling. If pupils are learning a foreign language, English spelling can often be traced to forms in the language from which the word was taken. However, even in the absence of study of foreign languages, dictionary listing of derivations ought to be regarded and discussed when bright children are studying both meaning and spelling.

Grammar and Usage

Except at the most sophisticated levels, usage is a matter of habit. A large proportion of bright children may be expected from homes where good language habits prevail. These children are not likely to make common errors in speech or writing. As a matter of fact, it sometimes happens that such a child will never consider using "he don't" until he is confused by the choice of right and wrong that confronts him in a workbook. Children coming from culturally deprived homes, however, may not be so fortunate, and their occasional lapses in usage are the more noticeable because of the obvious contrast between their thought and expression.

Learning rules of grammar is sometimes advocated as the proper procedure to correct poor language habits. Research does not support this point of view, probably because expression is more a matter of habit than of reason. Particularly in the elementary school, emphasis should be first on the right form and on tactful ways of correcting the pupil when he makes errors. If correction results in inhibiting expression because of the young child's sensitivity when he is just beginning to speak to a large group of other children or when he is beginning to write, the teacher has to "temper the wind to the shorn lamb" and seek expression first and correctness later.

For the gifted as well as for the average the recommendation of the National Council of Teachers of English carries meaning:

> *Concerted attack on individual items of usage in the intermediate grades helps greatly in clearing the way for more mature elements of speech and writing in later years. Crucial matters of literacy should come first. Niceties such as the distinction between* can *and* may *have no place in the program of pupils still saying* I seen it *and* I done it. *Labeling the parts of speech has proved in one research study after another, both in this country and in Great Britain, to be futile so far as its effect on speech and writing is concerned. Intermediate-grade pupils should have practice in the use of language, not in the classification of forms. This does not mean that the teacher may not refer to a word as a verb or pronoun and that some children will not use the terms after her. It means that instruction will be focused on improvement in the pupils' speech and writing.*

Of considerable value in teaching usage are the lists developed by Pooley and confirmed by the National Council of Teachers of English which distinguish among school levels at which certain forms should be taught and those at which these forms should be deferred for greater maturity.

As children grow in maturity, the "enriching" aspect of correcting usage and written language involves introduction to grammatical explanations of correct usage and language structure. There is no basis to suppose, however, that routine drills on parts of speech, the three types of dependent clauses, and diagramming of sentences will have any greater attractiveness to bright than to slow students unless they can see some usefulness in them – and unless their language concepts are advanced enough for them to understand what is being taught. After all, it is not the slow or average student who turns up in college, having forgotten all that was taught to him as "grammar," and claiming that he was never taught it. It is the verbally superior student who is admitted to college. Even for the above-average group, formal instruction in grammar apparently does not succeed. Grammatical concepts have to justify a place in the curriculum on the basis of correcting errors or enriching the language of the pupil, not simply as a value in themselves. The teacher who finds a meaningful approach, however, is more likely to succeed in teaching this abstract material to bright students than to others.

Speech and Listening

Most frequently used of the language arts are speech and listening. The teacher can make a genuine contribution in these areas to the education and life of academically talented pupils. Concern for speaking ranges all the way from correction of mechanical speech defects to developing self-confidence in speaking before the child's own class and larger groups of children and adults.

Most bright children in elementary school have a speaking vocabulary, a sentence structure, and a speech pattern which is related to their mental advancement. Some few, however, will be found with infantilisms at age five and six and even later. Many need to learn voice projection. Lisping, labeling, and stuttering are not eliminated by the simple fact of intellectual giftedness. Because speech is a matter of habit, the elementary school does well to attack these problems as early as it can effectively do so. It must, however, start with the purpose of developing interest in oral activities and a sense of adequacy in children as they try to express themselves in speech. As in writing, emphasis must be on content rather than on form. The young child is not limited in speech activities as he is in writing by the need to learn a new medium that makes both conceptual and muscular demands. He has been speaking words since he was one year old, sentences soon thereafter. The bright child who has not been culturally handicapped can already express himself with considerable skill in kindergarten. The school draws him out, provides experiences that challenge oral expression, stimulates creative ways of saying what is on the child's mind, and finally (not least, but veritably *last*) builds an idea of standards of expression.

Throughout the elementary school there is gradual development of speech activities. "Sharing periods" in the primary years grow into more ambitious reports on individual activities and projects in the intermediate grades. Dramatic play and creative dramatics help to bring shy children out of their shell since more attention is focussed on the situation and the group than on the individual child and his speaking skill. Choral reading should start when children can first speak simple poems in unison and should grow into more finished productions that draw out the full drama and music of the poem or play. Skill in conversation grows as children are permitted to work and speak together informally.

Discussion skills start in small group activity, perhaps springing from a reading group, perhaps from the job of a committee working on one aspect of a class unit. By and large, the teacher recognizes the need for small groups and small audiences to provide maximum participation for each pupil and to afford a setting for speaking which is more natural than speaking before the entire class. Taking part in "buzz" groups, serving as the discussion leader, and reporting for the group, help to develop specific discussion skills.

Speech defects ought to be ferreted out for correction as early as possible. Until the child develops some confidence in himself, it is often hazardous to focus attention on errors. When the teacher senses that the child possesses enough assurance, efforts should be undertaken to correct infantile letter substitutions, harsh, thin, or nasal voice quality, lisps, lalls, stuttering, careless articulation and the like. If a speech correctionist is available, referral is often desirable. Whether a correctionist can be called or not, the teacher must assist in the process of correction. Care should be taken to avoid embarrassing the child who needs help. If defects are extremely noticeable and even painful to the listener, other children have to learn to be patient, understanding and sympathetic. To ignore poor or inadequate speech patterns, however, is extremely unfair to the gifted child whose general verbal excellence may be eclipsed by a speech problem.

Particular attention should be given, too, to the child from a culturally limiting background. One of the most obvious signs of cultural handicaps is to be found in the child's speech pattern. Generally slovenly or illiterate speech may grow in English-speaking homes; unidiomatic, poorly inflected speech may reflect a non-English speaking home. For the child who has unusual intellectual capacity, an inadequate language pattern can become an insuperable handicap. Often the school is the only agency that can help. Too often it is an oasis where children make their only contact with appropriate English.

Because of the verbal nature of our culture, listening, viewing, and observing are basic methods of learning. The child listens with varying degrees of participation. Sometimes he is barely conscious of what goes on around him; sometimes he half listens, as to Mother's eternal demand that he pick tip his toys or clothes. Sometimes he seems to be absorbing what is said but not reacting. At other times he responds by digging into his own experience in order to relate what is said to what he has knowledge of. Sometimes he goes farther; he asks questions, voices his own opinion, or starts his own line of independent thinking. The later activities represent more sophisticated levels of operation. In this direction all children, but especially bright children, should be guided through discussion.

To develop this kind of thoughtful listening, the teacher will find a variety of techniques useful. He may provoke thought by asking questions. He may organize activities that demand knowledge of what has been said or read aloud. He may ask for creative elaboration on a theme that has been set forth. He should never be satisfied with mere parroting back of material.

There are other aspects to listening beyond the classroom. Children spend long hours with the mass media, particularly television. While the effect may often be intellectually soporific, guidance can make the experience more stimulating. Without disparaging the child's choice of programs, the teacher can encourage thoughtful reaction to what is shown. He can call for inventive parody of what is seen and heard. He can go beyond this to class discussion of what makes a "good," an "exciting," an "informative" program for boys and girls. Ultimately, by recognizing the child's right to choose childish programs, he may help the pupil to choose the best of the fare that is offered and to move in the direction of more mature choices. In addition he may succeed in encouraging children to consider the balance of time spent on television viewing, outdoor play, and free reading. Comic books, motion pictures, and radio may be approached in the same way as television.

Language Arts in Secondary Schools

The language arts program in secondary schools is of fundamental importance to the gifted both because of the basic necessity of communications skills for persons in leadership and because of the potential of the gifted to profit from advanced instruction in utilitarian and aesthetic elements of the program. In 1953 the National Council of Teachers of English established a Committee on English for High School Students of Superior Ability which stated special objectives in language arts for the intellectually gifted student:

> *Since many academically talented students will find themselves in positions of responsibility when they are adults, the English teacher anticipates their language needs in public speaking, discussion, research, professional writing, and other areas requiring communication skills of an advanced nature. Therefore bright students are taught the history, structure, imperfections, and beauty of language. They are taught to consider how the context of time, place, and medium can affect the meaning of words and how audiences with diverse interests may react in different ways to the same words. Pupils are taught the devious techniques by which some speakers and writers use language to conceal their intent, to distort truth, and to prevent straight thinking. In brief,*

language instruction helps these pupils to do creative and original thinking, as well as to communicate ideas accurately and honestly.

Emphasis is placed on the development of communication skills and on refinement of thought processes. In addition, the superior intelligence of the gifted student makes possible the appreciation at higher thought and higher aesthetic levels of literary and informational reading. The challenge falls to the teacher of the gifted to place emphasis on these objectives which are relevant to the ability of the superior pupil. In meeting this challenge the teacher will find the report of the Committee on English for Students of Superior Ability, published as the bulletin on English by the National Education Association Project on the Academically Talented Student, a useful guide. Of particular interest to the English teacher should be the chapter by Cohen and Coryell, "English Studies," in *Educating Superior Students*. The committee of the English Council makes a number of recommendations for organization of programs for students with special ability in English. These include:

1. Ability grouping, with small seminar groups for students in the top 3 per cent
2. Limitation of drill on routine correctness as determined by early administration of diagnostic tests
3. Setting of more advanced goals and more rigorous standards of expression for the gifted
4. A literature program that is characterized by reading of original works in their entirety, by attention to broad cultural goals, and by integration of objectives in reading and literature
5. A goal of effective expression with appropriate emphasis on both creative and expository writing and speech.

Differences in school philosophy from community to community and differences in school size ensure the coexistence of homogeneous and heterogeneous grouping for all of the foreseeable future. The individual teacher is not able to make such decisions himself but faces the group he meets, of narrow or wide ability range, intent upon doing the best he can for each student. The goals that have been stated can be met for the bright student under either type of organization, and the English Teachers Committee itself admits that there is no research evidence to establish definitively the superiority of either type of grouping

If special classes are established, Gordon and Freudenreich suggest one criterion that applies universally-"the factor of eagerness to take the course, not to get the credit, but to do the work. Such eagerness indicates more than ambition; it indicates the consciousness of needing and being ready for a more challenging course of study." This readiness is evinced, they say, in avid reading, in familiarity with the classics, in writing, in contact with the performing arts, museums, and lectures.

Independent work and small group activities are to be recommended under both types of grouping. So, too, is the organization of broad units which encourage students to pursue their interest in a particular field as far as their ability will take them. There is considerable agreement among authorities in the teaching of English that the study of literature should be organized around broad themes, that a particular play or novel or essay should be studied in relation to some fundamental ethical idea or social problem or in comparison with other literature of the same type. *Julius Caesar*, for example, may be studied by a bright class in conjunction with plays having similar themes; or, it may be studied in the context of struggle for power and compared with Robert Penn Warren *All the King's Men*.

The broad unit calls for class, small group, and individual planning which challenge the bright student's ability to contribute. Group and individual projects that are part of the unit call for independent work and for leadership in small group activity. Individual competence can be developed and expressed through oral reports, dramatization, creative writing based on group or individual activity, and panel discussions on particular aspects of the work studied. When the class is relatively homogeneous, a consistently high level of performance may be expected. In heterogeneous groups the range of performance may mirror the range of ability, and there is no need, if properly guided, for ability to remain hidden under the proverbial "bushel."

Failure of Old Methods

Two major social concerns of recent years have placed in sharp focus the quality of school efforts to identify and develop the high potential of gifted students. One of these is the sharpened sense of challenge from the Soviet Union, arising primarily from its scientific success in atomic and space technology. The other is an awakened national conscience disturbed by the failure of an affluent society to root out poverty and ignorance. With respect to scientific competition with Russia, schools are asked whether they are discovering all students of intellectual promise and whether they are stimulating them to adequate performance. As regards underprivileged segments of the population, schools must answer whether they are identifying talent that is hidden by the effects of poverty, and whether schools are compensating through their programs for these effects.

The tasks of developing talent and providing opportunity for the disadvantaged are not new assignments for the schools. The urgency of present needs places new emphasis on these long-established functions. As never before, schools must look about them to define new requirements, to formulate new plans, and to set in motion new programs.

Since 1950, a wealth of reports has accumulated in areas such as creativity, motivation and achievement, guidance of the gifted, the potential of underprivileged groups, characteristics of the gifted, application of new teaching methods, and employment of new curricula in the schools. Much of this research is still fragmentary and suggestive rather than conclusive, or on too small a scale to warrant definitive conclusions. However, so much has been reported that it is time to try to relate theoretical research and demonstration of practices in actual situations to problems in education of the gifted. New problems are not solved by applying old formulae which were discarded because they did not work in the past. An enhanced education of the gifted depends upon fresh perspectives tested in a crucible of objective research.

The goal of teacher is to implement the new methods for searching the intelligent students. The teacher is not able to make such decisions himself but faces the group he meets, of narrow or wide ability range, intent upon doing the best he can for each student. The goals that have been stated can be met for the bright student under either type of organization, and the English Teachers Committee itself admits that there is no research evidence to establish definitively the superiority of either type of grouping.

Reading in Junior and Senior High School

In the long sweep from the seventh to the twelfth grade superior students ought to make striking gains in their reading ability and sophistication. The basic reading skills should be well established, and so should an interest in reading. Where this is not true, the teacher should look for causes of underachievement and attempt to remedy the situation. In a few cases the cause of reading retardation may be simple and "mechanical," and limited work in remedial reading may suffice. Certainly it is worth trying again if there are signs that somehow the student has new motivation and is ready for a fresh and more promising start. Generally, however, the intellectually gifted student who is not reading well represents a more serious problem, and the help of a reading specialist and a psychological case study may well be in order.

Where lack of motivation is at the root of the problem, the teacher may make some contribution by helping the student to recognize the value of reading (and other language arts). But more specific to the student's perception than the general goals of English are daily assignments; English specialists urge emphasis on the purpose and importance of every assignment which is given. This emphasis should include suggestions on how to study and how to read the material assigned. Supervised study periods provide opportunity for observation of and work with individual students. Consultation with other teachers may reveal special interests that may serve as a focus for improvement in English. The teacher can help the student set goals for his own improvement so that he competes realistically with himself rather than futilely with the budding Hemingway of Lincoln Junior High School. Conferences with parents and enlisting the underachieving student in extra-class activities are also recommended as techniques to improve motivation and performance.

For most gifted students the need is for development rather than remediation. Reading skills, even in the junior high school, should be incorporated into the literature program and should not be used to justify time spent on material of dubious literary value. Such integration may be attempted in recognition of the fact that not all work of literary merit need be difficult. Some of Saroyan's short stories and Jack London's dog legends, for example, may serve the dual reading-literature needs of bright students in the seventh and eighth grades. Distinction among reading approaches for different types of reading material and different purposes in reading is one of the lessons to be learned in secondary school years. The appreciation of literary qualities and critical analysis while reading fall to the English teacher. To teachers in all other subject areas fall responsibilities for teaching the specific vocabulary and concepts of their areas and particular reading modes that are relevant to their subjects.

Reading by gifted students makes possible relatively sophisticated analysis and discussion of the material read. Certainly there is no literary gem in the secondary school curriculum which must be read for its own sake only, for the particular pearls of wisdom that are found therein and without which a cultured life might not be worth living. Various schools report instead emphasis on philosophical, semantic, social, and ethical elements as well as literary qualities. The Mt. Lebanon High School (Pennsylvania), for example, distributes to a special class studying *Moby Dick* a reading list organized around these themes: The Problem of Evil, The Consequences of Sin, A Search for Faith, The Sea, and other allegorical works. Some schools introduce units on semantics for bright students in various high school grades. Many agree on gearing their study of literature to an understanding of contemporary society, of psychological motivation, of the development of the cultural heritage, and of other cultures past and present. Some few schools suggest to students for individual reading books that may have personal value in understanding and facing their own problems. Witty encourages and describes this process in relating reading to the developmental tasks of adolescents. An excellent source book for teachers in helping young people to choose reading of value and interest to them is Hanna and McAllister *Books, Young People and Reading Guidance.*

Advanced Placement programs in English normally center around the study of literature. Materials are generally selected from one or more of the college-level anthologies, sometimes a textbook on rhetoric, and these are supplemented with selected individual titles and paperback anthologies, generally of poetry. While there seems to be a drive to gain academic respectability by emphasis on the older classics, authors studied range all the way from Aeschylus and Homer through Shakespeare and Bacon to Ibsen and Tolstoi, James Joyce, and Hemingway.

In brief, the literature program for bright students should aim at personal values in enriching the life of young people through reading; it should seek utilitarian values in improvement of reading skills; it should focus upon more general intellectual values in emphasis on the thinking process.

Expository and Creative Writing

The English teacher has a special interest in the boy or girl who shows some spark of originality and creativity in his writing. He has a responsibility to nurture this spark whenever it is found but also to develop competence of all verbally gifted students in workaday, expository writing that is essential for school and college work in all subjects. In addition, he may make some contribution to expository skills on a high level for students who may some day be reporting scholarly work in their special area of interest.

Perhaps the most important thing the English teacher can do is to build and maintain interest in writing. Too commonly high level personnel loathe the prospect of any writing assignment. There is room for suspicion that severe blue-pencilling in high school days and routine writing chores contribute to this distaste for written expression. To the English teacher falls the delicate job of synchronizing student interest and adult standards. Primary focus of adolescent student and professional adult alike is on the content of what is said and not upon form. On the contrary, what distinguishes the English teacher's job is precisely his role-concept which puts emphasis on correct— or even exciting-form. Yet, to maintain the adolescent's interest in improving his style and technique the teacher has to indicate primary interest in the content of a theme and his desire to help the student say more effectively what he wants to say.

Using Grammar to Improve Writing

The Council of Teachers of English holds out hope to the teacher of the gifted who sees in grammar a tool for improvement of writing:

> *Knowledge of systematic grammar is likely to prove most useful, not to the less able students, but rather to the more able. To learn systematic grammar, he has to apply the principles to his own speech or writing and to the speech or writing of others. Such ability to grasp principles and to apply them readily to new sets of facts is stronger in some students than in others. In the brightest student, this ability is often his most noticeable characteristic.*

However, the Council of Teachers of English warns, the brighter students are usually those who have the least trouble with problems of good English usage, and diagnostic testing early each year should eliminate from study and drill items which have already been mastered.

At the secondary level, therefore, systematic grammar teaching assumes a role different from that in elementary school. The greater maturity of the student and his increased reading and linguistic experience justify more concerted attention to the structure of language. In addition, his verbal gifts give promise that grammatical analysis may be employed in practice as he writes and speaks. Furthermore, the demand of the foreign language teacher for familiarity with grammatical terms begins to make sense for both student and teacher. The student is now able to apply knowledge of structure to a different language. The teacher of a second language needs gradually to draw more on knowledge of the structure of language. Yet there is still no justification for teaching, out of context, formalized, routine drills that apparently have no direct usefulness.

Instead of learning grammar as a dead and perfect science, the student can experience a more valuable study if the teacher will approach grammar as the structure of living and changing language. How rules of grammar were developed, the mistakes that grammarians have made in formulating these rules, how language grows and develops, the growth of structural linguistics— these topics will stimulate greater interest in linguistics and the nuances of language than workbook exercises. Hugh Sykes Davies ' *Grammar without Tears* and Pooley *Teaching English Usage* contain stimulating material on this subject for student and teacher alike.

The Secondary Speller

In the teaching of spelling to bright students in secondary schools, principles of operation at earlier levels may be extended. Early diagnosis should eliminate study of words, rules, and approaches which represent no genuine problem. While individual "demons" may need to be studied as single words, students in junior and senior high school should be employing clues from phonetic and structural analysis and from a growing understanding of morphological changes and relationships that stem from a word's derivation from another language. While spelling in English often appears capricious, students should accumulate a stock of information and understanding which serve to explain the surface peculiarities of English orthography. Some study in context of Latin roots and how these roots change in transformation to English seems essential to good spelling which is not restricted to memorization of individual words alone. Boys and girls studying either French or Latin can assume leadership in study of differences in structure when the word is derived directly from Latin as compared with words coming from Latin via French. The dictionary is the basic resource for words coming from the multitude of languages that provide a smaller proportion of roots. The dictionary should be used not simply to find correct form but to discover how English spelling copies and differs from the language of a word's origin. In this way use of the dictionary accounts not only for a greater number of words but for enriched understanding of the spelling (and meaning) of words studied.

Except for the small number of words that are commonly misspelled, at the high school level, any given word list has little utility. The only values of such lists for bright students lie in the way in which they may be used. These values accrue if emphasis is placed on the process of looking words up, on understanding the reasons why a word is spelled as it is, and on developing a habit of being *sure* about spelling of a word rather than being content with guessing. However, the same values can be built through the maintenance of individual spelling and vocabulary lists. These approaches may ultimately have more meaning for the student than a few thousand words selected by the teacher or curriculum director from the half million or more that make up the English language.

Writing, Typewriting and Stenography

As children grow into adolescence their muscular coordination improves. This coordination, added to accumulated writing experience, should produce a higher level of penmanship. While improvement is made and should be demanded, the desire and need of the student to get his ideas onto paper rapidly often results in almost illegible scribbling. Some students find continued use of manuscript of value, and this ought not to be discouraged if the student can maintain legibility and develop adequate speed. At least a modicum of legibility, neatness, and aesthetic appearance ought to be demanded in handwriting since the bright student will need to do considerable writing in high school, college, and adult life.

On the other hand, there is no justification for condescending attitudes toward typewriting and stenography as school experiences for bright children. The college student who cannot type with reasonable efficiency is handicapped to some extent. The college student who can use some kind of shorthand has a definite advantage in the many note-taking situations required of him. Unfortunately, in many junior high schools bright students are shunted into still another academic class when typewriting might have greater ultimate value in learning academic subjects at a later date. Stenography is generally reserved for students in the commercial curriculum and is regarded as vocational only.

Actually, there is need to re-evaluate offerings in both these fields. Some schools differentiate between typing that is meant as pre-vocational and typing for personal use. Perhaps the framework in which secondary schools operate where the Carnegie Unit establishes every subject as a daily period every week for a school year (or half a unit for a semester) accounts for the small number of bright students who receive instruction in these areas. It is hard to refute opinions that such a course represents an inordinate proportion of the bright child's school year. What is needed in typing is some sort of compromise which gives the student a few periods of instruction in typewriting and then provides for practice in free periods or at home. Because of the need to maintain skill, a typewriter at home is an essential, and assistance to a poor student in securing a machine may be no less significant than other, more ambitious scholarship aids.

In shorthand also there is need to reconsider conventional offerings. The student who is going to become a stenographer may well need one of the systems which uses its own symbols and requires a fairly long period for development of skill and speed at a high level. The college bound student will need to write quickly but not at the same speed as the professional stenographer. Some colleges have made available to their students courses on methods which employ the conventional alphabet for the most part. Six or eight weekly lessons generally suffice to give the student the basic knowledge. Concerted use in taking notes from lectures and from readings generally suffices to develop a speed of eighty words or more per minute. There is no obvious reason that militates against offering such a voluntary course in free periods or after school in secondary schools as well.

Creative Writing

Adolescence presents a concatenation of circumstances that encourages creative expression as in no other period of life. On the technical side the young person is at last developing enough competence in mechanical skills to be able to express himself on paper. Psychologically, the adolescent is in a period marked by wonder, sensitivity, and idealism. While more aware than the child of attitudes of others toward him, he is less self-conscious than the adult. The need to assert himself as an individual, to tell all the world he is growing up, may also encourage self-expression. Many lyric masterpieces in world literature have come from youths in their late teens.

The English teacher in junior and senior high may accordingly look for both interest and marked achievement in creative writing. Some few young people will be found with a particular interest in writing for its own sake, with motivation toward writing careers, whether realistic or not. A larger number of bright students will respond to stimulation toward creative expression as amateurs— just for the fun of it or for the therapeutic values of self-expression. The need of the adolescent to "find himself," to locate his own position in the wide universe, to develop a sense of values may be explored through writing— narrative, lyric, dramatic, or expository. Some of the perplexing but pressing problems of the adolescent provide the dramatic or philosophic stuff of literature: conflict between generations as the child grows up in his own family; the individual caught between desires to conform and to rebel; the young person struggling to find meaning in life; the effort to establish spiritual as well as economic independence; relations with brothers and sisters and relations with peers outside one's family; the advent of romantic love; alertness to social wrongs; loyalty to community, to region, to nation, to humanity.

Since these concerns are so often the themes of the world's great literature, one can readily see the desirability of relating the reading to the writing program. The good reader will find provocative parallels in *The Bible, The Way of All Flesh, Of Human Bondage, Hamlet, The Grapes of Wrath, A Farewell to Arms, Arrowsmith, Joseph and His Brothers,* and a host of volumes available in paperback reprints as well as on library shelves. In this area, as in many others, the distinction between education for all and education for the gifted is the same. The difference lies in quality rather than in kind; deeper understanding, greater sensitivity, and more articulate expression may be expected.

To encourage this expression secondary schools use various devices. One is to provide for publications channels— school and class papers and literary journals which invite creative expression and reward it through recognition. A second is to provide for interchange among interested students. This may be a small writing group in an individual class with whom the teacher meets periodically— sometimes while the rest of the class is otherwise engaged, sometimes in free periods, after school, or in the homes of teachers and students. A third is to provide an established forum for exchange of ideas— a writing club, poetry club, playwrights' company, journalism group, radio and television workshop. Many schools provide elective courses for students in English in their junior and senior year so that they may choose, if interested, a Creative Writing or similarly named class. Some schools cooperate with interested writers in the community who are willing to sponsor off-campus junior writers groups. In many communities the public library serves as the meeting place for aspiring writers, and a librarian utilizes his knowledge of books to further the taste of young people for writing. The essential elements are common to all: an adult who can stimulate young people to write and who can give some guidance in expressive techniques; a forum for exchange of ideas and mutual encouragement and cross-fertilization; a method of publishing or at least reading aloud the products that ensue. Regular English classes in the high school can conceivably meet these conditions, too.

Speech

The verbal felicity of the intellectually gifted may make a section on speech seem superfluous. Yet it would be fallacious to assume that a reading-writing program is adequate to the needs either of those generally gifted or of those with special talents in the language arts. Speech programs for the gifted run the gamut from corrective and generally developmental programs to the offering of highly specialized training for boys and girls who show promise of genuine talent in public speaking, dramatics, and radio and television presentation. A basic competence in self-expression is essential to performance in a variety of fields that attract the intellectually gifted. Superior ability in verbal presentation and in discussion skills contributes to leadership in the same fields. Thus, a high standard of speech effectiveness has to be set for bright students in general and not simply for those who may specialize in speech activities.

Speech patterns, of course, reflect the family and community background of the student. If the school is indeed discovering all the high potential in its student body it will include boys and girls "from the wrong side of the tracks." An especially difficult problem is found here since the pattern which teachers regard as simply adequate may be viewed by the adolescent, his friends and family as overly elegant or even sissified. The student may need to develop two modes of language— one for school and one for his neighborhood. Such bifurcation requires greater sophistication than may be generally expected of children and adolescents. Even if the youngster tries hard to develop an acceptable speech pattern for formal situations, his customary use of undesired standards militates against real change.

In junior and senior high school oral communication plays an important part in the transactions of every class, in school activities, and in social life outside the school. Many classes are almost completely oral events. Reciting, debate, committee activity, reports, and panel discussion are to be found in almost all subjects. The teacher expects oral participation to reflect superiority in the area he teaches. The opportunity is present for spoken expression in each field of strength. In English and speech classes greater emphasis can be placed on the improvement of oral effectiveness whatever the speech situation. In this way, the teacher of speech contributes to achievement in all areas. Choral speaking, reading plays and other literature aloud, and various forum type activities represent opportunities for both corrective and developmental work.

The importance of small group discussions in all spheres of life puts emphasis on skill in group process. Participation in "buzz" sessions, leading discussion groups, recording and reporting for one's group are skills that depend upon practice at all school levels.

More extensive oral projects in the class challenge higher levels of expression. Putting on a play, staging a debate, presenting an assembly program, reporting to other classes or to parents on particular experiences, conducting a club meeting, simulating a radio program or, in fact, presenting a program on radio or television— all these activities are within the ken of junior and senior high school classes within a very wide range of maturity levels. Some of these activities are carried on outside of class. In senior high school, co-curricular activities, honors classes and electives in speech activities provide an emphasis that is often not available in the "regular" English class.

A fundamental concern, however, in education of the gifted in secondary schools is the special competence in speech needed by the scientist, the historian, the lawyer, and the physician as well as by the person whose vocation lies in speech fields. The student aiming at the former careers is likely to be so wrapped up in his own field that he is not likely to enroll in special speech activities, curricular or otherwise. To such a student opportunities for oral presentation and group discussion have to be available both within his special field of interest— for he has to learn to express himself well in that context— and within the regular English class where somewhat more attention may be given to form because of the English teacher's special training. On the one hand is the need for improvement of technical speech; on the other, emphasis is needed on expression of thought, on organization of a topic, on stimulating and maintaining interest, on "reaching" one's audience, on creative and imaginative expression even in purely expository speech.

Foreign Languages

Foreign languages have found their way into elementary and secondary programs for intellectually gifted students via two routes. One is the search for "horizontal" enrichment— the addition of new material at the elementary level that would not entail acceleration ("vertical" enrichment). The second has been a response to demands for foreign language training to fill a gap in national skills. Both approaches have, ultimately, to be interpreted in the light of contributions they make to the development of individual potential and creative living.

The "classical" elementary programs for the gifted have offered foreign languages in early grades for many years. These include Cleveland's Major Work programs and the Hunter College Elementary School. In the latter, French or German is studied one or two days a week with a special teacher starting when the children are seven years old. All instruction is given in the language that is studied. A conversational approach is used. Instruction is continuous to the end of the sixth grade. At that point boys and girls may continue with the same language in junior high school. Because they are grouped with students coming from other elementary schools not offering foreign language instruction, articulation is difficult for these and other children with previous language training. The youngsters have the benefit of greater readiness and knowledge, but it is not generally possible to build directly upon it in terms of the secondary school curriculum. If the arguments of foreign language specialists hold, these children are far more likely, because of early exposure to conversational use, to master thoroughly a second or even a third language.

Sumption, evaluating the Cleveland program, reports initial enthusiasm of boys and girls in the Major Works Classes for their foreign language. When novelty wears off and the need for sustained practice begins, interest apparently declines. By the third year, one-third of the students remain devoted, one-third begin to object, and one-third are slightly uninterested. Gifted or not, the children are part of a broader environment which makes little use of other tongues.

What may seem "enriching" to the teacher or administrator, may not prove, in practice, to enrich the life of an eight-year-old.

One caution, then, ought to be observed. Foreign languages may be of considerable value and interest to many pupils in elementary and secondary schools. It is doubtful whether the statement can be extended to *all* students, or even to all gifted students. Specialization of intellectual abilities argues against prescription in languages as it does against required programs in science or mathematics. We should be interested, therefore, in foreign language programs offered as a matter of choice, rather than as a matter of course, to gifted students. Of some assistance to teachers may be the new Modern Language Aptitude Test developed at Harvard University which is apparently being used with a measure of success to predict ability to master a second language.

A committee of the Modern Language Association and the NEA Project on the Academically Talented Student prepared in 1960 a bulletin on teaching foreign languages. The group recommended a ten-year program beginning in grade three, with an alternative six-year program beginning in grade seven, and a four-year program beginning in grade nine.

The ten-year program begins with an audio-lingual program in grades 3, 4 and 5 for fifteen minutes each day. In grade 6 the fifteen-minute period turns to formal structure drills without grammatical explanation. Grade 7 provides a full period three times a week, brings in grammatical elements, an organized reading program and introduction to writing. Laboratory facilities are recommended at this level, too. In grades 8 to 12 the program is intensified and extended in the direction of full competence in speaking, writing, and reading, including literary materials.

The six- and four-year programs attempt to follow the same organization, except that less time is left for the conversational introduction in the longer program. The ten-year program is preferred for two reasons: "It results in a notably higher degree of linguistic control and it exposes the student, for ten highly formative years, to concepts of another culture and civilization".

From the point of view of the linguist, the early beginning is essential, "preferably not later than the third grade." The skill to learn unfamiliar sounds by imitation with an accent as good as the teacher's declines, it is claimed, at about the age of ten. In addition, a program in grades 3 to 5 may provide the best kind of screening device for selecting students with the necessary language ability to go ahead and students with extraordinary ability who ought to be urged to expend special effort. A major drawback after the glitter of novelty has tarnished is lack of opportunity to use the language. Another is the child's sense of personal involvement which may not be as great as that of the teacher who is straining to meet national manpower needs in international affairs.

Conversational approach to a foreign language requires a higher level of teacher competence than does the older focus on reading knowledge, grammatical structure, and translation. The purpose of early instruction is to establish authentic speech patterns. The importance of the teacher as-model is basic. If a teacher who can "speak like a native" is not available, the program may be self-defeating. Personnel may be recruited from outside the school or school system. A person not trained as a teacher may work with the teacher in giving language instruction. A special language teacher may be needed even in schools that adhere to the self-contained classroom otherwise.

Since 1958 foreign languages have been taught in special classes for intellectually gifted children in grades 4 to 6 in a score of elementary schools in New York City. A guide based on the experience of the first teachers in these classes lists the following aims:

- To pronounce foreign sounds correctly
- To understand simple expressions in the foreign language
- To say simple things in the foreign language
- To follow directions given in the foreign language
- To acquire a vocabulary of five hundred useful words
- To sing a half dozen familiar songs.

The approach in the program is conversational, making use of objects, pictures, and charts. Writing is restricted to keeping a record of new words in a notebook. Spoken language is used almost exclusively, with much reliance on songs and games. The basic learning technique is imitation and frequent repetition of the spoken model.

Certain aids are available to supplement the efforts of a competent teacher. Publishers are experimenting with a series of motion pictures making use of native speakers or highly fluent American teachers to provide an example and to lead pattern drills. Printed text material, in other cases, has been organized to accompany recordings or tapes. The Modern Language Association is sponsoring some materials of this kind.

An increasing number of schools may be found with fully equipped language laboratories. Basically these laboratories are facilities for playing tape recordings of language instruction, for recording the student's response, and for playing back to the student his own speech in the new language. The fully equipped laboratory provides for group instruction as well as individual practice. It has a library of tapes that permit the student to move ahead at his own speed. However, any school can provide the basic components inexpensively. Tape and disc recordings are readily available for purchase. Playback equipment and a tape recorder for the student to record his own voice are the minimum essentials.

Other types of assistance are found in the mass media. Foreign language broadcasts or lessons via commercial or educational television channels provide additional practice for the student. As students increase in ability, they may gradually learn from and appreciate the fine motion pictures produced abroad. Many of these films provide a realistic picture of another culture in its native habitat; in addition, they are of value in teaching the language.

Ideally the language laboratory, television, and motion pictures supplement the teacher who speaks the foreign language with an authentic accent. Unfortunately there are not enough teachers of foreign languages available to supply all the high schools in the United States, let alone junior high schools and elementary schools. Where the fully competent teacher cannot be found, consideration should be given to use of these other media as substitutes.

Certain issues in teaching foreign languages remain unresolved. One of these is the selection of languages to be taught. As an aid to mastery of particular disciplines, a small number of western European languages traditionally taught seem to be adequate. The Soviet Union's giant strides in scientific fields argue for introduction of Russian. The language as a tool for scholarship, however, is only one purpose. Problems of international understanding and the needs of diplomacy and commerce argue the case for all of the languages that may be found in the universe. School systems have to make choices; they are restricted by the training of their personnel or by availability of additional personnel in doing so. Their only consolation is the claim of linguists that learning a second language makes learning of still other languages an easier matter.

A second problem is the place of classical languages in the foreign language program. Conversational approaches tend to downgrade the study of Latin. Claims of classicists as to the fundamental nature of Latin are in apparent conflict with advocacy by modern language specialists of early study of currently spoken languages.

A third problem is the place of general language courses and the approach to foreign languages as a study of the structure of language. This approach focuses more on linguistic study and understanding of other cultures than on the mastery of a single language. However, its customary exposure of students to a smattering of several languages sometimes helps the student select the language he will later study with some persistence.

In education of the gifted, one should distinguish between foreign languages as a special area of study and foreign languages as "enrichment" to fill the time of students who have time left over from prescribed studies. There is little point in denying the importance of study of foreign languages in their own right. As an automatic addition to the diet of every intellectually superior student, however, foreign languages should be subjected to the normal criteria of aptitude, interest, and even utility. The bright student with little aptitude for foreign languages should not have to struggle with them as a stumbling block in the way of other studies.

Summary

Language arts are of fundamental importance to the intellectually gifted student. They occupy a large fraction of the time spent in formal education. They represent both a means to achievement in other areas and an area for accomplishment in themselves. For the gifted student basic concerns must include establishment of fundamental learning, progress at a pace consistent with the learner's ability, development of tastes and interests, as well as skills and techniques. The teacher of language arts has the opportunity to help youngsters build necessary competencies for achievement in all areas and a cultural background that may enrich all of the student's life.

6

Motivation and Underachievement

Introduction

Numerous compilations have been made which attest to the failure of able young persons to exploit their talents. Warner, Havighurst, and Loeb estimated that the number of students with requisite ability who do not attend college equals the number of students with lower ability who do enroll in the ivied halls. Their judgment is that half of the students who do not enter college exceed in ability half of the students who do attend. Wolfle, making a survey for the learned societies, found the following percentage of college graduates among the indicated levels of ability:

Level	Per Cent Graduated from College	
Top	0.1	per cent 69
Top	1	per cent 59
Top	5	per cent 49
Top	10	per cent 42
Top	20	per cent 34

In general, all students in these distributions are considered capable of completing a college course; yet only 1 in 3 graduated. Other studies paint pictures that are similarly bleak.

A number of alternative explanations may be made. One of these is that intelligence scores and high school grades are not adequate predictors of college success. The chapter on intelligence testing reports studies that cast considerable doubt on popular testing instruments. The omission of important factors in intelligence tests (creativity and social leadership, to mention but two), the neglect of conative factors (persistence and motivation, for example) support the following thesis. While many students possess relatively high verbal capabilities, they may not have the total qualities necessary for persistence and success in college. In brief, because of high verbal ability, they are overrated. This explanation probably applies to some "underachievers," but it does not seem adequate for the large number of cases of low achievement.

Economic Determinism

A second explanation that has more currency centers upon financial limitations. College attendance is expensive. Costs for tuition and room and board continue to rise. In low income families there is a sacrifice of potential income from the youth who goes to college rather than to work.

Do these obstacles in fact deter able students from attending college? The evidence is circumstantial and contradictory. On the one hand we know that high school graduates who must live away from home to attend college enroll in smaller proportion than do graduates who are able to live at home while attending a commuting college. We know that tuition-free institutions enroll a larger proportion of children from low income families than do colleges with moderate or high fees. Millett, reasoning from the effect of veteran scholarships after World War II, discovered no greater increase of college attendance among low income groups than among more favored groups as a result of government assistance. Mulligan also found cultural factors more influential than economic factors. He noted that children from white collar and skilled groups who fail to go on to college are frequently the victims of economics, but that children of farming, semi-skilled, and unskilled groups are more likely to be deterred by cultural tradition than by finances. Apparently the aspirations of a group are more effective than socio-economic status in motivation toward academic achievement and college attendance.

Cole study of able students revealed a large percentage who attributed their failure to enroll in college to financial handicaps. On the other hand, Cole indicated greater relationship between parental occupation and college attendance than between socio-economic status and further study. Questioning the top 30 per cent of almost 33,000 high school seniors, Cole discovered that 12 per cent of those not going to college gave finances as the reason. A much larger proportion, 25 per cent of the high ability boys and 45 per cent of the brightest girls indicated simply the lack of a college goal in their plans for the future. Almost one tenth of the boys and one fifth of the girls said they had no interest in higher education.

Havighurst presents two statistical tables underlining a relationship between social class and college attendance rather than the desired relationship between ability and college enrollment:

Percentage of Social Class Groups Entering College

Social	*Class*	*Per Cent of total group*	*Entrants to college (percentage)*			
			1920 (est)	*1940 (est)*	*1960 (est) male*	*female*
Upper,	upper middle	10	40	80	85	70
Lower	middle	30	10	20	55	35
Upper	lower	40	2	5	25	18
Lower	lower	20	0	0	10	5

The first table shows marked differences among social classes in college attendance but is hopeful in terms of the increasing proportion of lower class students enrolling. The second table reveals 10 per cent of graduates in the bottom half enrolling in college while 43 per cent in the top half do not. Both tables show clearly the smaller proportion of girls who enter particularly girls of high ability and low social class.

Intellectual Ability and College Entrance

Quartile of Scholastic Aptitude	*Percentage*			
	Enter College		*Do Not Enter College*	
	Male	*Female*	*Male*	*Female*
I (top)	19	14	6	11
II	15	9	10	16
III	4	3	21	22
IV	2	1	23	24

(*In* Shertzer, 1960, pp. 228 and 229)*

The first table shows marked differences among social classes in college attendance but is hopeful in terms of the increasing proportion of lower class students enrolling. The second table reveals 10 per cent of graduates in the bottom half enrolling in college while 43 per cent in the top half do not. Both tables show clearly the smaller proportion of girls who enter particularly girls of high ability and low social class.

A study of high ability high school seniors in New York State not planning to attend college showed comparable but not coinciding results. Among the top 20 per cent, the father's occupation rather than the child's ability "appeared to determine in large part who would go on to college after high school, who would attend a four-year degree-granting institution rather than a junior college and who would select a local college rather than one located outside the State". In all occupational categories girls cited lack of interest more than financial problems as their reason. In lower socio-economic groups, however, boys indicated lack of finances more frequently than lack of interest.

Bowman cites Liddle's study of the high school records of graduates from two elementary schools, one serving predominantly a lower class neighborhood, the other a middle class population. In the high school no student from the lower class school made an "A" in an academic subject over a three-year period, but 45 per cent of the students coming from the middle class school made "A's". On the other hand, no graduate of the middle class school made an "F" in the three year period, but 44 per cent of the lower class school graduates drew "F's". These differences exceeded the variation found by Rosen among children representing different ethnic groups. Edwards and Wilson found similar differences in contrasting eight elementary schools in Berkeley. In upper occupational households, 90 per cent of the children were reading at grade level. Only one-third of the children of semi- or unskilled manual laborers were doing as well. The teachers' judgment of students' achievement, when related to occupational status, was parallel to scores they earned on standardized tests.

In sum, there is no question that economics plays a role in determining college attendance. Academic achievement is no doubt related to socioeconomic standing. However, the father's occupational classification apparently makes a greater impact than does his bank balance. And more important than financial ability, socio-economic, or occupational status is motivation – perceiving college as a goal.

Ethnic Influences

Studies of differing achievement levels and variations in college attendance among individual ethnic groups confirm the significance of value patterns in motivation. Contrasts among groups are very much reduced when individuals with the same values are found in the groups being compared. Strodtbeck has provided a valuable insight in his analysis of differences in achievement among second generation Jewish and second generation Italian families in New Haven. When members of each group adhered to the group's typical scheme of values, differences were marked. The greatest differences in values between the two groups were found in respect to individual endeavor, family behavior patterns, and belief in the reign of order rather than luck. But achievement in both groups was equally high when individual families held the same values. If Strodtbeck's studies are valid, there is no reason to accept a biological determinism in estimating the level of ability to be expected from any ethnic group. Achievement is seen as culturally rather than biologically determined. The school, the family, and other community institutions may be effective in stimulating greater achievement if they find productive ways of influencing the values children hold.

In human affairs, of course, it is never fully possible to disentangle the twisting threads of multiple causation. Edwards and Wilson surveyed patterns of achievement in eight elementary school zones in Berkeley against a background of social and psychological influences. They found high socio-economic status, high occupational classification, membership in an ethnic minority, high ability, high aspirations, and high achievement all associated. Conversely, low ratings in all these categories went together. Which is cause, which effect? They noted with interest, however, that regardless of socio-economic and occupational status, the tendency was to regress to the norm of a particular school. The low status child in the school in the "good" neighborhood did better than his compeer in a "poor" neighborhood. Similarly, the child of the professional worker in a "poor" neighborhood did more poorly than his compeer in a "good" one. Membership in an ethnic minority appeared to yield different results. Negro children in a heavily Negro school did better than in a more heterogenous situation. Edwards and Wilson hazard the guess that minority status in a heterogeneous group can be discouraging. Perhaps "a socially segregated minority can generate and maintain higher hopes than when integrated." The authors make the guess that in a group where they are dominant, the minority is "not demoralized by continuous tokens of imposed inferiority".

The School's Effect

The fact that aspirations and achievement of children regress toward the norm of their school suggests the importance of the school itself— as an environment— apart from its personnel and curriculum. This item would seem to negate Edwards and Wilson's effort to explain higher achievement in the kind of segregated school situation existing in Berkeley.

Teachers apparently adapt their expectations to a particular school population. Because they attempt to deal with the class as a group, teachers "contribute to the strata differences in achievement, and may also affect the students' aspirations". But fellow students as well as teachers have a profound effect upon the pupil. "The ubiquitous quest for popularity and respect among one's associates leads to a homogenization of values". Considerations like the preceding contributed to the Supreme Court orders for racial desegregation in the schools. "Separate but equal" was regarded judicially to be anomalous.

Sex Differences and Academic Motivation

The individual's sex is found to have bearing upon achievement just as socio-economic status, the parents' occupational status and ethnic derivation do. A study in Indiana in 1959 of almost two thousand high school graduates highlights the failure of our culture to attract capable girls into the professions. Of girls in the top decile 36 per cent do not enter college. Nor do girls who enter have a high record for persistence. Women earn only one-third of the bachelor's and master's degrees, only one-tenth of the doctorates. Doctorates tend to be concentrated in "women's fields" – education, fine and applied arts, English, journalism, and foreign languages. Relatively few women earn degrees in the natural sciences, mathematics, law, or medicine.

Once again, the culture and its values seem to be at the bottom of differences in this case as in the others. The small proportion of American women in dentistry, medicine, and the physical sciences is in sharp contrast to larger proportions of European women in these fields. Not differences in native ability, but differences in cultural expectations, may be found to underlie differing achievement of the two sexes in these and other fields. Despite the sharp rise in careers for women outside the home, girls in secondary schools and colleges follow a course of aspiration, thought, and action which center upon marriage and homemaking as an exclusive concern. In studies where boys indicate basic interest in achievement, girls put their interest in social accommodations that they believe pave the way to successful marriage. "It's dreadful to be taller than a boy but fatal to be smarter" is the archetypical remark of the very bright girl. The critical element in differential motivation toward achievement between the two sexes is, as in other cases, not native ability but the values through which each sex sees the world.

New research by Lesser and French is directed at determining patterns of academic motivation among girls and women in a variety of college situations. A study by Lesser, Krawitz Packaawitz at Hunter College High School revolved around efforts to increase achievement motivation. High achievers and low achievers responded differently to these efforts but related probably to different perceptions of their sex role. The girls were asked to respond to pictures showing men and women in poses of achievement. The high-achieving girls responded favorably to pictures of women as achievers; the low achievers responded favorably to pictures of men as achievers. One is led to presume that girls may be induced to strive for success only if they regard such a pattern as consistent with their concept of the female role.

A general consensus prevails among researchers on motivation. They do not deny the obstacles that economics, ethnic derivation, and sex may place in the way of the superior student. However, they cite the much greater impact of value systems of the sub-culture and the force of individual motivation.

Motivation from a Perceptual Point of View

The importance of motivation has not been overlooked in massive efforts under way to improve the output of underachieving bright students. Counseling, curriculum adaptations, improving the cultural climate of the community are all coming into their own as ways of stimulating greater interest in intellectual achievement. To the extent that they transform the way in which the student looks at himself and his world, these mechanisms may be effective.

To a large extent, however, proposed solutions represent manipulation of the environment. There is good reason to identify motivation as an aspect of personality rather than the environment—as existing within rather than outside the individual. We may find ourselves on the threshold of a hopeful approach to problems of motivation in the perceptual psychology of Maslow, Rogers, Moustakas, Combs and others. These writers start from the premise that the key to behavior is in the individual's immediate perception of the situation and his current self-concept. They take an ancient philosophic viewpoint that we do not see things directly but through a system of perception which includes psychological as well as sensory perceptors. The important thing in motivation, then, is not to manipulate the environment but to help the individual to see himself and his world more positively.

In this process we are aided by the view of human nature which this group of psychologists advocates. They posit a will to health as characteristic of the normal human being. We are born with potential abilities and with a will to use them. We are not born to the idle life (to shirking assignments, to seeking the easy way out, to satisfaction with C's if easier to come by than *A*'s); we find joy in achievement. Since man is both a social and an intelligent creature, he does not express these tendencies directly. Social interaction and intelligence serve as mediators. The individual's evaluation of the total situation and of his place in it determine whether or not he will follow a healthy path toward achievement and self-expression.

George Herbert Mead spoke of a "self-other" process to explain the way in which an individual learns his own identity. He sees himself only through the reactions of others to him. In like manner the phenomenologists describe development of the self-concept. The individual meets himself only as he perceives the reaction of others. If he is encouraged to think positively of himself he finds more encouragement in the reaction of others; if he has been led to downgrade himself he meets the reactions of others with suspicion. If teachers help Johnny to appraise his efforts as generally, though not always, successful, he views himself as an achiever and may seek ever higher standards for himself. If teachers are perpetually critical, Johnny loses faith in himself and gives up easily in the face of difficulty.

An interesting example of this hypothesis may be found in the Horace Mann-Lincoln Institute of School Experimentation research in New York City at DeWitt Clinton High School. Working with a group of underachievers the Institute found some effectiveness after long exposure of the group to a warm, supportive, sympathetic teacher who combined the roles of homeroom and social studies teacher. When the same boys were assigned in a subsequent semester to a teacher who placed greater emphasis on meeting academic standards than on emotional support, the boys drifted back to patterns of poor achievement. The habitual pattern of self-abasement was apparently open to some modification, but in the face of opposition, and with support removed, the boys returned to their previously established self-concept.

From this point of view, then, motivation is not a matter of external stimulation, not a matter of the carrot or the stick. Motivation is simply a characteristic of the person who is self-actualizing, of recognizing one's powers and putting them to use. Combs, Rogers, and their colleagues describe the self-actualizing person as one who is open to experience. Such a person trusts himself and trusts life. He goes out to meet life joyously and unafraid. He is not fearful of himself and, therefore, forever on the defensive protecting himself against life and new experience. The self-actualizing person is also described as one who identifies with his fellows. His positive self-concept leads to constructive relationship with others. In Combs' words, "The feeling of oneness with one's fellows produces in the truly adequate person a high degree of responsible, trustworthy behavior" and "a deep sensitivity to the feelings and attitudes of others". Because human beings live in a culture, the truly adequate person also has "a field of perceptions, rich and extensive enough to provide understanding of the events in which he is enmeshed and available when he needs them". If motivation is to be regarded as a characteristic of a fully functioning personality, those who seek to build a desirable level of motivation must look to the components of the self-actualizing person: a positive view of self, openness to experience, identification with others, and possession of a rich perceptual field. The perceptualists regard all these qualities as learned. The school is one arena in which such learning can take place.

While the school is interested in all of the external factors that affect motivation, it may find more fruitful results in working within its own realm to help pupils fulfill themselves. The school can do little to influence patterns of family interaction or basic value patterns in the home. It can work mightily, however, in the directions suggested by the perceptualists. The 1962 Yearbook of the Association for Supervision and Curriculum Development devotes itself to ways in which the school can help students develop a positive self-concept, explore new experiences hopefully, relate more freely to other people, and build a rich background of meaningful information and understanding.

The Underachieving Personality

Many studies have been made of the opposite of the self-actualizing person. The person who does not fulfill himself is called the underachiever. In academic terms he is generally defined as the student whose achievement is markedly inferior to his tested intellectual ability. If one is willing to use the intelligence quotient as the criterion, the underachiever may be regarded as any student whose achievement record in a particular area is more than one standard deviation below the point which might be expected on the basis of his IQ.

Beasley has brought together the findings of a considerable number of studies of underachievement. From a number of studies she reports a positive relationship between personality difficulty and low academic performance. Findings of inferiority feelings are somewhat more frequent among underachievers. "Maladjustment and/or radicalism" show a negative effect on achievement. She is not, however, impressed by the evidence cited in the reports:

> *The evidence from the above findings, though indicative of slight group differences on various measures of adjustment, is insufficient to conclude that differences in adjustment are a major factor in scholastic achievement, especially since other studies fail to differentiate the underachiever group from the normal or overachieving population on personal adjustment scores, the heterogeneity which apparently exists within and among groups of various achievement levels would seem to negate the adjustment factor as the sole basis for differences in scholastic functioning.*

Beasley substantiates her conclusion that personal adjustment is not related to achievement by citing studies showing little difference in personal adjustment scores between (1) college men on academic probation and those of superior achievement, (2) men in the highest and lowest deciles of college ability, (3) gifted high school students failing two or more subjects and those with good academic records. She presents studies by Griffith, Morgan, Owens and Johnson, Ryan, Leibman, Pearlman, Monroe, Montalto, and Conklin which yield results showing striking similarity in personality adjustment scores. Many of the recognized tests available were used: the Bell Adjustment Inventory, the Minnesota Multiphasic Personality Inventory, the Darly and McNamara Personality Scale, the Rorschach, and detailed clinical studies. Beasley's conclusion:

> *The inconclusive and somewhat contradictory evidence on the relationship of total adjustment to achievement may be due to the*

problems inherent in assessing personality functioning, the types of instruments and inventories available as well as the varying definitions of underachievement. Or it may be a spurious notion, indeed, that adequate school performance necessarily correlates with the commonly accepted standards of good adjustment. Stanger suggests in view of the lack of linear relationship between objective measures of personality and either academic aptitude or academic achievement that personality influences achievement in an indirect way *by affecting the degree to which use is made of the individual's potentialities.*

Numerous efforts have been made to describe characteristic personality traits of underachievers. Beasley, following these in detail, reports considerable disagreement, contradiction, or failure to find significant differences between high and low achievers. The careful study by the Quincy Youth Development Project, coming since the publication of Beasley's review, may have some promise however. Pierce and Bowman report the effort to assess motivation of high school students in the tenth and twelfth grades by using the following instruments:

- Unconscious need for achievement (McClelland's n-Achievement test)
- Conscious value placed on success (Strodtbeck's V-scale)
- Overt emphasis placed on achievement behavior (deCharms' V-scale).
- Strength of educational motivation (interview with student).

Personal and social adjustment were measured through the California Psychological Inventory, a sociometric test, and a behavior rating by teachers. Other comparisons included measures of value orientation, socio-economic status, religious activity, family background, parental value orientation, and attitudes toward children and the teacher's value orientation. High-achieving boys and girls at the two grade levels were compared with low-achieving students of the same sex at each level. The following distinctions were found to characterize the high as compared with the low achievers:

- Parents were better educated.

- Parents of boys placed early emphasis on responsibility and independence training.
- Both boys and girls showed more responsibility and independence.
- Parents placed value on the child and his intellectual achievement; parents held higher educational and occupational aspirations for their child.
- Children came from smaller families; were more often first-born children.
- Children identified more with parents, had similar values.
- High achievers were more involved in more activities in and outside of school, had somewhat more friends and more leadership positions.
- Achievers were more strongly motivated toward education; more of them went to college.
- Boys had stronger unconscious needs for achievement.
- Both boys and girls were better adjusted socially.
- Achievers valued school-related concepts more highly.
- Girls in particular placed high value on achievement.

Some important sex differences were noted:

> *High-achieving boys had mothers who held democratic attitudes; mothers of low-achieving boys showed attitudes of interfering, controlling or fostering dependency. On the other hand, high-achieving girls had mothers who were authoritarian, controlling and strict, but who believed in equalitarianism. Low-achieving boys were aggressively more maladjusted than low-achieving girls. Their sex role adjustment was also poorer.*

In the development of a school program, the time when underachievement begins to manifest itself would seem of prime importance. Shaw and McCuen, studying "*The Onset of Academic Underachievement in Bright Children,*" in two large city high schools, compared male and female achievers and underachievers. They discovered significant differences in achievement for boys starting in the third grade. For girls, differences did not become significant until the ninth grade. Shaw and others also reported that achieving boys see themselves as stable, realistic, and intelligent, while underachieving boys are more negative in their self-concept. Achieving girls were more ambitious and responsible; underachieving girls showed ambivalence in feelings toward themselves.

Strengths of High Achievers

As already indicated in studies reported above, one method of investigating the characteristics of underachievers is to note the countervailing strengths of their achieving classmates. Nason, in a study of 237 superior high school students in Long Beach, California, pointed to a pattern of circumstances accompanying high performance. These included:

- Satisfactory social and personal adjustment
- A plan for college in the future
- A fairly specific vocational goal
- Expectation by their parents that the students would go to college
- A sense of inspiration, a source of inspiration, or encouragement to succeed.

Gowan also uses a contrast between high and low achievers to describe the student who does not seem to be performing up to his potential. He notes "the underachiever lacks all of the personality traits essential to succeed":

- Clearness and definiteness of academic and occupational choices
- Strong ego controls
- Social interaction (as compared with withdrawal)
- Good use of time and money
- Reading and arithmetic ability
- Positive character integration as compared with psychotic and neurotic tendencies
- Permissiveness, intraception and creativity as compared with authoritarianism in the parental home environment or in the student himself

- Parents who provide motivation as compared with autocratic or laissez-faire parents
- Goals which are clear and possible to attain
- Maturity, responsibility and seriousness of interests
- Awareness and concern for others
- Dominance, persuasiveness and self-confidence
- Enthusiastic socialized activity; an oriented view of life as compared with apathetic withdrawal.

Bowman posits five elements as factors in motivation. First is Murray's concept of an unconscious need for achievement which apparently varies greatly from individual to individual. It is the need which McClelland and his associates have attempted to measure through projective use of pictures in their *n Ach test*. A second factor is the "need to know," a value set on learning for its own sake. This value was one of the common characteristics noted by Anne Roe in her study of fifty-nine outstanding scientists. Third are the social values of the family and neighborhood. Strodtbeck's studies already discussed shed light upon the importance of this factor. The fourth factor is "the way we perceive other people." Bowman cites studies including his own research in Quincy which show that students who achieve well are those who feel the approval of their parents and teachers. Also, the teachers selected as most inspiring by pupils perceived themselves and their students very much more favorably than did other teachers. Finally, self-perception plays apparently a highly significant role. High achievers have a much more positive view of self than do underachievers.

Bowman summarizes:

> *There are surprisingly few contradictions in the picture of the underachiever as painted by the various studies. The characteristics that distinguish the underachiever are not superficial ones; they involve the deepest roots of personality. One could generalize that most of the characteristics of the underachiever can be accounted for by either an intellectually sterile background in the home and early grades or an emotionally frustrating background arising from interpersonal tensions at home and at school.*

Bennett suggests there are two types of variables — internal and external which may account for differences in motivation and achievement. Internal factors include "an intrinsic love for learning which cannot be precisely defined," and a personal need for achievement such as Murray has set forth. This need for achievement is believed to be related to the age of beginning training, to severity of training, to training in the home for independence, and to the home's cultural values.

External factors include family, society, peers, and adult models. The influence of family, society, and peer attitudes toward intellectual achievement have already been discussed. A number of studies agree on the absence of adequate father relationships for many underachievers. Gowan indicates little identification with adult models in general. Gough and Gowan, in studies of underachievers, are investigating the assumption that underachievement may be interpreted as failure of the child to adjust to prevailing cultural demands. The achiever, on the other hand, has learned what is expected of him and adapts readily to producing what is required.

Davidson, Greenberg and Gerver, studying achievers from a severely deprived environment, support Gough and Gowan's thesis. They found the school achievers to be "relatively controlled, cautious, but with a degree of originality and creativity." They generally conformed to adult demands and had a positive view of authority and self-confidence. They showed superiority in analytic and organizing abilities and processes requiring convergent thinking. Poor achievers showed opposite performance and contrasting attitudes toward authority, adult demands, and self-confidence.

Research on Motivation

Influence of Teachers and Peers: A considerable body of research is growing on factors influencing educational motivation. Zander, Curtis and Rosenfeld have reported a study on the influence of teachers and peers on the aspirations of youth. They discovered that teachers had greater impact on aspirations of their students when students identified with them (when students wanted to be like them) than when they tried to coerce students with threats of punishment. Students were more susceptible to the teacher's efforts to raise their aspirations when they felt that the teacher was fair in his treatment of them. They also responded to perceived expertness on the part of the teacher. Students were more willing to work hard if they regarded the goal as within their reach, i.e., if their level of aspiration was within hailing distance of their percept of their own ability. Indiscriminate rewards and punishment correlated negatively with aspiration. This research supports long-held beliefs that the most effective teachers impress their students as being expert and equitable in their treatment of students. The importance of the teacher as a model is also underlined.

A second part of this research inquired into the effect of peer influences. By and large, peer relationships reflect the same principles as teacher influences. When students identified with their peers, they were more highly motivated than when they were coerced by their peers. Also, they found peers in the friendly situation more attractive than peers who might hold coercive power over them.

Standards: Third, the researchers inquired into the results of reported failure on a test and the influence of standards in evaluating one's own behavior. Students who were given a set of standards evaluated their performance more rigorously and were motivated to greater effort than did students who had no standards to apply. A control group who were given high scores on the test were more favorable to all aspects of the situation and to themselves than were low scorers. This research corroborates other studies on the effects of success on aspiration. It also supports the establishment of standards to assist students in self-evaluation.

Barwick and Arbuckle throw further light on the relationship between parental acceptance and academic achievement in a study of eighth grade adolescents in a suburban junior high in Massachusetts. High-achieving boys perceived their fathers as more accepting than did their low-achieving peers. The former believed their fathers and mothers to be equally accepting. Average- and low-achieving boys regarded their mothers as more accepting than their fathers. Among girls there was a correlation between perception of acceptance and achievement.

Non-intellective Factors in Motivation: Since the achievement of all students scoring high on intelligence measures is not consistent with their apparent potential, two explanations are possible: that the intelligence measures are inaccurate or that non-intellective factors play a major part in achievement. Efforts to improve identification instruments have been discussed in Chapter 4. A considerable amount of research activity currently centers around efforts to discover non-intellective factors and to determine their effect. McClelland and a research group at Yale University have been proceeding in this direction for some years. Their volume, Talent and Society, reports several studies they have undertaken.

McClelland starts with H. A. Murray's assumption of the existence of an unconscious need for achievement , and he has developed projective tests to measure this need. In an earlier volume, *The Achievement Motive*, McClelland reported on his research with his new instrument. He provides the following definition in relation to the response of subjects confronting stimulus pictures in a projective test:

> *By achievement goal is meant success in competition with some standard of excellence. That is, the goal of some individual in the story is to be successful in terms of competition with some standard of excellence. The individual may fail to achieve this goal, but the concern over competition with a standard of excellence still enables one to identify the goal sought as an achievement goal. This, then, is our generic definition of n-Achievement.*

In general, McClelland found a significant relationship between projective technique protocols and various indexes of achievement and vocational interest. The researchers then looked to the home background of persons with high and low *n-Ach* scores. Achievement motivation apparently developed most strongly where there was "emphasis on the independent development of the individual. In contrast, low achievement is associated with families in which the child is more dependent on his parents and subordinate in importance to them". The parents whose children develop strong achievement motives may be either autocratic or democratic, but in either case "they still act as if the child exists as an individual worth developing in his own right". The low scorers are more likely to come from homes where they must subordinate their interests for the sake of the family.

Sex differences in motivation scores are apparently closely related to social expectations. "Women have achievement drives which are tied up with getting along successfully with other people, whereas men have achievement drives associated with 'getting ahead' (i.e., getting a good job, being cleverer than other men, leading others, and so on)". It is not surprising, then, that men's achievement motivation falls off with age. More of them have "arrived," and now they temper further achievement more and more to reality.

Other writers also reflect the widespread belief that motivation is more a matter of personality than intellect. Marshall R. Jones, summarizing a symposium on cognitive factors in motivation, concedes that "cognitive change has no corresponding effect on non-cognitive motivational components," but notes that "*some* non-cognitive components will be affected". Since the primary mission of the school, as assigned by society, is cognitive, one may expect a certain inevitable amount of frustration as efforts are made with intellective tools to root out non-rational bases of underachievement.

The Larger Culture

Motivation is not solely an individual and family matter. Perhaps more pervasive is the culture's attitude toward achievement. Riesman's provocative speculations on the development of personality types as a function of the total social structure provide some clues. Nineteenth century America with its desperate needs to produce developed a type which Riesman calls "inner directed." It adopted standards, internalized them and clung fiercely, rigidly, perhaps neurotically, to them. Twentieth century America has by and large solved the bread-and butter problems of production. Now we find ourselves with leisure on our hands to contemplate each other and to set consumption rather than production as the criterion of success. In this kind of culture we compulsively keep up with our neighbor's standard of consumption. We are "other directed." Stress is not on what we can make and what we can do, but on what we can use up and how we can manage with a minimum of effort. In place of these two types, Riesman idealizes a third, the "autonomous" personality which is driven neither by tyrannical inner standards nor dictatorship of the Joneses. Instead, he finds his *raison d'etre* in what Maslow calls "growth motivation." This is the "will to health," the drive to employ powers, and competences which clamor to be used — Veblen's "instinct of workmanship," Murray's "need for achievement."

As part of the larger culture, adolescent society is a powerful influence on the motivational drives of young people. The detailed study by Cole man and the values patterns reported by Tannenbaum are important sources of information, albeit discouraging in their general findings of low academic aspirations among adolescents.

At this time there are signs that our culture may be awakening from the doldrums of the post-depression, post-war period. The strenuous struggle against "fear itself" in the 1930's was followed by the all-out mobilization of World War II. A longing for "normalcy" was to be expected, but Russia's gains in the fifties have apparently galvanized a new will to move onward, to broach "new frontiers" in the sixties. Apart from the stern and grim realities of the Cold War, the national mood may be one which is more conducive to achievement, especially by the gifted. "To strive, to seek, to find, and not to yield" may replace "playing it cool." The style of the Kennedy administration was expressed in an inaugural address which placed a premium on what America, as a people had to give, rather than on the blessings it had already received. The proposal of an idealistic youth Peace Corps found ready acceptance throughout the country and a multitude of responses from young people.

Productivity, Commitment and Independence

This shift of emphasis may signify the passing of the baton from the "cool" to a productive type described by Hobbs. Hobbs cites two intriguing differences between young persons he regards as productive and those he describes as non-productive. First is the intensity of commitment. Not the sheer number of activities, but the "concentration of effort and intensity of purpose," distinguishes the two groups. Second is the extent to which the productive group "regard themselves as relatively autonomous, goal directed people." The nonproductive subjects tended to depend on others, mostly parents and teachers for rewards, admonitions and guidance. "By adolescence, the high productive youngsters have their own built in system of reinforcement". New national goals, new values appear to make this productive type the model for emulation. If so, the gifted are likely to find sources of stimulation in the whole national mood.

By teachers and parents two cues may be found in this concern with the gifted. One is the need to develop challenging goals and a sense of deep commitment to these goals for their own sake. Another is the admonition to wean the young from their parents and teachers— and, in return, the adult preceptors from their students and children! Tasks requiring independent action, and goals set by the student himself leading to self-imposed tasks— these would seem to have more meaning than additional scholastic burdens imposed by the teacher.

Competition and Motivation

One of the frequent attacks laymen make upon schools to explain underachievement centers about the alleged failure of current programs to stimulate competition. Vaughan and Diserens, in a summary of the literature on competition, find little support for a doctrine of competitive activity to enhance education of the gifted. Most studies of competition have involved very simple learning tasks. The simpler the task, the greater the effect of competition. The less the threat of failure, the greater the impact of competition. And most important, the less gifted the learner, the more effective are competitive activities. Precisely for the group in question, the gifted, is competition less promising, and precisely with the kind of learning that is most important— judgment, reasoning, interpretation.

Freehill states effectively the case against undue reliance on competitiveness:

> *Some children have little need to compete, others are fearful to compete, and not all who compete truly make progress. Students may neglect appropriate subjects or participate in less useful activities in order to secure prizes. They may concentrate on trivial but popular aspects of a particular course. The student involved in a science competition may bend all his efforts toward making an attractive display and pay little attention to genuine scientific thought or ingenuity. Such pupils become competitors intent on prize-getting and are devoid of social responsibility or self-criticism.*
>
> *The intentional use of vigorous competition is most frequently rejected because there are negative by-products. Losers withdraw from the very activity which competition is supposed to promote. Planned competition may also interfere with the development of social morality.*

Of vital concern, too, is the effect of competition on creative endeavor. Creative activity depends upon absorption in a problem because of its intrinsic interest. It demands total commitment. It involves a willingness to experiment, an openness to experience. To these qualities the prospect of failure must make no difference. Competition normally is viewed in relation to others. The seeker of the prize cannot afford to experiment with the unknown. He is constrained to stick with the tried and the true.

Our culture places high value on competition in certain situations. Certainly gifted students should be prepared to cope with this emphasis. They can apparently complete some simple learning more effectively when competition is part of the picture, but different persons respond differently to competition as a stimulus. Where complex learning and creative work are sought, the weight of evidence is against competition.

Pressure from Adults

The studies by the McClelland group at Yale support other research on the positive influence of families which set firm standards for their children. Inquiring further into the effects of parental pressure on children at the University of Chicago Laboratory School, Haggard discovered that "one can have too much of a good thing." Haggard investigated the relationships among socialization, personality and academic achievement in a longitudinal study of forty-five children from grades 3 to 9. Included in his definition of "socialization" was parental pressure upon children to achieve academically.

Haggard found striking differences among the high general achievers as they matured. In grade 3 they were "sensitive and responsive to socialization pressures." They accepted adult values, got along better with teachers and parents than with peers. They were "more tense, competitive, aggressive." By grade 7 the high general achievers were "still responding to the socialization pressures of adults, but had developed strong antagonistic attitudes toward adults, a marked increase in anxiety and a corresponding decrease in intellectual originality and creativity." They were also "more aggressive, persistent, hard driving, competitive, willing to be aggressive and destructive to defeat and win over other persons" than were the lower-achieving peers. Haggard notes that the values of parents act as strong pressure even without any overt activity on their part. He concludes, "On: can have too much of a good thing and, if carried to excess, socialization pressures may serve to cripple the child, both emotionally and intellectually. Our findings indicate that the best way to produce 'clear thinkers' is to help children develop into anxiety-free, emotionally healthy individuals who are also trained to master a variety of intellectual tasks".

Bronfenbrenner arrives at parallel conclusions in a discussion of "the changing American parent," and his new techniques in disciplining his child. The basic tactic in the contemporary middle class home appears to be withdrawal of love— a technique which seems to be more lenient but is actually more compelling. Children from these homes tend to excel lower class children in self-control, achievement, responsibility, leadership, and adjustment in general. However, Bronfenbrenner warns that achievement is not all, that the prospect of a society organized to maximize achievement drive "is not altogether a pleasant one. True, children from achievement-oriented homes excel in plan fullness and performance, but they are also more aggressive, tense, domineering and cruel. It would appear that education for excellence if pursued single-mindedly may entail some sobering social cost".

Research on Correcting Underachievement

Recognition of prevailing patterns of underachievement has led to considerable research on solutions to the problem through guidance, grouping, and curriculum adjustment. No definitive findings can be enunciated but some clues may be found in recent reports.

A research team from the University of Illinois worked with Evanston Township High School in the late 1950's to determine the effect of group counseling on academic and personal adjustment of underachievers. An eight-week period of group sessions was undertaken. Within the treatment period no startling improvement could be identified. Nor at the time of an eighteen-month follow-up did the subjects improve their grades significantly. However, the research group reported:

> *With varying degrees of depth each client discovered: (1) that expressing his own real feelings about people, things, and ideas helped him to understand himself and the forces that disturbed him; (2) that at least one adult could accept him and that this adult, the counselor, wanted to understand him; (3) that his peers had problems too; (4) that, in spite of his faults, which his peers wanted to help him correct, his peers could accept him; (5) that he was capable of understanding, accepting, and helping others; and (6) that he could learn to trust others. When a client discovered that others accepted him, he found that he could better accept others, and eventually, that he could better accept himself. After he began to accept himself, then, and only then, could he accept the fact that he was gifted, and make plans which required him to use his great potentialities. All of this takes time (and more than eight weeks).*

The investigators at Evanston saw the underachiever as one who "tends to feel rejected by the important others in his life." He does things which deserve rebuke since this is the only way he knows how to get attention. Rebuke lowers the self-concept and, in a cycle, causes more negative behavior. The remedy, we are told, lies in a cooperative effort of counselor and teachers to understand the gifted underachiever and help him build a more realistic, more positive self concept. Three of the four groups "made significant growth," but the team agreed with other investigators "that underachievement is not a surface phenomenon which can be easily changed".

Another investigation of group counseling for remediation of underachievement was conducted by Sister Mary Viterbo McCarthy in the greater Boston area in 1956 and 1957. Twenty-four boys were selected from seventeen high schools on the basis of high IQ (125 and over) and low achievement (school average under 75 per cent). An experimental group was exposed to six one-hour counseling sessions revolving about discussion of twelve case studies highlighting problems of underachievement and the outstanding traits of the group members. The counselor maintained as non-directive a role as possible in the group situation "affording the experimental members maximum opportunity to ferret out the problems in each disguised case, to diagnose the failures, and to plan remedial measures."

Members of the experimental group were compared with members of a control group through pre- and post-counseling test results. Unfortunately, significantly greater changes did not occur in the experimental group. Sister Mary Viterbo suggests two hypotheses to explain the failure to make significant growth. One is the short time available to produce a change in a relatively deep-seated condition. The other hinges on the non-directive nature of the counseling. The students revealed in the group sessions a need for information about the self. Had the counselor been permitted to provide desired information concerning ability, aptitudes, interests, and goals, Sister Mary Viterbo hypothesizes better results.

From Sister Mary Viterbo's study two points stand out. One is the old refrain of "too little and too late." Underachievement has to be caught early. Whenever caught, it is likely to respond only to a sustained program of some length and depth. A second provocative suggestion is the need for more directive counseling where underachievement is involved. In this counseling, information about the self may be a primary need.

Guidance Plus Teaching Method

The Talented Youth Project of Teachers College, working cooperatively with De Witt Clinton High School, an all-boys high school in New York City, undertook a study with two objectives: (1) to determine social and personal factors related to underachievement, and (2) to experiment with school procedures which might improve the performance record of gifted underachievers. Underachievers were divided into experimental and control groups of thirty-five each and they in turn were compared with a group of high-achieving boys. The experimental group were placed with a home room teacher who was warm and outgoing, interested in the problem and able to combine flexibility with the maintenance of high standards. The study aimed to discover whether substantial improvements in school attitude and performance would result if these students were grouped together, if they shared each other's problems, and if they identified with and received support from this teacher.

Pre-tests of the high and low achievers yielded highly comparable IQ, reading, and arithmetic scores. The major academic difference lay in the wide difference in ninth year grades. There were also large differences in socio-metric ratings in favor of the high achievers. Of the low group one-third had been enrolled in special progress classes in junior high school, of the high group about 45 per cent. Goldberg remarks in her report, "These findings (supported by similar findings from the junior high school records of subsequent groups) suggest that during the elementary and junior high school years most bright youngsters, regardless of classroom performance as reflected by school grades, acquire considerable mastery of basic skills and knowledge."

The study of personal characteristics indicated closely similar patterns for high and low achievers— with respect to appraisal of their own abilities and characteristics, their occupational aspirations and their family background. However, one noticeable exception supports findings from other studies. Broken homes were far more frequent among the underachievers. As a result, Goldberg expresses the theory that underachievement among boys, twice as great as among girls, "may be related to inadequate identification with a father figure". High achievers were more satisfied with their school performance and stated higher expectations than did the lows.

In the first year of the study the homeroom teacher worked with the experimental group in the twenty-minute homeroom period and for a full class period as their social studies teacher. No gain was shown over the control group in the first semester, but by the end of the year, the experimental group outdistanced the control group in most respects. Goldberg credits no single incident such as praise or complimentary remarks to a parent. "It was rather the entire range of experiences, interactions and every-day relationships which the teacher saw as responsible for bringing about improvement in many of the boys. A carefully planned social studies program, an expression of interest and concern with problems of both a personal and academic nature, a friendly, and in general, more supportive and flexible teacher role combined with the support that students in the special group seemed to give to one another, all contributed to help many of the students gain the maturity and confidence necessary for successful school work".

In the following year (eleventh grade), the experimental group remained with their homeroom teacher but were assigned for the first semester to an honors course in social studies with a woman teacher who was accustomed to demanding high standards of her honor students. The loss of a male figure with which to identify combined with rigid application of standards resulted in poorer academic performance and misbehavior in class. The initial improvement was thus not sustained when the group was returned to a more conventional situation and held to "uniformly high standards, both of conduct and achievement." Being rouped together was not enough. "The important element is, apparently, the performance of the teacher in utilizing the group spirit constructively". In the second half of the year, the group was placed with another man teacher who utilized the experience of the two previous teachers and did not maintain his usual honors class standards. He attempted to create a warm and accepting climate, allowed leeway in performance standards, and showed interest in students' individual problems. He also concentrated on teaching much needed study skills. Once again the average performance of the experimental group improved. In both the experimental and control groups "improvers" and "non-improvers" were identified. Those who were able to make strides during the two years when compared with the others showed higher scores on the Iowa Composite and Correctness of Writing tests. Other differences did not reach the level of statistical significance. These included for nonimprovers a greater gap between perceived and wished-for abilities, more divorces in the family, fewer decisions reached as to vocational goals, and fewer siblings in college who might act as models. Goldberg concludes with the conviction "that academic underachievement is a symptom of a wide variety of more basic personal and social problems." By the time they have entered high school some students have passed the point where any help can be given profitably by the school. Unfortunately, criteria for earlier prognosis are not available. For students who can profit, Goldberg points to two crucial factors:

- Identification with a teacher who is constantly interested and supportive
- Assistance in mastering skills of learning which may not have been developed at the usual time

Havighurst ties together guidance and curriculum revision in underachievement. He bases his approach on the assumption of four factors in motivation:

- Need for achievement
- Identification with persons who have gone to college
- Social pressure coming from parents, teacher and friends
- Intrinsic pleasure in learning.

Having posited these factors, Havighurst suggests the following procedures to increase motivation:

For boys:

Counseling to identify able boys not well motivated for college

Giving awards, extra-curricular and community recognition; building social prestige of scholastic attainment

Making school work more interesting

For girls:

Parent-counselor conferences to encourage academic aspirations of girls

Contacts with professional women as intellectual models Assistance by counselors to girls in understanding how a career and homemaking role may both be pursued.

Basic Skills and Underachievement

While underachievement is often rooted in broad family, community, and national values, the school cannot evade responsibility for functions within its realm. The NEA invitational conference on identification of the gifted underlined a number of school-connected factors in poor academic attainment. Some of the more important problem areas follow:

- In some cases the desire to think and to know is not fully stimulated.
- Often the pupil sees no meaning or purpose in subjects he is required to study.

- Sometimes the student is keenly interested in one field to the exclusion of others. Below the graduate university level, schools are not prepared to permit such specialization of interest and generalization of ignorance.
- At times the student overestimates his own knowledge and is not helped by the school to look beyond his limitations.
- Inefficient reading and study methods are a frequent handicap.
- The influence of the peer group may be antagonistic to school achievement.
- Poor relationships with teachers may discourage interest

To these, Edwards adds his observation that low expectations on the part of faculty coincide with low aspiration levels on the part of students. Schools can make positive efforts to correct such conditions. Where causes are more deep-seated, these efforts will not always succeed. It is the school's responsibility, however, to make sure that school-related causes of low motivation are kept to a minimum.

A common characteristic of underachievers is inadequate performance in the basic study skills— reading, writing, listening, arithmetical computation, problem solving, and independent study. Most frequently these failures are symptoms of low motivation, emotional problems, or deprivation of some kind. In addition, they almost always induce failure to make progress at higher school levels. School personnel recognize that these failings are often symptoms, not causes. They justifiably do what they can to help identify the causes. However, the expected role of the teacher is to work in these basic areas, not on the causes underlying failure in them. The teacher may therefore *refer* the underachiever for assistance at a psychologically deeper level, but he must work with the student at the academic level. Of course, he must avoid aggravating emotional problems and reinforcing psychological blocks. However, he may be able to reduce underachievement if he can alleviate to some extent even the symptom.

Because the school's expected role is in the academic realm, schools give major attention in approaching problems of underachievement to remedial work in the foundation areas. The

Demonstration Guidance Project in New York City, for example, put its major in-school emphasis on small remedial classes in language arts and mathematics. To this were added the counseling services of psychologists and social workers and the stimulation of attendance at cultural activities in the community. While one may protest the weight of attention given to a symptom rather than a cause, no amount of psychological and social service work up can substitute for remedial learning that is generally necessary. The teacher who works alone without such services, however, should have no illusions about the difficulty and probable futility of his efforts.

NCA Project on Guidance and Motivation

In 1958 the North Central Association of Colleges and Secondary Schools established its Project on Guidance and Motivation of Superior and Talented Students primarily to investigate causes of, and to correct, the situation in those schools where fewer than half of the high school graduates were entering college. One hundred such high schools were identified and participated in the program, studying their students and inaugurating practices that might, hopefully, result in increased academic motivation. In a bulletin to participating schools, the Project defined three problem areas:

- Problems dealing with goals, aspirations and self-concepts
- Problems dealing with peer group, family and community attitudes
- Problems dealing with studying, reading, listening, and self-appraisal skills

In the first area, the following problems were identified:

- Influence of immediate, rather than long-range goals
- Helping students realize they have special abilities
- Preparing students for realistic thinking about educational goals and plans
- Assisting students to plan for an appropriate occupational choice

Lack of interest or desire to achieve; lack of understanding of the personality qualities that are "musts" in maximum development of talent peer group, family and community attitudes included these problems:

- Competing for grades rather than developing an interest in the material for its own sake
- Reluctance of students to enter a new program or special classes
- Evaluating work of students in special classes
- Parents who do not wish children to attend college
- Increasing the school's power to hold capable students who are potential drop-outs
- Financial need preventing college attendance
- Negative attitude of students toward high achievement or scholarship

Study, reading, listening and self-appraisal problems include improvement of these four skills. In addition, the lack of supplementary materials in the school and a dislike for writing represent academic obstacles. To attack these problems the Project makes a series of recommendations in a booklet, Guiding Superior and Talented High School Students. A number of suggestions are made for these purposes:

- Promoting community understanding
- Early identification of superior students
- Special provision for counseling

Special provision for challenging and stimulating activities through the curriculum:

- Recognizing and honoring academic achievement
- Special cooperation by business and professional leaders
- Special cooperation by colleges and college students
- Securing understanding and cooperation by parents

Summary

The burst of research activity in the late 1950's on motivation and underachievement has a dual significance: (1) It developed an awareness of the magnitude and importance of the problem. (2) It disclosed a recognition that we do not yet know why individuals react differently to environmental stimuli, personal handicaps and native ability. Financial limitations, low socio-economic status, minority group membership, being born female – all of these interfere seriously with college entrance, but more powerful than all of these is motivation to succeed. Lack of such motivation outweighs favorable circumstances of birth, economics, or neighborhood.

Investigators continue to work assiduously on factors in motivation since the will to achieve appears to overshadow all external conditions. Unfortunately, research has thus far yielded contradictory findings with respect to the personality of underachievers and their emotional and social adjustment. Certain conditions may characterize underachievers taken as a group, but they may also describe a significant proportion of high achievers as well. Competition is not viewed as a great spur to motivation, nor is strong pressure from parents. Instead, motivation is seen as a normal facet of a healthy personality. A healthy self-concept is viewed as leading to positive relations with others, openness to experience, and the development of a store of accurate perceptions. This perceptual field – information, understandings, concepts, generalizations-serves the individual well in facing immediate problems. It also begets further growth. The more one knows in a particular area the more one wants to know, the more one needs to know. In this view, motivation is not imposed from without; it is instead an expression of a healthy personality seeking wholesome experience with other people and with objects in its environment.

There is some agreement that strongly motivated persons have an unconscious need to achieve; that their families value training for independence; that they define their career objectives at an early age; that they are encouraged by their parents in plans to go to college; that they have an adult figure with whom they can identify; that they have mastered basic learning skills; that they take pleasure in learning for its own sake. They come infrequently from broken homes. Many children who show signs of high ability do not have these favorable factors in their background. Some become "underachievers." Even their "ability" or "aptitude" scores begin to decline. The school has to do more than point regretfully at the circumstances surrounding failure. It has a responsibility to circumvent the obstacles that keep potential Milton s mute and inglorious. A few large-scale efforts have been made; more are in process. One approach is to assume the need for greater personal guidance. A number of projects have centered on increased personal, academic, and vocational counseling. A second approach is to adapt the curriculum. These efforts have included modernization of subject matter and utilizing practical applications of theoretical studies and intensive programs to bring the underachiever "up to grade level" in fundamental learning skills. Exposure of students from culturally impoverished environs to the many faces of metropolitan culture represents still another curricular approach. Some efforts have been made to combine guidance and curriculum emphases. Unfortunately, the phrase "no significant differences" pops up with disappointing frequency in these researches. The investigators in their conclusions underline the stubbornness of underachievement, its deep-seated and long-term character. The school is often working alone on a problem which is steeped in community and sub-culture influences. Repeated investigations into the nature and etiology of underachievement put stress on the same theme: the complexity of the phenomenon and its resistance to remedial efforts. Academic underachievement and low motivation for scholastic performance seem to be closely related. Efforts to raise the student's academic aspirations may, hopefully, produce higher achievement. The following means find support in raising motivation levels:

- How the student sees himself is of primary importance. The school can help able students build positive self-concepts. The student who shows academic promise should be helped to see himself as a collegian. Negative criticism should be avoided; instead, parents and teachers should help the young person build a feeling of personal worth.
- Community, neighborhood, and peer-group attitudes toward intellectual performance have a powerful influence on motivation and school achievement. The school must know what these attitudes are, help develop these in desirable directions, and assist the student to identify with constructively directed groups. School authorities, other youth agencies, the local press, service clubs in the community and local businessmen should be invited to examine their

programs for signs of attitudes that encourage, overlook, or actually discourage intellectual distinction. General policies of the school affect motivation. Are students given opportunity for independent academic work? Do they develop a sense of commitment, a feeling of excitement, in their school work? Are sufficiently high standards maintained? Are competition and pressure from adults serving as stimulants or depressants? Current tendencies to look to the past for educational solutions deny the importance of independence and commitment in learning. High achievers generally have clearer vocational goals than low achievers. The school should examine its curriculum and guidance to determine whether individual students are securing early and realistic help in planning for careers. The underachiever is obviously not adapting to the standard program. Curriculum adaptation is apparently needed. The school program must present a challenge. It must be flexible enough to avoid penalties for students with blind spots in particular areas. It should be adaptable to the non-conformist, providing opportunity for free effort, for undirected, and creative work. Free use of laboratories, workshops, studios, and practice rooms is called for. Contests, games, papers, plays, teams, and clubs represent devices that are helpful in stimulating interest. The curriculum has to be geared for gifted students who do not fit the "able and ambitious" standard. The most effective and direct efforts that the school can make lie in its traditional realm. No bright student should remain handicapped by early failure to learn fundamental tools. Small classes and personal attention appear necessary for effective remedial teaching in reading, mathematics, speech and social studies skills. Curriculum and co-curriculum should aim at widening the students' cultural perspective. Frequently, the unmotivated student is also culturally underprivileged. Attendance at concerts, plays, museums, libraries, and college functions often helps the student begin to see himself in a new light. Guidance services are potentially a strong arm in redirecting the underachiever. Individual and group efforts should be directed at helping the student assess his potential and then to exercise it. Personal, educational and vocational guidance are all needed.

Counseling parents with respect to their children's abilities and needs seems especially necessary for the underachiever. While no environment guarantees high achievement or consigns the student irrevocably to low achievement, greater problems will be found in certain economic sectors, ethnic groups, social classes, and geographic areas than others. The school should be close enough to its own community to recognize such factors which predispose to success or failure. As unobtrusively as possible, it should make particular efforts to prevent underachievement among children in disadvantaged groups. The feminine gender presents a special problem. The average superiority of girls in the lower grades gradually declines, and fewer girls of high ability go on to college. Far fewer go on to graduate work. Girls of superior ability should find help in recognizing the possibility of combining a professional career with a feminine role in life. Of considerable importance is the identification of the gifted child with adults who serve as appropriate models. Children often set their aspirations after beloved or admired members of their family. Teachers often cast a longer influence through example than instruction. The teacher's own professional activity, his interest in students, and the warmth of his personality combine to invite emulation by students. The school provides still another source of inspiration by introducing students to other adults with whom they may identify readily. Similarity with the student's background, relative youthfulness, reputation, or a particular career choice are factors in such identification. Underachievers apparently perform more successfully with teachers who are supportive than with teachers who are simply demanding of high achievement. The choice of teachers is especially important for the able student who is not fulfilling his potential. While underachievement is not primarily economic in its source, financial assistance is necessary for some students. Knowledge by the family that such help is available may avoid early rejection on financial grounds of dreams of higher education for their children. Scholarships may include not only tuition costs but supplementary items while the student is still in tuition-free schools. These items include various instructional materials and cultural opportunities outside the school. Sometimes, the symbol of interest by others in the child is more important to the young person and his family than the financial aid itself. No finding is more ubiquitous in research on underachievement than the need to start early. Underachievement, like envy, seems to feed on itself. A poor start snowballs into chronic failure, possibly because of immediate influence on the child's academic self-concept. For this reason early identification of giftedness and early discovery of failure to achieve as expected are essential. Concerted efforts to relieve underachievement have generally failed of their purpose when delayed of inception till the senior high school. A continuous program of guidance, diagnosis and identification needs its beginning apparently in the primary grades.

7

Science and Mathematics for the Gifted

Introduction

The era of atomic energy, rockets, and space satellites has made the nation acutely aware of science. The ubiquitous competition with Soviet Russia has accentuated pressures on schools to upgrade their programs in science, particularly where students with scientific ability are concerned. As a matter of fact, practically all new proposals in science and mathematics in recent years have centered about curricula suitable mainly for the highly gifted. In one respect these demands have been healthy: they have placed in sharp focus the need for curriculum reorganization in science, a notably weak field prior to 1950 in elementary schools, and in mathematics, a field in which teaching at the secondary level had not changed materially for two centuries. These same demands, however, have not been quite so wholesome when they have tended to impair a balanced educational diet. Nor can these pressures be viewed with equanimity when they impose the same program on all students nor when they "guide" into shortage areas all students of moderate ability whether they have superior interest and competence in other areas or not.

Identification Of Science Aptitude

Considerable research has been done in the identification of scientific aptitudes in young children. Lesser summarizes efforts to define talent in science, noting differences among investigators as to (1) the existence of scientific aptitude as a definable entity, and (2) the components of this aptitude if it may be defined. Some investigators are convinced that science talent is not a single trait but that it is an "aspect of high general intelligence which emerges through environmental stimulation and available opportunities for development." Others believe such a trait exists but disagree as to its components which include some of the following: "sensitivity to problems, ability to develop novel ideas, and the ability to evaluate"; "specialized and persistent curiosity, alertness in detecting inconsistencies, and a high degree of mechanical-mindedness"; "industry, devotion to work, energy and initiative"; and "spatial visualization, manipulative ability, ability to plan and design a study, and ability to communicate".

Biographical approaches have also been used in efforts to identify elements in scientific achievement. Roe studied elements in family background and individual development of eminent scientists. Knapp and Goodrich checked on educational backgrounds of individuals listed in *American Men of Science* and discovered unexpected proportions of scientists coming from particular undergraduate institutions. One may infer from these data that individual abilities tell only part of the story, that stimulation in particular educational programs is of great significance. Brandwein, studying high school students, established three categories which suggest bases for identification. These include, first, "genetic factors" – high level verbal and mathematical ability, and adequate sensory and neuro-muscular control. Second are "predisposing factors" – persistence, willingness to work on a task overtime, to withstand discomfort, and to face failure; and "questing," a search for new ideas that comes from marked dissatisfaction with present explanations of how the world works. Third are "activating factors" – opportunities for further training and the accessibility of an inspiring teacher. The first factors are constitutional – cognitive and physical abilities that are "natural," rather than acquired. The second factors are conative – emotional, motivational. The third factor is environmental— the contribution of the culture to the ability and the willingness of the individual. By providing students with opportunities to work independently at Forest Hills High School in science activities, Brandwein and his colleagues set in motion a mechanism for self-identification which is regarded as one of the more effective types of selection. These opportunities include working in laboratories in free periods during school hours or before and after school, preparing instructional materials for teachers, assisting the science teacher, helping maintain a science museum and vivarium, joining in such co-curricular activities as science clubs, and preparing a science journal. Early identification of students with aptitude in science is commonly advocated. Since interest and self-direction seem to be important elements in science achievement, University School at Ohio State University made a study through student autobiographies of factors in the development of science interests. The study identified the following as important factors:

- Attitude of teachers and parents toward the child's questions
- The influence of family and friends
- The value of mass media of communication, trips to museums, hobbies and games, books, chemistry sets and other materials, particularly as provided for in the home
- The child's own curiosity, desire to create, ambition and determination
- The role of organizations and special events
- The content and structure of the science program or individual courses in science
- Methods and activities employed in the science program or in individual courses
- The role of the laboratory and its equipment for use in experimentation and the development of special projects, both in and out of school
- The place of outdoor education
- The role of mathematics
- The concern shown for the high ability student
- The effectiveness of the teacher.

Definition of the adjective "early" in early identification apparently relates to the level at which the writer operates. At the Hunter College Elementary School, Davis and Lesser report on one project predicting science ability at the five-year level and on another testing for ability at the seven-to-eight-year level. In the year following testing, the tests appear to have had predictive validity. The research was not extended far enough in time to evaluate prediction over a longer period. Brandwein and Bloom, working in the senior high school, speak of "early" identification at the ninth and tenth grade level (ages thirteen to fifteen). There is no necessary conflict between identification at one age or another. It is noteworthy that Bloom and Brandwein place heavy emphasis on interest and self-selection. These elements no doubt reflect the same aptitude and environmental factors that produce high scores in the tests administered at earlier ages.

Objectives in Science for the Gifted

Objectives emphasized in science are found in the areas of information, attitude, skills, and application. Certainly an important goal in education of the gifted is understanding the world we live in from a scientific point of view. Small bits of information are learned and interpreted in the light of concepts, generalizations and principles. The bright child may be expected to accumulate a larger store of information but also to have greater facility in handling the abstractions to which this information contributes and by which the details are explained. Learning scientific attitudes and methods contributes a major outcome both for the future scientist and the future layman. While teaching critical thinking with verbal materials is basic in social studies and language arts, in science critical thinking takes concrete form where experimentation and more direct cause-to-effect relationships can be seen. DeHurd suggests ten skills that should accrue:

- Reading and interpreting science writings
- Locating authoritative sources of science information
- Performing suitable experiments for testing ideas
- Using the tools and techniques of science
- Recognizing the pertinency and adequacy of data

- Making valid inferences and predictions from data
- Recognizing and evaluating assumptions underlying techniques and processes used in solving problems
- Expressing ideas qualitatively and quantitatively
- Using the knowledge of science for responsible social action
- Seeking new relationships and ideas from known facts and concepts.

Throughout, emphasis should be on concept formation rather than accumulation of information per se, and on discovery as a primary method of learning. Schwab expresses this point of view eloquently in "The Teaching of Science as Enquiry," stressing the tentative nature of scientific knowledge and the dangers of presenting information in science as permanently established and unassailable.

Motivating Interest in Science

An important problem in a society that is more entranced by technological wonders than by the science which makes them possible is motivating interest in science careers. Based on its biographical study of young people with an interest in science, the Ohio State University School committee listed the following implications for school personnel:

- Students must be permitted and have sufficient opportunity to ask questions; parents should be encouraged to adopt a healthy attitude toward their children's questions.
- The teacher needs to know his students' home background and its impact.
- Field trips, mass media, publications should enrich the program.
- The school program should aim at promoting and developing the student's curiosity, desire to create, and determination to succeed; early experiences are essential.
- The science program should provide an outlet for the student's desire to be creative, utilizing in-school and out-of-school organizations and events.

- Methods and activities should provide for actual experiences in problem solving, independent discovery, drawing conclusions, using the library and other resources.
- Participation should be encouraged in outdoor activities, such as camping and hiking.
- The science and mathematics programs should work together to assure developing interest in both fields.
- The high-ability student should feel either through method within a course or through program organization that he is moving along and accomplishing worth-while things.
- The teacher is a key person in fostering and developing interest and talent and should be carefully chosen for teaching assignments.

An important element in experimental programs at elementary and secondary levels is the effort to stimulate interest in science as a field of study. Bloom, Brandwein, and others stress opportunities for first-hand experience, for actual handling of the materials of science and for student exposure to experiments that are truly open-ended. The essence of science is not in following a laboratory manual, cookbook style, but in reaching for what is still— to the student— unknown. The efforts by Roe and others to categorize the backgrounds of working scientists is an effort to seek out environmental factors which motivate commitment to scientific work.

Elementary School Science Programs

Rapid strides are being made in improvement of science education at the elementary level. School districts with the necessary resources recognize the inadequate preparation in the past of most teachers for the teaching of science. Accordingly, summer workshops and in-service courses in science during the school year have been offered in many places and have been generally well attended. Colleges of education, moreover, have been stepping up their science requirements for elementary school teachers and providing instruction in methods of teaching science. Under the auspices of the National Science Foundation, special summer workshops have enrolled elementary as well as secondary science teachers in the study of new subject matter and teaching techniques.

In one sense, then, elementary science education may be said to be improving. General betterment brings with it improved offerings for the gifted. In another sense, a basic problem in elementary school science remains unsolved. It is idle not to recognize the feeling of inadequacy that many elementary teachers continue to feel in this area. Actually the problem is dual in nature, involving both limited background in science and inadequate preparation in science education. Not having studied the problems of science teaching, such a teacher is likely to confuse science information with science education. Science in his hands becomes simply another set of facts to be absorbed. All students, gifted or not, depend upon much improved programs of science preparation for teachers.

A good science program at the elementary level takes steps toward achieving the various objectives of a science program anywhere. Nowhere do children exhibit more curiosity than in the elementary school. Helping children to find answers to their many questions of how things work and why they work as they do is the beginning of an organized view of the scientist's universe. Guiding them in small experiments aims not only at discovery of a solution but also at appreciation of experimental method and critical thinking. A basic purpose running throughout the teaching of science should be the stimulation of interest in science as a subject and as a method. Obviously the most effective teacher is one who is himself interested and who is himself well equipped to guide scientific inquiry.

Blough and Blackwood in publications of the U.S. Office of Education suggest numerous experiences of value at the elementary level, and they list easily available, inexpensive material that may be used in experimentation. Other suggestions are to be found in publications of the National Science Teachers Association. If the gifted child is to see more in science than just another variety of book-learning, facilities for scientific exploration are essential. Movable science tables are available which are equipped with their own water and gas supply and with electrical outlets that may be connected to a wall socket. Flat surfaces such as long tables and wide window ledges are needed to set up projects. Finally, space has to be provided for storage of the students' uncompleted projects as well as for the teachers' supplies.

In addition to regular classroom work in science, the student with a special interest in science has opportunities to participate in science fairs that have sprung up in the wake of the Science Talent Search. Here again, required participation by every child in the class waters down rather than enriches the program. Everyone is urged to bring in a project, and the teacher has little time, accordingly, to work with a handful of students instead. If the teacher were to concentrate upon the few children truly interested, he might draw them out, discover their special areas of enthusiasm, and suggest to them ideas for projects which they might then push farther. In the absence of such guidance, children too often depend upon parents for the idea and for its execution, too.

In viewing elementary science patterns, the committee preparing the National Society for the Study of Education 1960 Yearbook on science defined behavioral objectives related to (a) knowledge and understanding, (b) skill and competence, (c) attitude and interest, and (d) action patterns. The committee explained:

> *With respect to* knowledge and understanding, *a primary-grade child is able to generalize in simple terms about seasonal changes; their effect upon the way people eat, dress, and live, and their effect upon plant and animal life. An intermediate-grade child has knowledge of electrical phenomena and understands the uses of common appliances. An upper grade child should have an understanding of the universality of change and some of its causes.*
>
> *Regarding* skill and competence, *a primary child should be careful in crossing streets, should play safely, and should know how to deal with fire. In the intermediate period, a child is able to use simple scientific apparatus. In the upper grades a child knows how to repair a variety of appliances and simple machines....*
>
> *As to* attitudes and interests, *a primary-child should exhibit inquisitiveness with regard to all aspects of his environment. In the intermediate grades, children should be interested in learning the simple scientific principles of sound, light, heat, electricity and magnetism.*
>
> *Finally, in the* action pattern *of a primary child, there should be evidence that he asks sensible questions as he seeks to satisfy his*

> *curiosity ... The intermediate-grade child goes to reliable sources of information and collects data. He helps keep home and school premises clean, sanitary, and orderly. In the upper grades, for example, a child uses scientific information in a broad range of activities about the home relating to appliances, equipment, gardens, furnace, ventilation, and conservation.*

Starting from these premises for all children, the committee expresses an expectation that gifted children will learn more science quantitatively, but that qualitatively purposes remain the same. Emphasis on individual differences, however, will capitalize on "rare opportunities to challenge children of varying intellectual abilities and interests. *If there is one unique purpose* in teaching bright children, it is to keep their interest in science alive so that many of them will choose to pursue careers in science, mathematics, and engineering".

Basically, elementary science helps the child to find answers to his questions about the environment. But science *asks* questions as well. Children of ability should be encouraged to ask *why* a given answer is correct so that they may build an understanding of basic concepts and principles. Generalization, conceptualization, and abstraction are a peculiar forte of the intellectually gifted child. To allow learning to fall short of this stage is to neglect the culminating step in the bright child's learning. Obviously, however, principles and generalization represent a last step, not a first step, even in the exploration, discovery, and concept formation of the gifted.

Mechanisms in this process are the science curriculum of the elementary school, the science corner in the classroom which invites reading and experimentation in science, clubs that form through interest in space, electricity, or plant-life, participation in science fairs, building science museums, and laboratory work within and outside the curriculum. To staff such programs, a few schools provide a special science teacher or borrow him from the secondary schools. In the Hunter College Elementary School a special science teacher meets every child from age six up in a specially equipped laboratory once or twice a week. Classes are divided so that the teacher is able to conduct a genuine laboratory program with a group of twelve to fifteen students. A major problem is the limited time each student has for science in this kind of organization. Some schools find able science teachers on their regular staff and free these persons at stated times to work with children showing special interest in science. Some school systems provide science consultants who serve individual schools either as experts working with the teachers or as itinerant special teachers working directly with groups of children. It is indeed short-sighted, however, not to recognize the inadequacy of the average teacher's preparation for an active program in science marked by genuine student exploration and discovery. And such an active program should certainly take precedence over a book-oriented program which simply stresses mastery of science information.

The availability of leadership personnel often dictates the organization of science opportunities. If a special teacher is available, a project room can be maintained full time in the elementary school. Children can be scheduled to work in such a room as part of their regular program. They can also visit the room to work on individual projects as their class program may permit. If no one teacher can give a major portion of his time to science instruction, a club period once or twice a week may make it possible for the teachers especially interested in science to guide boys and girls who choose to join the radio, electricity, astronomy, or greenhouse club. If an outside consultant visits a few times during the week, children with special interest may be excused from their regular class activities to work with the consultant. If the consultant works with teachers only, provisions for individual scientific activity should be made in the framework of the class daily program. Any of these alternatives can be effective if sparked with the enthusiasm and competence of personnel assigned to it.

Junior High School Science

At the junior high school level, the student is ready for an organized approach to science. Recent recommendations urge a two-year general science program in grades 7 and 8 and the beginning of a specialized science course — earth science or biology — in the ninth grade. A committee in New York City, seeking to replace a two-year accelerated program with a three-year enriched program in the junior high school recommended such an organization but placed equivalent stress on method. The committee urges the "open ended" approach to laboratory work, describing it in these words: "It will involve having pupils themselves recognize the problems needing to be solved, delimiting the problems into smaller problems, and then their suggesting laboratory procedures for seeking answers to these problems". They recommend not only school activities but small experiments at home, field trips, and reading of accounts of original research that are of appropriate simplicity. Such accounts are to be found in the Alembic Club reprints. A good example of methodology in a problem-solving experiment in junior high school is provided in the report.

The conventional club program in junior high school provides administrative opportunity for special interest activities that are science-related. Hobbies such as radio and photography are obvious centers for club organization. If the school has (or can acquire) such facilities as greenhouses, gardens, or observatories, these facilities can attract groups of pupils into clubs. In addition, all such activities can be incorporated into a single club, if personnel and equipment make it possible for students to work simultaneously on a variety of interests. The club, however, should make project and experiment activity possible; it should not be limited to discussion of experiences outside the club or to an academic study of science information. The basic purpose remains that of building firmer interest in science activity and study.

The strengthening of programs in elementary science is leading to speculation as to its eventual effect on the junior high school program. It is conceivable that practically all the general science customarily taught in junior high school will be covered in the elementary school. Many science educators question moving high school type courses in biology, physics, chemistry, geology, or astronomy to grades seven and eight. It is apparent that continuing examination of the junior high school science curriculum will be needed. The effort to provide a program that relates scientific information and scientific method to the child's life and environment will probably be continued. Greater emphasis on problem solving by the students themselves is suggested as one way of upgrading the program while retaining the same general approach. A second would involve more advanced probing into the applications of science. A third would put more stress, for bright children at least, upon theoretical elements that come closer to the systematic approach of conventional high school science.

Science in Senior High School

At the senior high school level, experimentation with course offerings is bearing fruit in biology and the physical sciences. The professional associations in these fields in the late 1950's gave new attention to revisions that would bring science offerings up to date, and simultaneously provide more challenge and interest to the gifted. These programs are still experimental. They are marked by greater emphasis upon laboratory procedures that approximate more closely the work of the scientist in research where he is genuinely seeking an unknown result. Far more equipment and more extensive storage space are needed for student activity and student projects than has been planned even in the newer high school buildings. An earlier trend to replace student experimentation with teacher demonstration or motion pictures has apparently been forgotten. Emphasis is not upon *coverage* but upon depth of experience, appreciation of scientific method, and stimulation of interest in scientific activity.

Curricular offerings are marked in some places by differentiating science experiences according to the interests and abilities of learners. Chemistry, for example, is offered on several levels— an applied, layman's chemistry which is not intended for college preparatory students; a descriptive, somewhat theoretical chemistry which is meant for the college bound student who displays no special interest in science; and a rigorous quantitative, theoretical chemistry which will be directly preparatory for chemistry specialization in college. Similar adjustments are made in some schools in biology and physics. Where possible, special project classes are offered to students so that they may work with some independence in small numbers under the guidance of a teacher competent to direct research activities.

Sad experience with the conventional, unimaginative, science programs of the past argues for a high degree of ability grouping in the future. Before a full commitment is made to ability grouping, it is necessary to explore more attractive and meaningful programs with a broad spread of ability. The lifeless courses that imitated college types have, over the years, repelled high school students. Because a year or more of organized "laboratory science" was required, many schools watered down their science program in an effort to help students "pass" courses which were not inherently meaningful. A better solution might have been to upgrade courses by individualizing the approach within each class. In addition content might have been modernized. The objectives of science education as indicated earlier ought to have stimulated development of courses no longer imitative of higher level programs.

Few efforts of this kind have been made. Some exploration, however, has been attempted in diversifying courses, using ability grouping as a basic principle. Distinctions have been made in some cases between science-for-the-citizen and science-for-the-scientist offerings. Such an approach has the merit of providing a sufficiently challenging program for the more able who are already identified. For those not identified, however, the school may find itself providing a less stimulating course that prevents later self-discovery by the student or identification by the school.

A number of patterns are to be found. Pupils showing little aptitude in science take general science through the ninth grade, followed by a one-year elective in what purports to be a "laboratory" course in biology, physics, or chemistry. The less able students, if grouped together, are likely to have more demonstration and less experimentation. "Laboratory" exercises often turn out to be cook-book type practices where the student is required to produce the results called for by the "recipe" in his workbook. A few schools have substituted advanced general science for physical science requirements. Some have instituted courses of some interest in the applied physics or applied chemistry area.

Providing for the non-science student in this way, schools have felt free to provide more rigorous courses for the more able. A common approach is to omit ninth grade general science and to plunge directly into an organized program of biology or earth science. In a sense this procedure represents acceleration. In addition, the selected grouping apparently makes more feasible a course that is more quantitative and theoretical. More laboratory work is also offered. Some schools are working with "open ended" experiments rather than the cook-book type. In addition to the usual kind of college preparatory science courses, honors courses are offered in the larger schools to students of exceptional ability and interest. These courses may simply delve more deeply into college level work, but frequently they provide opportunity for individual exploration, project work, library research and the "open-ended" approach. Brandwein describes features of such an "operational approach for science-oriented students": honors courses in biology, physics, and chemistry, advanced science offerings, career guidance and extracurricular activities in science. Activities include "original" research, laboratory techniques, operation of laboratory equipment, skills in shop work, library research, mathematics, exhibits, reports of students' own work, seminar sessions, participation in the Science Talent Search and Advanced Placement work.

Club programs provide additional chances for students to share burgeoning interests in science. Programs normally include opportunities to pursue individual projects, presentations by experts on the faculty and from outside the school, participation in competitions such as science fairs, and reports on research in special areas of interest.

At the senior high school level the growing competence and accumulated knowledge of the exceptional student in science make possible a number of first-hand experiences in science. Some schools stimulate such students' participation in science by permitting them to serve as laboratory assistants in unassigned periods. Some school science rooms are enriched with models, diagrams, and collections that superior students have made. In some cases students have marked nature trails in the wooded sections of the school grounds, of adjacent city parks, or of nearby hillsides in rural and mountain areas. School camps provide unusual opportunities for junior naturalists, foresters, zoologists, botanists, and geologists. All of these activities may be regarded as informal kinds of work experience. A more advanced kind of work experience is found in actual placement of students, during or after school or on Saturdays, with clinics and industrial research departments, in the offices of physicians and health departments, and in science laboratories in the community.

Visits to science facilities in the community — university, governmental, or industrial — are used to stimulate interest and develop some basis for understanding. Bringing science resource personnel into the classroom can provide both stimulation and new learning.

Statements made by New York City high school science chairmen in 1935 continue to hold true: "Growth in physical science is chiefly made through contact with science apparatus and inspiring, sympathetic teachers." "pupils in physical science need, more than all else, firsthand experience with science materials and scientific literature... opportunity to do individual work in verification, problem solving, and research work within their abilities".

Curriculum Proposals by Professional Groups

The resurgence of interest in high school science in the 1950's, stemming from international crises in the emerging "space age," found expression in fundamental reconsideration of course content by science and teacher groups. Professional associations in physics, chemistry, and biology as well as the National Science Teachers Association brought together scholars and teachers to update curricula, to refresh teacher backgrounds in science, and to develop material both for students and for teacher training. These programs are of particular concern in educating the gifted since their primary emphasis is on college-preparatory science and on the higher ability within this selected group.

The group that got its study off the ground first was the Physical Sciences Study Committee, starting in November 1956 with a grant from the National Science Foundation to Massachusetts Institute of Technology. The Committee related its work to that of a committee of the American Institute of Physics, the American Association of Physics Teachers and the National Science Teachers Association. In the course of its activities, the Physical Sciences Study Committee prepared a series of new texts and motion pictures for use by high school students, a syllabus and monographs for teachers, and a number of annual institutes (supported by the National Science Foundation) for physics teachers. Twelve such institutes for familiarizing teachers with new developments were operated, for example, in the summer of 1960. A result of this concerted activity was that six hundred high schools were already using PSSC materials in 1960-61.

The National Science Teachers Association has made available a considerable quantity of publications to assist teachers in enriching their program. These include material at both the elementary and secondary level such as science project pamphlets, bibliographies, lists of free and inexpensive materials, and clearinghouse pamphlets on teaching suggestions. The last include *New Developments in High School Science Teaching* and the annual STAR (Science Teaching Achievement Recognition) abstracts which report selected successful teaching techniques each year. Teachers of the gifted who are seeking ways to enrich science programs may look for considerable assistance to their professional associations.

Parallel developments have taken place in biology and chemistry. Supported again by the National Science Foundation, the American Institute of Biological Sciences organized the Biological Sciences Curriculum Study in 1958 and by 1960 had developed textbooks for trial use in secondary schools attempting three different organizations of biological material. The American Chemistry Society has produced a chemistry course on 16 mm. film which should have value in those schools not able to secure adequate chemistry personnel, and in other schools as a stimulating supplement to competent teachers. Two new curricula are available in Chemistry – the Chemical Bond Approach and the Chemical Education Materials Study. Commercial publishers have produced texts for all these new programs.

Advanced Placement Science Courses

In Science as in other areas, considerable experimentation has been done with Advanced Placement Courses. The Advanced Placement Bulletin carries the following remarks concerning work in Biology and Chemistry:

> *An advanced course in biology may be either a single intensive course or a second course presupposing an earlier beginning course. In any case, it should provide a more mature presentation of content and more extensive laboratory experience than is usual....*
>
> *The following important considerations should shape the presentation of an advanced course in biology. The fact that*

> *fundamental principles apply to both plants and animals should be emphasized. The overall approach should be dynamic, making constant reference to functional morphology. Evolution should be a fundamental theme or framework of the course, and the interdependence of organism and environment should receive constant attention with stress on animal adaptations and behavior. Living materials, and field work if feasible, should be an integral part of the laboratory work.*
>
> *The advanced chemistry course should be planned to meet the objectives of a general chemistry course on the college level... Beginning general chemistry (in college) is conceived as an introduction to chemistry. It concerns itself with the fundamental assumptions and the* logical structure *of chemistry.*
>
> *The students should attain such a competence in* dealing with simple chemical problems *that they will feel a* justifiable self-confidence *within these fields.*
>
> *The emphasis is on chemistry as an intellectual subject and on the rigorous training in fundamentals needed in preparation for future work in it or in related fields.*
>
> *The advanced work in chemistry should not displace any other part of the basic curriculum for any student. Some secondary schools have successfully given the advanced level chemistry as the first course, allowing 10 to 12 periods of chemistry per week.*

In physics, the Advanced Placement Program distinguishes among three different types of physics courses at the college level – a descriptive physics course which is aimed at the student who will probably take no additional courses in the area; a second course, more quantitative and more rigorous, depending upon algebraic and trigonometric handling of principles in physics and a third type which is still more rigorous and depends upon the methods of calculus in formulating physical principles and applying them to physical problems. Advanced Placement work is suggested to offer the second type of program at the high school level. But students who may specialize in physics or engineering are advised not to take Advanced Placement work in physics, but rather to "place primary effort upon preparing themselves for the Advanced

Placement Examination in Mathematics (which includes calculus)". Since Advanced Placement courses are intended precisely for the kind of student who would need the third type of course, secondary school teachers and administrators might do well to capitalize on the candor of the Advanced Placement Bulletin and look to other fields for accelerated college work.

Other Provisions for the Gifted in Science

Various alternatives to the Advanced Placement Program are found in secondary school offerings. In addition to the four-year sequence for grades 9 to 12, some schools offer electives so that interested students may take two science courses in their third or fourth year or both. Electives suggested by the National Science Teachers Association committee working on the NEA Academically Talented Student Project include microbiology, field biology, advanced general chemistry, atomic physics, electronics and electricity, geophysics, a fourth year of mathematics, history of science, astronomy, earth science, and geochemistry. Of a different type are suggested science seminars or science research courses which permit variation from the typical course pattern and perhaps greater personal involvement of the student in scientific endeavor.

The committee of the National Science Teachers Association participating in the NEA Academically Talented Student Project declares that there is no one best curriculum, no one best way to organize subject matter. Instead the committee suggests "nine fundamental guidelines for the selection and organization of subject matter." These guidelines follow:

> *The content should be developed in the light of contemporary scientific thinking and theorizing. As often as possible, pupils should glimpse the frontiers of scientific investigation. They should come to understand that neither our knowledge nor our understanding is static.*
>
> *Content areas should be developed in depth. To this end, a few well chosen areas should be studied, and the emphasis should be on better quality of teaching and learning rather than on covering a great diversity of subject matter.*

> *The over-all science program for the talented should be planned carefully to assure continuity of the program from the elementary school through college. Such articulation should avoid the needless repetition of subject matter.*
>
> *Science content should be developed in such a way that pupils have many opportunities to work with science materials, equipment, and apparatus. The choice and development of content areas should be planned to reveal the relationships among the sciences....*
>
> *The science program should be planned for the early and increasing application of mathematics to the precise formulation of scientific relationships and to the application of scientific laws and principles.*
>
> *The teaching of science should be concentrated increasingly on the development of the concepts, principles, broad generalizations, and great issues of science rather than on the accumulation of unrelated facts.*
>
> *Full advantage should be taken of the science resources of the community for enriching and supplementing the science program for talented students.*
>
> *Science should be taught in such a way as to reveal the influence of science in such other areas of culture as politics, economics, world outlook, standard of living, and the influence of these areas in the development of science. Recognition of the social responsibility of science should be developed.*

The bulletin setting forth these guidelines illustrates from topics in junior and senior high school science how these suggestions may be carried out in practice.

Resources for Science Programs

Bricks, of course, are not made without straw. The teacher needs the material and the time to do a stimulating job. In addition to the usual science materials, if students are doing individual projects, the teacher needs a budget and a petty cash fund for ready purchase of necessary items. He needs work space and storage space for students. If these can be provided apart from the regular laboratory, individual projects and independent work will not conflict with the normal school routines. Some of the tools typically found in a wood shop or machine shop are also needed for construction in science research projects.

At the elementary school level, Martin and others recommend adequate space for children to work, read, experiment, set up, and leave occasional long-term projects or exhibits. They call for a work counter with storage cabinets beneath it, electric outlets, running water, bulletin boards, and a display case. Some source of beat is also needed.

At the secondary level, Martin suggests locating science rooms in close proximity for sharing of common teaching materials. Movable furniture and placement of utilities along the sides of the room provide desirable flexibility. Space is needed for storage as well as activity. Project areas should be equipped with proper tools and supplies for construction and repair of science apparatus. Facilities should include areas for reading of printed material. Auxiliary rooms should include storage-preparation areas, a darkroom and office for the science teacher.

Not all science work is done in a laboratory. In the upper grades there may be increasing employment of library resources. Science reference materials and books dealing with the history of science have an important place either in the school library or in a special collection housed in the science rooms. Books like those in the Traveling High School Library of the American Association for the Advancement of Science, the Alembic Club reprints, and scientific periodicals should be included.

If the science teacher is to carry a normal number of classes, he needs assistance in the laboratory, both for preparation of his regular classes and for the supervision of students doing independent work. The previously noted committee of the Science Teachers Association suggests that "competent, paid laboratory assistance may be drawn from the ranks of qualified members of the community, such as retired personnel, housewives, and college students, or from among qualified high-school students". Even with such assistance, the teacher who would like to guide individual experimentation cannot give the necessary help when his class exceeds the recommended limit of fifteen to twenty students.

Non-School Programs

One source of assistance comes not inside but outside school hours and the normal school framework. Concern on the part of governmental, scientific, and industrial leadership has led to development of programs after school, on weekends and during the summer which provide science experiences both for students and teachers. Several universities extend such informal assistance—speakers, seminars, organized courses, summer programs, and after-school laboratory experiences— to neighboring school systems or to individual high school students. The largest summer program for high school students is sponsored by the National Science Foundation which supported intensive experiences in science and mathematics for approximately 7,500 high school students on college campuses throughout the United States in 1964. Additional programs of a similar type are sponsored on Saturdays during the academic year. The Joe Berg Foundation has mobilized industrial scientists in a number of communities to provide in-school or out-of-school leadership for young people of scientific bent. Science institutes are offered to teachers by the Federal Government to update their training; at Oak Ridge a program is geared to the teacher who wants special background in nuclear physics. Some industrial firms provide work experience in summers for science teachers as well as for students. In larger communities the teacher can often find such assistance already organized. In smaller communities the teacher may be able to mobilize unused resources, or he may find ways of joining with teachers from other schools to organize regional seminars during school days or on weekends for students in sparsely settled areas. Such a program in rural New York State, for example, has been able to provide an unusual Saturday morning experience in science and mathematics for students in all of one county, drawing upon qualified leadership personnel who are willing to undertake the necessary travel on the weekend.

Mathematics

The mathematics program in education of the gifted has suffered from two factors in the educational scene. One has been the static nature of secondary school mathematics in the United States for approximately two centuries and an unimaginative approach to arithmetic in the elementary school that was confined to routine drill on computation. The second has been a greater loss for bright students in mathematics than in other areas as a result of broadening the population base in schools without individualizing instruction. Both of these factors, fortunately, are now the subject of intensive treatment.

Elementary Programs

Elementary mathematics in the past quarter-century has benefited from the "meaningful" mathematics approach. Emphasis placed on understanding of mathematical processes rather than on computation alone has moved elementary programs in the direction most valuable to intellectually gifted children. Their ability to comprehend, apply, and generalize, and their lesser need for drill combine to support a program that places stress on mathematical and social meaning. Some recent programs are "getting out from under" an exclusive stress on social applications. Instead, greater balance and more challenge result from putting primary emphasis on the meaning of the mathematics itself— the number system and the processes employed to utilize number. Certainly, in the case of the gifted child, the school cannot rest satisfied simply with accurate manipulation of numbers; more important for present appreciation and later development is understanding of why and how number systems "work."

Authorities in the field distinguish among four levels of pupil operation: manipulation of objects in quantity; "laboratory" procedures in discovering and understanding arithmetical processes as a result of working with real or representational objects; symbolic learning that bypasses the slower handling of real objects; and the use of short cuts and equivalent operations to arrive at solutions. Obviously all children need some of all four of these approaches to learning, but the gifted child should not be kept busy with idle manipulation when he is ready to move on to more abstract functions. The bright child may be expected to advance at an earlier date to symbolic operation alone, but this "early date" may not arrive much before junior high school.

A word of caution is necessary before plunging too rapidly into advanced studies with the gifted child. It is a truism that not all of a child's intellectual powers develop evenly. Verbal, mathematical, reasoning, spatial and other factors have been identified as distinct functions, and correlation among them are not always high. What, then, if a child has been identified as an intellectually gifted youngster on the basis of the Binet? The test is admittedly heavily weighted toward verbal ability. What happens is what might be predicted. In special school programs where admission depends upon a high Binet score, mathematics is the area where children are most likely not to perform at anticipated levels. High ability in *mathematics*, accordingly, is not always present in the high IQ child. A combination of factors is needed to predict this ability; these include the intelligence quotient, but also reading ability and interest, vocabulary, previous arithmetic achievement, and such general characteristics as intellectual curiosity and perseverance.

Education of the mathematically gifted child, then, takes on two facets: education of the mathematically gifted leading possibly to careers in mathematics, and education of the generally gifted to have as much appreciation of mathematics as possible for the intelligent layman. If children are selected for special attention on a general basis, a wide variety of mathematical abilities will be present and a variety of content and method will be necessary.

Emphasis on *useful* mathematics in the years before World War II led to development of curricula that were limited by the uses of mathematics observed in children's or adults' activities. Such a program drew immediate protest from some quarters. Not what uses are currently made, but what uses *might* be made if adults knew more mathematics-this was the criterion that critics suggested. Schools should be concerned with enriching life, not with maintaining an impoverished status quo. Brownell experimented with first and second graders and came up with an impressive list of useful mathematical topics within the range of six- and seven-year-olds if they were but exposed to a richer mathematical environment.

The gifted child's superiority in abstract operations make the more recent approach in organizing the mathematics curriculum especially relevant. Emphasis is placed on the role of mental discovery by children of the meaning, nature, and structure of the number system; on arithmetic as a language of quantitative thought and action; on the mathematical meanings involved in computation; on mental analysis and computation; on the development of "self-imposed standards of critical thinking and accurate computation" both in and out of school. An important objective is a growing "appreciation for and interest in arithmetic as an indispensable language and functional resource in industry, commerce and the sciences". The School Mathematics Study Group, having initiated its program of revision at the secondary level, has more recently turned to elementary programs starting at the fourth grade. Other groups and individuals working at a number of centers are also giving their attention to introducing the language of modern mathematics in the elementary school.

Enrichment

Enrichment in mathematics involves both the introduction of new topics and acceleration through earlier study of topics normally taken at a higher grade level. To some extent introduction of new topics also anticipates work at higher levels and results in acceleration as well. Holling worth insisted that the bright child could learn the usual elementary school curriculum in one-half the time normally provided, the very bright child in one-quarter the time. The surplus one-half or three quarters can be used in various ways. One is acceleration. A second is enrichment through increasing the number and complexity of applications or enrichment through introduction of related but different topics.

A third is to be found in the intensification of the learning experience. Some authorities distinguish among three levels of teaching in mathematics – for appreciation, for understanding, and for mastery. Since the mathematically oriented child is capable of the third level, one may well assume that the surplus of available time will go partly toward developing mastery. Such a statement should not be interpreted to justify long periods of involved drills. The child should be able to perform basic operations, to understand their rationale, and to compute without making errors. Beyond this point, further drill brings diminishing returns. Gradually, slide rules, tables, logarithms, and mechanical computers should be introduced.

Review of recommended programs of enrichment reflects agreement that topics should come largely from modern mathematics. There is little tendency to increase complexity of problems and intricacy of manipulation in conventional areas. Excellent sources for the teacher are the Twenty-seventh Yearbook of the National Council of Teachers of Mathematics which deals with enrichment in elementary and junior high schools and the Twenty-eighth which treats enrichment in senior high school and the transition to college mathematics.

Enrichment topics in the elementary school should be related to overall goals of the mathematics program. Grossnickle recommends the following attainment for the gifted in mathematics by the end of the sixth grade: fundamental principles governing structure of the system of numeration; commutative, associative, and distributive laws; inverse processes, meaning of reciprocals, representation of division as a fraction; identity elements. Flagg lists the following topics as the content of a special program in the fifth and sixth grades (later extended to seventh and eighth as well) for gifted children in the laboratory school of the Illinois State Normal University: "(a) historical topics; algorithms formerly used, development of numerals, other numeration systems; (b) exponents – meaning, use in analyzing place value and in scientific notation; (c) bases other than the ten; analysis of place value, operations; (d) sets and sentences; equalities and inequalities; (e) number systems; natural numbers, integers (positive and negative), rational numbers; laws governing operations; (f) number line representations and graphing; (g) prime numbers and factors; (h) tests for divisibility and why they 'work' ". Flagg also indicates that gradual extension of the "new mathematics in elementary schools is beginning to preempt some of these topics for the general program for all students. As a result the Illinois Normal program for gifted children changes as needed to maintain a high level of challenge for the special classes.

At the junior high school level, topics recommended overlap with those of the elementary school because of the need for more sophisticated treatment of these topics and because of a generally fluid situation arising from current introduction of new approaches in mathematics. Some topics suggested include history of numbers, numeration in bases other than ten, prime and composite numbers, inverse operations, statistics and graphs, probability, set theory, rational and irrational numbers, and phases of plane geometry.

New curricular proposals in elementary mathematics include experimental materials which should be helpful to the teacher of gifted children seeking direction. The following programs are of particular interest:

- School Mathematics Study Group project on elementary mathematics; Director: E. C. Begle, Stanford University. Materials published by Stanford University Press.
- University of Illinois Committee on School Mathematics; Director: David A. Page, University of Illinois. Materials published by University of Illinois Press.
- Syracuse University Madison Project; Director: Robert Davis, Syracuse University.
- Geometry for Primary Grades; Director: Newton Hawley, Stanford University.
- Sets and Numbers (Primary Grades) and Experimental Project in Logic (Intermediate Grades); Director: Patrick Suppes, Stanford University.
- Greater Cleveland Mathematics Program; Director: George Baird, Educational Research of Greater Cleveland .

Supporting the flourishing activity in curriculum development has been a surge in the printing of materials for students and teachers by professional organizations and commercial publishers. The National Council of Teachers of Mathematics has prepared a number of books and pamphlets, some for teachers, some for students, some for both, which present new topics and curriculum developments. L. W. Singer and Webster have published series of booklets for use by students. RowPeterson has prepared a group of 16 page pamphlets for pupils in grades 3 to 6. Other publishers are reorienting their textbook series in keeping with new developments. In addition, there is a rapidly growing list of supplementary books for students on the themes of "fun in mathematics," mathematical puzzles, paper folding (topology), codes, numeration, and mathematical history. These materials potentially build understanding and a background of information while contributing a sense of wonder and excitement to students independently pursuing their interest in mathematics.

Acceleration

The most commonly observed characteristic of gifted children is their precocity in handling abstractions inherent in mathematics. One may expect, therefore, earlier readiness of many bright children for mathematics at all levels. Since mathematics is probably more sequential in its organization than is any other subject, it would seem likely that more rapid progress through the sequence is appropriate. Enrichment in mathematics at the elementary level necessarily entails acceleration in learning both the processes and social arithmetic of the first eight grades. In many schools and in most textbook series, careful gradation has been planned. It would seem perfectly proper to follow the sequences that have been laid out. It would seem equally improper to subject a child who already has a good knowledge of number meanings and a high level of mental arithmetical ability to the laborious tracing of numbers in the first two grades and the invention of "number stories" to illustrate their meaning. Similarly, a child who is already doing subtraction and addition with three-place numbers at home ought not to be limited to the addition facts with sums to 9 or subtraction facts with minuends to 6 because these standards represent optimum grade placement for the average. While readiness programs in reading and arithmetic are indeed important, the gifted child who enters school with experience in both these areas is likely to be discouraged and disappointed if his appetite to learn new things is ignored.

By and large, the child who is ready for multiplication, division, fractions, ratios, or decimals ought not to be held up simply because a given topic belongs to the next grade. The teacher of bright children, of course, is likely to get in curricular difficulties if he truly seeks to enrich the program in a district where the course of study is extremely rigid. If children with genuine ability in mathematics are to be given the opportunity they need, a more flexible view of curriculum has to be taken. This entails organization of small groups in the heterogeneous class that can move at a faster pace. It also calls for articulation as these children move to the next class so that they need not backtrack or tread water while the rest of the class catches up. Ultimately, the elementary school child will "run out" of elementary school topics, and ways of introducing junior high school math need to be found. The same cross over will be experienced toward the end of junior and senior high school where normal course offerings will be inadequate. In homogeneous groupings, the same situation arises, but the a typicality of an entire class may simplify necessary adjustments.

Various alternatives are open when the school needs to look to the next school level in order to provide suitable opportunities. Some communities make available the more advanced work in the lower school program, utilizing teachers with special background or borrowing teachers from the next higher level. Some communities say impliedly, "You've learned all we can teach you in this organization. Now we will transfer you to the next level at an earlier age." Some communities keep their bright children with their age group but provide them with a period or two in the building at the next higher level where they study their special interest with older students. Thus, some fifth and sixth graders may be found in the high school one period a day, and some high school students in a nearby college. In no subject is the problem more apparent than in mathematics because of the sequential nature of the discipline. There is a certain point beyond which addition of two-column numbers cannot be "enriched."

Teacher of Mathematics in Elementary School

Fundamental changes are taking place in elementary as well as in secondary mathematics. An important problem in instituting more challenging programs will be the preparation of teachers, particularly in elementary school where few teachers have extensive background in this area. Some school systems may be successful in updating the mathematics training of large proportions of their elementary teachers. Others may have to depend upon use of specialized mathematics teachers in elementary schools. Some may have to limp along until they have gradually replaced retiring teachers with new teachers who have themselves studied modern mathematics in high school and college.

Proposals in the 1960's to departmentalize upper grades arose, no doubt, in part from observation of the inadequacy in mathematics of many classroom teachers assigned to teaching all subjects. Before departmentalization is accepted as a solution considerable research data of a substantial nature are needed. A study by Gibbs and Matala does not support the use of special teachers either in urban or rural situations for science and mathematics in grades 5 and 6. Testing the use of special teachers in different communities, they reported "no difference in insights and understandings gained in science and in mathematics" as class organization and school systems were compared. The particular personnel available in a given school district, rather than a fixed policy on specialization, seems to provide the best guide, until further evidence is at hand, in determining the approach to be used in teaching mathematics to especially apt pupils. The teacher himself, rather than the type of organization, was found by Gibbs and Matala to be significant in changes of interest on the part of pupils. If children gifted in mathematics are to enjoy opportunities in newer areas, they will need teachers who are qualified to lead them in the study of new material. In-service workshops, graduate courses on university campuses or at extension centers, and reading of the multitude of attractive materials available offer avenues to teachers to update their training. School districts interested in their gifted students should provide resources and facilities to assist in this continuing professional growth.

New Secondary School Programs

Recommendations made in 1959 by the Commission on Mathematics of the College Entrance Examination Board promise considerable impact on secondary school programs. Following four years of study, the Commission presented the following "nine-point program for college capable students":

- Strong preparation, *both* in concepts *and* in skills, for college mathematics at the level of calculus and analytic geometry
- Understanding of the nature and role of deductive reasoning- in algebra, as well as in geometry
- Appreciation of mathematical structure ("patterns")— for example, properties of natural, rational, real, and complex numbers
- Judicious use of unifying ideas— sets, variables, functions, and relations

- Treatment of inequalities along with equations
- Incorporation with plane geometry of some coordinate geometry, and essentials of solid geometry and space preception
- Introduction in grade 11 of fundamental trigonometry—centered on coordinates, vectors, and complex numbers
- Emphasis in grade 12 on elementary functions (polynomials, exponential, circular)
- Recommendation of additional alternative units for grade 12: *either* introductory probability with statistical applications, *or* an introduction to modern algebra.

Leaving the construction of new programs in grades 7 and 8 to other committees studying the problem (School Mathematics Study Group with headquarters first at Yale and later at Stanford, the University of Maryland Mathematics Project, the University of Illinois Committee on School Mathematics, and curriculum committees of the National Council of Teachers of Mathematics), the Commission seeks at the end of the ninth grade:

Skills, concepts and factual knowledge covering:

- The number system and the decimal representation of numbers
- The elementary operations with integers, decimal fractions, and simple fractions
- The vocabulary and ideas of elementary intuitive geometry
- The use of algebraic symbolism in formulas and simple equations
- The beginnings of graphical representation of data, of formulas, and of simple equations.
- The Commission suggests a framework built on the established foundation:

Grade 9: "Increased attention to algebra...with an equally earnest recommendation that the point of view from which the material is presented be that of contemporary mathematics." "Introduction of instruction in deductive reasoning"

Grade 10: Geometry, with three-fold objectives: "acquisition of information about geometric figures in the plane and in space";

"understanding of the deductive method as a way of thinking"; "opportunities for original and creative thinking by students." To accomplish this, a reduction in the number of theorems studied; introduction of coordinate geometry; treatment of certain material in solid geometry "along with analogous content of plane geometry"

Grade 11: Material from advanced algebra and trigonometry: Continued work on basic concepts and skills; linear functions: radicals; quadratic function; quadratic equations; systems of equations; exponents and logarithms; series; number fields; plane vectors; coordinate trigonometry and vectors; trigonometric formulas

Grade 12: Three possible programs:

- "Elementary Functions, first semester; Introductory Probability with Statistical Applications, second semester.
- Elementary Functions, first semester; Introduction to Modern Algebra, second semester.
- Elementary Functions and Selected Topics: Elementary functions enlarged to a full year by additional topics."

Within these general outlines modifications may be made that introduce modern mathematics recommendations coming from various groups studying the problem. Suggestions in some detail are also to be found in the bulletin on mathematics of the Project on the Academically Talented Student.

While considerable pressure has been generated to increase greatly the number of students enrolled in advanced mathematics courses, Conant suggests the need for restraint. A high level of intellectual ability is needed for advanced study in mathematics. If more than 15 per cent of the students are enrolled in these courses, says Conant, efforts to extend such study will be self-defeating. The instructor will not be able to bring students along without diluting the challenge of the course. It might be wise to limit the group to top ability in mathematics and not to top intellectual ability if one gives credence to specialization in intellectual functions.

Such reasoning lends support to ability grouping in secondary mathematics programs. Grouping of this kind generally results naturally when students have choices between general mathematics and college preparatory programs at the lower grade levels. It is extended in the junior and senior years when elective arrangements provide for self-selection. However, requiring all college preparatory students to take three or four years of mathematics might swell enrollments and lower the quality of advanced courses. Such extension would result in an unhappy experience for bright students who are mathematically inept while impoverishing the courses for the mathematically talented.

In mathematics, as in other areas, experiences outside the classroom can spur individual initiative, study, and commitment. Some schools organize mathematics clubs and even mathematics teams which enter into friendly competition with teams from other schools. Emphasis should be placed on creative thinking and extension of interest rather than on competition for its own sake only. Students may develop mathematical exhibits which illustrate projects upon which they have worked, and these may be displayed in mathematics and science fairs. Some mathematics projects are listed in "Thousands of Science Projects" published by the Science Clubs of America. The Academically Talented Student Project also calls attention to the contests of the Mathematical Association of America and the Society of Actuaries, and to enrichment materials published by the National Council of Teachers of Mathematics.

New developments in secondary mathematics also require some fresh study and review by teachers of mathematics. The Talented Student Project advises the teacher of the mathematically gifted to "refresh his knowledge in the area of analysis (the calculus and analytic geometry) and to catch up with some work in modern algebra." Recommendations include such topics as elementary concepts of sets and their applications in elementary mathematics; logic and symbolic logic, especially as related to geometry; probability and statistics; the number system; a modern concept of functions; and topics in modern algebra, such as groups, rings and fields. Secondary school mathematics teachers will find considerable assistance in the volume of Appendices with which The College Entrance Examination Board Commission on Mathematics followed up its recommendations for a new program in senior high schools.

At this time a revolution appears to be growing in the teaching of mathematics. Almost all efforts in the 1950's have been in the direction of a more challenging program for mathematically talented students. Many of the new proposals are likely to seem hopelessly beyond the average student. The major asset of new recommendations, however, lies in the many new ideas that will be within the scope of gifted boys and girls. Another is the excitement it promises to teachers working with new materials and to the students who will be the beneficiaries of their enthusiasm.

Summary

Both science and mathematics education have made large steps forward as a result of large scale assistance provided by the National Science Foundation and other public and private agencies. This effort has borne fruit in proposals for significant changes at all levels in both these major areas. New curricula have been established, and they have been accompanied by new materials and special training of teachers, largely at the expense of the Federal Government. Of particular interest to those interested in the intellectually gifted is the focus of these programs on children with special abilities in each field. It is no longer accurate to charge that programs do not exist to challenge the mathematically and scientifically talented student. On the contrary, new offerings at the elementary, secondary, and collegiate levels provide enough material to stretch the powers of the very best students and sometimes, unfortunately, to overwhelm them.

The new programs in these fields have certain points in common. There is an emphasis on concept development. The programs focus upon developing the ability to generalize as well as upon the learning of important generalizations already established. Proponents of new approaches advocate the method of "discovery" in both science and mathematics. "Inquiry" is transformed into a system, methodology or strategy that may be transposed from field to field.

Distinction is also made between mathematics or science for the citizen and mathematics or science for the specialist. For the former, proposals include an understanding of basic concepts and of the structure of the discipline involved. For the latter, advanced programs once reserved for more mature students are offered at each school level.

Public interest in these fields is reflected both in special activities in the school and in new opportunities in the community. Science honors programs capture the interest of students in weekend and summer sessions. Business, government, and professional groups sponsor science fairs, mathematics contests, study groups, and seminars for students in secondary schools.

In mathematics and the sciences, opportunities for the gifted abound. Schools can give direction to these efforts through appropriate motivation and identification of talent, through revision of programs, and through stimulating the growth of their professional staffs.

8

Teachers for Gifted Children

Overview

Of all the variables in the teaching-learning process, none is more significant for the pupil than the teacher. Researchers in education are frequently humbled by the fact that variation attributable to individual teachers often exceeds variation due to the experimental factor chosen for investigation. A case in point is the New York City study of grouping in elementary school where the individual teacher and his influence were considered to affect student growth far more than the pattern of grouping.

Whatever the significance of the teacher to students in general, the influence of the teacher of gifted students is magnified by several factors. The teacher's most obvious role is direct instruction, and in this role he may confidently expect to secure unusual results with unusually able pupils. The teacher is also a primary pole for students in an interactive process that is basic to learning. Again, superior intelligence will function best in interaction with a stimulating teacher. Third, the teacher is inevitably a model. Because of the potential of intellectually gifted students, the teacher's role as a professional and scholarly worker is most significant.

What does one seek, then, in the teacher of the unusually apt learner? Are there particular traits of personality especially desirable in such a teacher? Is special training necessary; if so, are definably different components of academic knowledge and professional skill needed? Should such training be part of the total pattern of a teacher's preparation or should it be a specialty added onto the basic structure established for all teachers? What should school systems do to prepare teachers for special assignments with gifted students?

Current Patterns of Preparation

It is instructive as a point of departure to examine existing patterns in preparation and assignment of teachers for the gifted. Over a series of years Wilson surveyed programs of pre-service, graduate and in-service education for teachers of intellectually superior students. Since then more recent but limited surveys have been reported by French, Hawes and James, among others. In general, undergraduate work in teacher education makes little specific provision for the prospective teacher of the gifted. Excellence in the liberal component and academic specialization of a college curriculum is crucial in the basic equipment of the teacher of the gifted. Built upon these is the program of professional development which normally places primary emphasis on general competence of the beginning teacher prior to specialization for teaching the gifted, the retarded, or other specific groups. Extremely few undergraduate courses in curriculum, methods, or materials for the gifted appear as part of the professional sequence in education. Units are studied in some colleges that relate to variability in learning capacity and ways of dealing with the extremes in the range of ability. A small handful of institutions provide observation or student teaching with academically talented children and youth. On the graduate level, an increasing number of universities are offering at least one course in education of the gifted. Fewer than a dozen were offering more than one course as late as 1960. French reports the following composite of graduate courses in thirty institutions:

I. Introduction
   A. Work with the gifted child (present emphases, issues, philosophy, history)
   B. Definition of gifted and talented youth

C. Characteristics of the gifted child

II. Identification of the gifted child

III. Educational provisions for the gifted

A. Aims and goals of democratic education

B. Culture and community involved

C. Survey of specialized programs

D. Provisions for enriching the curriculum

E. Acceleration

F. Administrative aspects of curricular patterns

G. Development of curricular materials

IV. Adjustment of the gifted child

V. Problems of the underachiever

VI. Motivation of the gifted child

VII. Teacher and the gifted child

VIII. Parents and the gifted child

IX. Community and the gifted child

X. Research and evaluation

With the relative scarcity of specialized work offered, only a small fraction of teachers in special classes report any particularized preparation to teach gifted classes. Hawes secured responses to a questionnaire from 173 communities, population 5,000-24,999, known to have special classes for the gifted. "Fewer than half" of the 219 teachers so employed had had either undergraduate or graduate courses devoted to education of the gifted. Only 8.1 per cent had supervisors employed fulltime to service these courses. The same percentage (8.1) of school administrators thought that specific educational preparation was the most important single qualification for teachers of the gifted. Teaching experience (26.6 per cent) and personality (23.7 per cent) secured more support as the single criterion of most importance. However, Cole and Fliegler reported that in their sample 79 per cent of the teachers of gifted children regarded special preparation as essential.

To compensate for the dearth of college course work for teaching the gifted, some school systems offer workshops of limited duration, consultant assistance, in-service courses in cooperation with university graduate schools, conferences, curriculum development projects, visitation to other schools, and publications. Through a combination of pre-service, graduate, and in-service programs, a pattern for preparing teachers for the gifted has developed. Currently, however, these activities are so limited in number and extent that they should be regarded more as pilot programs than as a universally available pattern of preparation.

Qualifications of Teacher of the Gifted

Since the good teacher in general must be a paragon of pedagogic virtues, the teacher prescribed for the gifted by various authorities, pupils, and parents, turns out to be a paragon of paragons. Relevant questions to be asked in describing a teacher for the gifted are these:

What qualities of a good teacher are especially needed in teaching the gifted?

Are any qualities needed for gifted classes that are not generally essential?

Can one distinguish between "the best teachers" and "the best teacher for the gifted?"

Does a teacher of the gifted have to be exceptionally able himself in the same dimensions as his pupils?

These questions will be considered after summarizing qualities frequently mentioned as characterizing the teacher for gifted students.

Personal Characteristics

There is general consensus that the intellectually gifted child needs a teacher who is intellectually superior. "Intellectual stature," "intellectual acumen," "love of learning," "inquiring mind," "independence of thought," "a range of skills and accomplishments," and "versatility of interests" are terms used to identify cognitive qualities sought for the special teacher. This ability is to be reflected first in general cultural attainments – "a rich fund of information and cultural background," "well rounded to help students see the interrelationships of life," "a philosophy of life," "informed in areas other than his own specialty." Second, his intellectual excellence is notable in his field of specialization – "knowledge of his own and related fields," "special aptitudes and interests," "scholarship in academic areas."

Not only is the desired teacher intellectual; he is also creative. Expressions such as the following appear: "flexible and creative persons," "creativeness, originality, inventiveness," "productivity in a creative area," "creative thinking ability."

Good health, *mens sana in corpore sano,* is also prescribed, including physical superiority and athletic interests and activity.

The good teacher is not only intellectual, creative, and healthy. He exemplifies the best of human qualities m – "modesty, kindliness and concern for others," "psychological maturity," "responsibility in emotional and social development," "respect for the importance of individual personality," "fairness, tolerance, good will, alertness, attractive personality" and, a substantial sense of values. He participates as a member of the community.

Teaching Characteristics

As a teacher, he shows special characteristics, too. He is supportive, being alert and sensitive to pupil needs. He is liked and respected by children. He is willing to take extra time to listen to children's ideas, go places with them, and do things in which they are interested. This interest in his students is also enlarged to a sense of social and professional responsibility. The desirable teacher is able to stimulate and inspire his students. He is not jealous of superior potential apparent in some of his students, and he is able to take occasional correction from students, just as he is able to accept criticism from adults and make necessary changes in his pattern of action. Similarly, he has a capacity for self-criticism. He knows how to let others assume responsibility, and he challenges students to enrich their learning on their own initiative. Children with strong ideas of their own and highly developed initiative do not trouble him. Most important, he has an urge to do something over and above what is normally expected of him as a teacher. He *wants* to teach gifted children.

The good teacher also puts to effective use what he has learned from psychology. He understands children and accepts them, and he has a special sympathy for children with exceptional ability. Learning theory is applied in differentiating activities for the intellectually able. The teacher knows how to develop a classroom atmosphere conducive to good mental health. He has a knowledge and understanding of social and emotional problems that may be created for the gifted due to their accelerated mental development. The teacher displays skill in human relationships and sensitivity to children's problems in dealing with each other. Identification of special ability is a meaningful concern to him, and he has some competence in discovering talents of various kinds.

The teacher of the gifted is also a master of educational methodology. Of superior professional competence, he takes pains to modify curriculum and activities so as to release the creative energy of gifted children. He provides a rich environment for independent efforts in such fields as science, art, and music. Opportunities are found for students to work in groups in order to learn group-working skills. The best pupils are stimulated and challenged; they know that they are expected to achieve at their top level of ability. Standards are kept appropriately flexible. The teacher knows how to use laboratory and workshop methods. He is able to teach a problem-solving approach to learning, to apply this to independent study and research, and to teach children to evaluate their own progress. He is able to develop a flexible, individualized, enriching curriculum suited to individual needs and avoiding identical, stereotyped demands. Emphasis is placed in his teaching on social responsibility, a desire to serve society, and recognizing the work of others. In short, he is resourceful in developing teaching techniques. Finally, he knows how to work well with parents and others who are vital parts of the child's learning environment. Surveys have been taken in a number of cases to determine students' reactions to their teachers. Representative of these is N. Davis' list compiled from responses of gifted students who were graduates of the Cleveland Major Work Program:

- Sense of humor
- Encouragement of responsibility
- Knowledge of subject

- Firmness and fairness
- Understanding of children
- Enjoyment of teaching

While there is no unanimity, student responses cluster around the items in Davis' listing. Dressel and Grabow expand and reinforce Davis' items with the following criteria elicited from gifted students in Michigan high schools:

1. Arousal of students' curiosity
2. Insistence that work be redone until it is of high caliber
3. Insistence that students engage in activities requiring initiative and self-reliance.

Most of the items in the list of personal characteristics and list of teaching qualities might well be demanded for teachers of all children. One might argue strongly that some of these qualities are more essential for the average, slow, or handicapped child than for the gifted. It is difficult to maintain the viewpoint that the *best* teachers should all be assigned to the gifted, but it seems logical to ask that teachers who *work best* with the gifted be assigned to do so. In an effort to determine which teachers are most successful with this special group, Brandwein studied the background and personal characteristics of teachers whose students had won awards in the Westinghouse Science Talent Search. Of the twenty-two whom Brandwein knew personally, he classified eight as inspiring master teachers, "ten as superior teachers, and four as average." He observed that teachers of the gifted exhibit some of the same characteristics as do the students themselves: high intelligence, persistence, and "questing" – a restless searching for better explanations than presently exist of the natural universe. These teachers were well trained in their subject matter and active in professional pursuits such as curriculum development projects and professional organizations. They demonstrated a liking for children, particularly adolescents. All of them were experiencing enough satisfaction with teaching to indicate their intention to continue in the profession. They presented a father or mother image to their students, appearing to be people who were sympathetic to their problems and meriting their trust. In addition, however, these teachers held firm and high standards of achievement.

From the distinctive characteristics of intellectually gifted children, a number of qualities seem to be more needed for teachers of such children than for others. Respect for intellectual ability is essential in working with young gifted children. With adolescents, unusual intellectual acumen itself is essential. Second, scholarly attainment must have grown out of the teacher's superior ability. Not only must the teacher of the gifted be able to keep up with his students; he must also serve as a model of academic achievement. This should be notable both in general cultural background and in specialized study in a field or discipline. The teacher should be doing some creative work, preferably in his own field. He must be mature and secure psychologically so that students of high potential are a source of gratification rather than a threat. He must be "free" psychologically so that he can accept originality on the part of students and challenges to his own academic authority.

The teacher of the gifted must also be a master of the art of teaching. He must promote opportunities for students to assume responsibility and initiative in their own learning. The teacher must be able to relate to students both as a model of scholarly performance and as a supportive figure in Brandwein's sense of a father-mother image. He must be committed to a philosophy of individual differences in his appraisal of the teaching task. He must recognize the uniqueness of individuals and be able to adapt his teaching program to provide adequate challenge and assistance to each learner. Part of this recognition is a firm understanding of the nature of giftedness, the potentials residing therein, and the problems that individuals in our culture face because of intellectual uniqueness. The gifted child's pedagogue must be a master of teaching techniques, drawing upon old and new methods to secure maximum results for each child's hours in school. Fundamentally, he must like working with gifted children, rejoicing in their accomplishments, recognizing them as children with both usual and unusual emotional needs, and refusing to exploit their exceptionality.

A teacher who meets these requirements may not be the best teacher in the school system. He will probably not be the best teacher for slow, average, or handicapped students. What is needed is not the best teacher but the teacher who is best for working with a particular group of children; every child deserves such a teacher.

Preparing Teachers to Work with Gifted Students

The preceding paragraphs set forth the proposition that the teacher of academically gifted students should have some competencies which are different in kind or degree from those needed by all teachers. What experiences in college, graduate school, and on the job should contribute to these special abilities? A thoughtful discussion of a program of teacher education for the gifted is presented in the National Society Yearbook by Frank Wilson out of his long years of experience in preparing such teachers at Hunter College. James, Ward, Abraham and French also contribute important insights with respect to the various components of undergraduate and graduate preparation of the teacher who is to work with high-ability students.

Proper screening and selection of candidates is important in the preparation of all teachers. At the point of initial selection it is too early to predict whether a candidate will become a teacher of the gifted. Screening of all prospects should therefore be accomplished in terms of motivation to teach, a professional commitment, academic promise, social values, interest in working with young people, psychological maturity, personality characteristics and health standards. At a later stage, Torrance suggests that the student with an interest in teaching the gifted should demonstrate creative thinking ability. His range of interests, personality characteristics, and previous experiences should reflect creative motivation. Ward asserts that "the personality characteristics of the teacher of the gifted should be adapted to the particular types of stress and demand which arise in dealing with children who have marked initiative, strong and sometimes distinctive interests, and exceptional rational capacity".

There is general agreement that the teacher of the gifted has first to be prepared as a good teacher in general. At the undergraduate level the candidate needs a solid background of general education in order to ensure the breadth of preparation that truly gifted students should be able to draw upon. The candidate ought to develop a philosophy, values, and professional ideals which will equip him as a guide for the gifted students who should in turn set high store upon social service and concern for others. While such an outcome is not guaranteed by the required pattern of courses that go under the name of general education or liberal arts in most colleges, the faculty as a whole and the teacher education department in particular should be directing attention to the ends and not just the means of college education. Jacob has called attention to the general lack of success colleges have had in affecting student values, but he has also indicated the effectiveness of a few institutions in this regard and the worth whileness of the effort. Training for independence in learning is another important facet in preparing teachers of the gifted. Teachers who themselves have simply followed their professors' directions and bibliographies are not likely to know how to guide their students in independent work. Certainly, a student who wants to teach gifted children should have himself completed some independent study and honors type courses. A college endorsing a graduate for work with exceptionally able pupils should be able to point to scholastic independence reflected in the prospective teacher's academic experience.

Not only should the candidate's scholastic exposure be broad, but his immersion should be relatively deep. The current move by state education departments to require more concentrated specialization of both elementary and secondary school teachers should help to accomplish this aim. The specialization of the teacher for the gifted should be qualitatively, and perhaps quantitatively, deeper. A serious problem arises, however, in the differences between organization of disciplines in universities and subjects in the common schools. Teaching needs should take precedence over a narrow preparation for advanced graduate work. The English teacher with a field in literature limited to a single century is not well equipped to deal with reading skills, composition, mass media, reading materials for students, and linguistics and speech problems which are everyday realities in elementary and secondary schools. Botany and political science are too limited as major fields for the high school teacher of science or social studies, let alone the elementary school teacher in the "self-contained" classroom. For the sake of the teacher candidate it is desirable to redefine the discipline in terms of probable teaching assignments. Finally, the student needs a broad view of his field which is philosophic and historical as well as factual. He should have some idea of structure in his discipline (*the* structure, if agreement exists; *a* structure which gives meaning to his work, if there are multiple viewpoints). He should be able to explain to laymen and children the methods of his field. The science teacher should have some grounding in philosophy and history of science, and other majors should be similarly oriented to their fields.

The professional education of the teacher should be divided among undergraduate, graduate, and in-service phases. Most authorities agree on deferring specialization (as in teaching the gifted) to the graduate level. If appropriate time is to be given to general education and to development of major fields, the professional component in undergraduate programs is limited to the general preparation of the teacher. This is all to the good since more advanced work depends upon substantial teaching experience if it is to be meaningful. However, the laboratory experiences that characterize most strong programs of teacher education afford opportunities for young people to explore teaching the gifted. School visits that are often part of introductory courses should include visits to special classes for the gifted where such classes exist; otherwise discussion of some visits should focus upon the children of superior ability in classes observed. Tutorial work, big-brother arrangements, and work in community agencies are sometimes employed as adjuncts to courses in educational psychology. Here again, work with gifted students can be included for candidates who are so oriented. "September experiences," observation, and student-teaching also provide opportunities to study or work with bright children while first establishing general principles of operation for the teacher of all children. Certainly, educational psychology and methods courses should give strong emphasis to the doctrine of individual differences, to the identification of different levels of ability, to the respect of each individual as a person of dignity, and to the adaptation of teaching methods and curriculum in keeping with individual ability.

Maturity is an important quality of the teacher. Vocational and avocational experiences can make a strong contribution to development of psychological maturity. Teacher education students should be encouraged to seek out part-time and summer jobs or to participate in cooperative work-study programs. It is indeed desirable for students to have had some contact with the business world as well as with summer camps, day camps, after-school centers, community agencies, and other youth serving groups.

Graduate Work

Professional specialization for the teacher of the gifted begins at the graduate level. Some organized study of education of the gifted should be undertaken by every teacher planning to work with special classes. A composite course outline, developed from thirty institutions by French, has already been presented in this chapter. Problems of identification, curriculum adaptation, grouping, acceleration, enrichment, evaluation, guidance, underachievement, and motivation are highlighted, as are more general concerns with administrative provisions for educating the gifted, social issues, and the characteristics of exceptionally able children. Such a course should be built upon previous work on curriculum planning in general, on intensifying understanding of child development, on understanding the dynamics of human personality, and on measurement of ability and achievement. Where possible, a practicum in working with gifted children should be provided. This should involve opportunities to appraise ability, to develop special programs of study for individual children or small groups, and to carry out limited research projects with small groups of bright children. Some observation and demonstration teaching may also be included. Few, if any, universities offer such programs at this time, particularly of the graduate type described. Wilson cites the following primary needs where practical action is immediately possible regardless of course and program structures:

- Correcting "misconceptions about gifted and talented children"
- Developing "more realistically an awareness of the great range of exceptionalities and of the broad sweep of different capabilities"
- Providing "firsthand experiences with very capable children to enable teachers to understand them"
- Acquainting "students with basic resource materials which they can use constructively"
- Developing "familiarity with and practice in using community resources"
- Acquainting "students with classroom procedures particularly suitable for the full development of the children"

- Studying "administrative plans and instructional procedures in regard to the gifted."

The development of improved programs in colleges for teachers of the gifted depends upon a number of factors. First, there is need for a strong teacher education program in general which provides both a theoretical and experiential framework for understanding learners as individuals. Such a framework depends both upon the normal academic resources and upon the existence of teaching-learning laboratories in campus schools and affiliated public school systems. Second, there has to be a philosophical commitment to the development of the learner's full potential, including goals of academic excellence. Third, opportunities for cooperative relationships with other institutions and provisions for wide communication are essential to avoid a narrow provincialism in the development of pioneer programs. Finally, there is need for continuous experimentation and research "lest one good custom should corrupt the world." To do so, the institution must have ready access to school situations in its own laboratory school or in associated school systems. It also needs a staff with sophisticated research techniques to ensure rigorous evaluation of experimental projects.

In-Service Programs

While there may be great value in graduate courses in education of the gifted, direct action to improve actual programs for gifted children is more likely to come from work and study projects conducted within a particular school or school district. The university course offers academic resources and a scholastic regimen that facilitate concerted study of gifted children and their education. The university makes its contribution by enriching the insight of persons who attend. Actual development of programs, however, is more likely to ensue when teachers from a common background work within an administrative framework where action is possible. A single teacher returning from a summer workshop at State University may be enthusiastic to develop a meaningful program in his school or community, but he finds it difficult to convey the enthusiasm he feels to persons who have developed other interests which are equally legitimate. As a result, he is most often limited to improvement of the program for his own classes alone. In-service projects have the advantage of bringing together persons who normally work with each other, who recognize the problems of a particular school environment, and who can often join with each other to secure changes in desired directions. The most effective program may be a combination of university study, utilizing the resources and the perspective of such an institution, and in-service projects which capitalize upon factors which must be considered on the scene.

A number of channels are open for on-the-job training of teachers for the gifted. Some large school systems operate in-service courses. Ideally these courses combine the systematic approach of a university program with attention to a specific school system and its needs. Teachers preparing to work with the gifted in a school system currently operating programs for the bright children can derive benefit from such courses. Some systems provide for interchange of ideas among teachers with particular specialties. A newsletter on education for the gifted can serve such a purpose. Periodic meetings are held in some cities for teachers assigned.to special classes or interested in the program because of bright children in the heterogeneous classes they teach. In the New York City area the Metropolitan Association for Study of the Gifted provides a forum five times a year for teachers, administrators, college personnel, and lay people with an interest in the gifted.

Consultant service also proves an effective method of improving instruction of the gifted. The consultant may be a member of the central school staff or a visitor from a university or other school agency. He may work individually with teachers in developing plans, studying particular children, reviewing teaching techniques, locating materials for children, or finding resources in the community and outside. He may work instead with committees of teachers concerned about educating the most able youngsters, or he may combine the two approaches. The effective consultant provides in this way both professional and psychological support to the teacher who is trying his wings in a new element.

Another productive means for teacher education in any area is participation in curriculum development projects A genuine reappraisal of programs for the gifted or planning to develop new programs for bright children provides a dynamic center of interest for teachers who simultaneously improve their own competence and work on school-wide or system-wide problems. Such programs, of course, have to involve responsible administrative personnel if there is to be a good prospect for adoption of recommendations made by the study group. It is desirable, too, that provision be made for utilization of consultants from other schools, agencies or universities, in order to avoid dangers of insularity and ignorance. An essential resource is a library of curriculum materials and major publications concerned with the gifted and their education. In addition, finances should be available for visiting of other schools where programs of interest are underway.

The opportunity to see actual programs in operation can be most meaningful to teachers who are seeking new ideas and some direction as they plan programs for the gifted. Some districts are able to provide time and travel costs for a few teachers and administrators to visit other school systems, near and far. Some districts have tried to establish demonstration centers of their own. With assistance from the Illinois State Education Department, the Chicago Public Schools have provided such centers in one high school and four elementary schools. The main purpose of these centers is to facilitate observation and personal evaluation of instructional practices organized for gifted students in these schools.

Many school systems provide workshops of short duration or "institutes" before the opening of the school year in which teachers are given a brief exposure to problems in education of the gifted. If such programs are to be more than a momentary spiritual uplift, there is serious need for sustained attention to the problem over a long period of time. Some work and study structure has to be developed which outlives the institute. Workshops are useful if conducted long enough to yield serious study of a problem and working plans that teachers may put to work in the ensuing school year. Provision should be made for careful follow-tip activities of workshops as well as other activities of shorter duration. In education of the gifted it is especially apparent that the schools provide only part of the environment for learning. Widening use is being made of community personnel resources. In South Orangeburg, New York, for example, foundation support provided finances for employment on Saturday mornings of artists, architects, scientists, mathematicians, and other specialists living in the community, and the school district furnished compensation for school personnel who served as coordinating agents in particular areas. While providing an unusual service for interested high school youth, teachers were able to find fresh insights into certain fields of endeavor and to learn new ways of enlivening their classrooms during the week.

Finally, teachers and administrators can learn themselves while trying to add to knowledge available generally on teaching the gifted. Part of the in-service growth effort of the school system should be research which it sponsors in various fields. School personnel should be encouraged to participate in research on characteristics of gifted learners, identification procedures and instruments, development of creativity, teaching techniques in working with exceptionally able children, motivation, non-intellective factors in achievement, and the host of other problems in educating the gifted which remain to be studied. Some programs should be initiated by the school systems themselves. In other cases affiliation with university, state, or federal research projects may be possible. The teacher who is also a scholar not only builds his own background; he also serves as a model for emulation by intellectually superior students.

Specialized Personnel for Gifted Programs

Most advocates of strong programs for the gifted advocate separate budgets and special departments for the gifted in state and district school systems. Obviously, personnel organization is a function of particular situations, and what may work in one place may be unsuccessful elsewhere. The author, however, does not believe that such separatism is helpful except, possibly, in mammoth organizations where special programs may be overlooked unless specific provision is made.

Gifted students are not a breed apart. Whether special classes are provided or not, a significant proportion of high ability students will continue to be found in the "regular" classroom. Teachers and supervisors should not be misled by the establishment of separate organizations into a belief that the gifted are no concern of theirs. Supervisors with broad responsibilities can help prevent this compartmentalized point of view.

Education for the gifted cannot be set up 426 as.an elite program to com. Within this framework, such officers should earmark a substantial part pensate for a poor school program in general. It can be only as strong as the rest of the organization. It should enrich the whole program and in turn be enhanced by the larger part. This kind of operation calls for planning for the gifted as an integral part of the school system's total curriculum development, staff recruitment, supervision and budgeting.

Rather than look to separate organization, the school district should give serious consideration to assignment of staff and educational responsibilities. Supervisory personnel should have considerable freedom in assigning teachers as needs and interests change. No individual should be pegged irrevocably as a teacher of the gifted or non-gifted. Better than appointment of one firebrand director of gifted programs would be coordinated responsibility and action where the curriculum director, chief guidance officer, subject supervisors, and principals affirm education of the gifted as an identified and important part of their jobs. of their time, activity, and resources to planning and supervising programs for the exceptionally able. The top administration should require of these persons an annual accounting of their stewardship of the gifted as well as other programs.

Summary

The teacher of the gifted is essentially a good teacher but with some special attributes and qualitative differences. He is interested in intellectual achievement in young people with superior scholastic potential. He is excited about learning and is able to communicate this excitement to students. He is a warm human being and serves to some extent as a father or mother image, but he also demands that students attain high standards consistent with their individual promise. He recognizes the extremes of individual difference and has the professional competence to arrange the educational milieu to provide for these variations. He is psychologically mature and not troubled by the possibility that some of his students may ultimately exceed his own academic attainments.

Few teacher education institutions currently offer specialized work for the aspiring teacher of the gifted. Advocates urge that undergraduates learn to work effectively with individual differences but concede that specialized study is the function of graduate rather than undergraduate programs. A growing number of institutions are offering such work at the graduate level.

While formal course work has the advantage of providing more organized background for individual teachers, in-service activities in school districts give greater promise of developing planned programs for the gifted. Course work in the school district, curriculum development activities, workshops, conferences, and the use of consultants are major channels available for on-the-job study. A combination of graduate course work to provide organized background material and curriculum development activities in a school building or for the school system as a whole offer the best potential for special preparation of the teacher of gifted children.

Bibliography

Abraham Willard. "A Hundred Gifted Children." *Understanding the Child.* 6:11620, October, 1957.

Abramson David A. "The Effectiveness of Grouping for Students of High Ability." *Educational Research Bulletin, 38*:169-82, October 14, 1959.

Aikin Wilford M. *The Story of the Eight-Year Study*. New York, Harper & Row, 1942.

Allison Harold. "California Principals Study a Curriculum for the Gifted." *Bulletin of National Association of Secondary-Schools Principals, 43*:102-106, February, 1959.

Altus Grace T. "Some Correlates of the Davis-Eells Tests." *Journal of Consulting Psychology, 20*:227-32, June, 1956.

American Association for Gifted Children. *The Gifted Child.* Edited by Paul Witty. Boston, D. C. Heath, 1951.

American Council of Learned Societies. "Report of the Art Panel." *ACLS Newsletter, 9*:9:12-15, November, 1958.

Anderson C. Arnold. "The Dilemma of Talent-Centered Programmes: U.S.A." *The Gifted Child: 1962 Yearbook of Education*. New York, Harcourt, Brace & World, 1962, pp. 445-57.

Anderson Harold H., ed. *Creativity and Its Cultivation*. New York, Harper & Row, 1959.

Anderson John E. "The Nature of Abilities." In *Talent and Education*, edited by E. Paul Torrance. Minneapolis, University of Minnesota Press, 1960, pp. 9-31.

Anderson William. "An Attempt through the Use of Experimental Techniques to Determine the Effect of Home Assignments upon

Scholastic Success." *Journal of Educational Research, 40*:141-43, October, 1946.

Applbaum Morris J. "A Survey of Special Provisions for the Education of Academically Superior Students." *Bulletin of National Association of SecondarySchools Principals, 43*:26-43, October, 1959.

Arnold John E. "The Generalist versus the Specialist in Research and Development." *In The Creative Person*. Berkeley, Institute of Personality Assessment and Research, University of California, 1961.

Aschner Mary Jane. "The Analysis of Verbal Interaction in the Classroom." In *Theory and Research in Teaching*, edited by Arno A. Bellack. New York, Teachers College, Columbia University, 1963, pp. 53-78.

Association for Supervision and Curriculum Development. *Freeing Capacity to Learn*. Washington, D.C., The Association, 1960.

Hillson Henry T., and Myers Florence C. *The Demonstration Guidance Project, 1957-62: Pilot Program for Higher Horizons*. New York, New York City Board of Education, 1963.

Hobbs Nicholas. "Motivation to High Achievement". *Address delivered to Annual Conference of Association for Supervision and Curriculum Development, March, 1959*. Washington, D.C., The Association, mimeographed.

Katterle Zeno B., and Craig Robert. "Exposing an Academic Fallacy." *Washington Education, 34*:5:10-11+, February, 1955.

Keys Noel. "Should We Accelerate the Bright?" *Journal of Exceptional Children, 8*:248-54+, May, 1942.

Lehman Harvey C. *Age and Achievement*. Princeton, Princeton University Press, 1953.

Lombroso Cesare. *The Man of Genius*. London, Robert Scott, 1891.

INDEX

Q

R

S

T

U

V

W